AF423793

BAJAN IN BEIJING

कुनाल हेम्ब्रोम
Kunal Hembrom
Sujani
1.10.2018

*To Kunal Hembrom,
my sponsored son in
Jharkhand, India.*

Contents

Introduction

THIS BOOK SEEKS to tell the story of my journey to China (as its name suggests) and hopefully paint a picture of the passions, struggles, adventures and mishaps of the author. I wanted to come to China for a very long time, and had only recently rekindled my love for reading and writing. I decided to write about my life here, and maybe compile my meanderings into a book when my tenure at university was over. I wrote a little bit here and a little bit there, and it was only when I looked back and saw how much was written in the first year alone, that I printed a first draft. It was when my friends and classmates saw that I had a book written by my own hands, that I saw their excitement. They all pushed me to write more and to publish the book, and make it official. I am glad for their encouragement.

Before coming to China, I had worked as an Administrative Assistant at the Embassy of the People's Republic of China in Barbados. Before that, I had pursued a Bachelor's Degree in Linguistics and Spanish at the University in Barbados. I find that these experiences have been critical in my understanding of the Chinese language, and I thank God for them. Though I would be tempted to think that I should have been here earlier, I look around and see that it was actually a lot better for me to arrive here at the time that I did. The timing was perfect.

I started writing because I got tired of responding to people asking "so, how's China?". I wanted to write a document or two describing what I was doing or experiencing to send to those curious people. Well, those documents started to pile up, and soon, I was thinking to myself "hmm, what if I print out all of them into some kind of book...?" The next thing I know, I was having Kunal writing his name on the front of my manuscript. This, and plenty of encouragement from friends helped me to decide to take on this most enjoyable project.

The book starts out as a series of chapters that are more like diary entries. You would notice that the present tense is used quite often in the first half. As we go into the second half, you can almost tell when I made the decision to compile all the entries into a book. The chapters get more and more coherent. There is a chronological account of the first year of my study here at BLCU, and then, there is a series of trips that I made in my second year. This is the first edition. Maybe the second edition would have more of a sandwich-like structure with the trips in the middle, and the BLCU adventures in the beginning and end. As I continue, I would write more, and perhaps have two books, or one big compilation. Bear with me, as I decide.

HAPPY READING!

I believe in Christianity like how I believe in the rising sun. Not because I see it; but because by it, I can see everything else.

C.S. Lewis

Journey to China

OUR JOURNEY BEGINS in a small house on the main road of Belair, St. Philip. I, Stefan Lorde was lying in bed from 5:30 am, staring at the ceiling, and thinking about the great journey ahead of me. After what felt like ages, the time finally came to get ready for my flight. I was getting numerous messages on social media, congratulating me on achieving the scholarship to study in China. I had called the Chinese Embassy, and told Mr Zhou（周凤全）that today would be the day that I would be leaving for China. He was ecstatic to hear me, and wished me all the best in my studies and endeavours in China. After a few more visits from friends and neighbours, I headed down to the airport with my father. At the end of each visit from friends and well-wishers, there came the thought that I may be seeing some of these people for the last time. At the airport in Barbados, I went immediately and checked in at the counter. Though I mostly strive to remain within the constraints of the rules and regulations, the first thing which I asked upon reaching the counter was the price of overweight luggage. I knew that, as I was only carrying one bag (any more would have been $104.00) it would be best to keep the one, and simply pay the $50 for the overweight. It was over in a few. The passenger agent who was dealing with me was pleasant enough to get special mention in this document. After the check-in, I headed over to see my friends.

Many of my friends made their appearances to wish me well and to see me off. Mathious Willie was travelling with me, and I ensured that he got himself checked-in and ready. While I was with my friends, he went off with his family for something to eat. We only met up again when it came to board the flight a few minutes later. While he was not dancing in the departure lounge like myself, Mathious was just as excited to go to China to do his Master's Degree in Quantitative Economics, while my degree will be in Chinese Language.

When I passed immigration, another friend came from his post (he works at immigration) and shook my hand. He looked at me with a happy-sad look in his eye, and told me that it's hard to see me go. I smiled at him, though I was not that happy to leave him either. There was also one small moment in the departure lounge where I felt a tinge of anxiety, but I quickly distracted myself from it. Even as I was in the plane taking off, there was no pounding nor fidgeting of my heart. I felt as calm as when I ever travelled before. I don't know how Mathious was feeling, but I know that he was still just as excited as I was.

Our first stop was in Toronto, Canada.

We left the aircraft, Mathious and I, and we went through the normal procedures for visitors to Canada. As young people in an age of technology, the first thing we looked for in the airport wasn't our luggage; but the free Wi-Fi. While I got on with a certain level of ease, Mathious wasn't so fortunate. I wasn't too sure why his phone didn't get on at first; but it did eventually, and he was able to connect with his family. After baggage claim, my travel buddy immediately regretted having packed the two bags he had. Me? I left Barbados knowing that I'm going to the place where everything is made. Therefore, I thought myself clever to pack one suitcase (not only because I was too cheap to buy a second one).

From baggage claim to the money exchange; from the money exchange to the 7-eleven, to the taxi. I took the time and coins to re-familiarize myself with beef jerky. I got some shrimp flavoured chips too, but they weren't as tasty as I would have hoped. The thought of eating all manners of food when I arrive in China usually makes my mouth salivate with excitement. Mathious' diet, on the other paw, isn't as diverse as mine, as he is vegetarian. I found myself having to retract statements made with regards to food, because he wouldn't be able to appreciate the little comments I make regarding things like Teriyaki beef and seafood. After spending some cash, we left for the taxi.

The taxi ride home was as short as I had estimated, having been to Canada many times before. The price was around the same amount, and my cousin's place was just as neat as I had remembered. Though she had left the country for a European tour, (she was in Rome at the time of my arrival, gotta remember to let her know that all went well) she left her key with the landlady, and I had to call the landlady (here and after known as Amanda) to let her know when I got in. As prayed, all went smoothly, and we got to Amanda's house, and settled down —and by "settle down", I obviously mean get the Wi-Fi password from Amanda. After a few minutes of eating and drinking our spoil, the thought hit Mathious and me to thank the good Lord for our smooth journey. Like clockwork —or like other devout religions- we knelt on opposite sides of the bed and prayed together. My mother had put some credit on my phone, and hence called to 'set her heart at ease'. After catching up on our social media and families, I set my clock to alarm, and hit the ground for rest.

At 4:45 the next morning, I woke before my alarm —figures, and lay there on the ground (not that my cousin didn't have a bed, but we thought it best not to disturb anything) and let my thoughts run. When the phone finally alarmed at 5, I got up and called the taxi company. They had a 'cab' over there in 10 minutes. I, being quite impressed that I could get a taxi at that hour, emerged from my cousin's place, and put her key where Amanda and I had arranged (shhh! It's a secret). Further regret came upon Mathious when he tried to fit his overweight, oversized luggage into the cab car, and he had to sit in the back with one of his gargantuan bags upon his average sized lap. The Lester B. Pearson Int'l Airport is so large that the distance from arrivals and departures is $13 difference in taxi fare.

By the time we got to the airport, the sun was somewhat risen, and Mathious could get a good eyeful of this magnificent country which he had never seen before. For your friendly neighbourhood Grammar-Nazi, it was all second nature to me, not only as frequent traveller, but as a frequent traveller to Canada. To my great surprise, I spotted a Bajan lady who was just coming back from China. I knew her because I was the one who gave her *her* Chinese visa while I was working at the Chinese Embassy. I find it a remarkable act of Providence that I happened across her in the airport. My flight to Vancouver from Toronto was at 7:05 am, and I made my way to the check-in kiosk to sort out my boarding pass. Unfortunately, I was then told that I had to also print baggage tags, which weren't printing at the kiosk. This appeared to be the plight of many a traveller, and I ended up at the back of a line so long, that I thought that this flight would be made by a hair's breadth if I made it at all.

For you Christians reading this, trusting God isn't just something that you do when you're in a desperate situation. It isn't an app that you activate when you need it. Trusting God is something that you have about you all the days of your Christian walk. When you hear Christians saying "I started trusting God in this time or that time", it would mean that there was a point in time when they weren't trusting Him. From the time I put my soul in God's hands, everything else is trusted for by nature. Sure, sometimes it's "hard as neck[1]" to trust God, but in Him we must trust if we believe that He holds the whole world in His hands.

All the above was mentioned because I noticed that it was getting on to seven o'clock and Mathious and I were still in the line for our baggage tags. If we continued at this pace, we would be left here for sure. We finally got to the counter at 5 minutes to seven. I told my buddy that it would be highly unlikely that God would bring me from 2012 when I first heard about the Scholarship, to now and I miss my flight by 5 minutes. *Nonsense!* The passenger agent checked the system with great urgency, and told us with a sigh of relief that flight was actually *boarding* at seven, as opposed to leaving at seven. This gives us until 8 to get to the plane. I was not surprised, as I knew that something would have

---

1   …as neck: Bajan parlance, "as ever"

worked out for Mathious and me. We took some more videos to send to various persons, and even liaised with some of the other Barbadians studying in China to make way for us. Suddenly, there were loud cheers erupting from behind us. Turns out, the Canadian Olympic athletes were returning, and their fellow Canadians cheered them on heartily as they made their way through the airport. Quickly afterwards was security and soon, we were on the flight to Vancouver. When I got seated, I saw one of the athletes. He had the Olympics symbol tattooed on his left bicep, and fully decked in track gear. Of course, your friendly neighbourhood Grammar-Nazi asked him some questions, and took a selfie with him. We talked a bit about swimming, and then, seeing the tiredness in his face, I let him go back to his seat.

This time, Mathious was 20 rows in front of me on the plane, and I sat next to Kirth, who is an American-born Canadian national of Indian descent. *Get a load o' that!* He spoke with his relatives with an Indian dialect (I can't imagine the number of dialects in India) He speaks quite a few languages, therefore, and thus got my attention. I got his by telling him about Kunal. Did the conversation then extend to talking about the love of God? No. At the time of this paragraph, he was rolling his head about in sleep. Unable to bear seeing him like that, I snuck my hand across to his armrest, and pressed the button. I then used my elbow to ease his seat back, and noticed an immediate change in his comfort. His head no longer rolled about. As any traveller does when he has connecting flights, I sat in my seat and counted the hours to my various destinations. I left Toronto after 9 o'clock, and from where I sat, I had in mind that my flight to Beijing would be between 12 and 2. If my flight were at 12, and it takes 4 and a half hours to get to Vancouver, I did and re-did the calculations in my head when it hit me, the most fascinating thing that occurred to me all day. I looked at the screen in front of me and noticed that the time in Vancouver was 6:12 am when we had taken off. Vancouver, therefore is three hours behind Toronto. This, then makes it impossible to miss any connections, because I am literally going back in time to catch the next one. If at any time I felt like "Dr Who", that would have been it. I looked from my window and beheld the Purcell Mountains, south of Calgary. Travelling 3500 km/s is not as glorious as it sounds, but I pride myself in knowing that I travelled not only space, but time as well.

But, what does a budding linguist and aspiring polyglot like myself do to occupy 4.5 hours of his time? Well, there was small talk between the passengers around me (3 minutes tops), there're movies which I've taken the liberty of downloading. There was also one of my favourite television series: Fringe, but the ones that I had downloaded were too far ahead of that which I've seen. Certain characters were not even present anymore. I've read a few chapters of John Bunyan's *Pilgrim's Progress*, and it has proven to be most highlighting of the ebbs and flows of the Christian life.

In Vancouver, the time passed a lot quicker than I had anticipated, and in no time, I found myself standing in the line to enter flight AC 029 to Beijing, China. As Providence would have it, Mathious and I found it impossible to find someone willing to exchange with, in order to sit together. I wasn't expecting any success, though, as I figured that people are returning home, and are most likely travelling with family. After what seemed like 45 minutes on the flight, all the shades in my section were pulled down. It would seem that everyone was that tired from travelling, because half the people were sleeping after the first serving of light food. At hour four or thereabout, I went to look for Mathious, and we chatted for a bit. It wasn't hard to do, seeing as we two were the only persons of that darker persuasion on board.

One moment that I hope I will always remember was when I went to the bathroom. I was waiting outside the lavatory when I saw a man coming from the back with a flask of hot water. As he tried to cover it, some spilled on the floor for it was a full flask already. With a smile on my face, I said quite mildly "太多了" (it's too much). He nodded his head in agreement and responded in kind without looking up. After another step, he froze shockingly in his tracks. He shot me a glance so intense, that if his chi was any stronger, it would have knocked me out the rear end of the plane. I gave him a moment to come to grips with what was happening, smiling at him all the while.

The following conversation ensued in Chinese:

Him: oh wow! Your Chinese speech is really good.

Me: oh no no no. it's not that good (keeping with the cultural custom of politely refusing compliments)

Him: where did you study Chinese? Did you study Chinese in China?

Me: in my country of Barbados, at university.

Him: oh wow! Your Chinese is really very awesome.

Me: no no. It's not that good

Him: YES YES, it's that awesome!!!

Me: okay okay, thank you.

After he left, I stood there with Mathious talking about other random topics, and recounting the journey we've made thus far. Suddenly, the plane began to shake violently, and all who were standing froze in our tracks. The shaking was violent enough that things began to fall from their shelves. I grabbed the nearest handle, while still trying to keep the tray next to me from toppling over. It was the most violent turbulence I've felt in a long while. Looking back, it didn't last that long, but when it was happening, it certainly heightened my senses. It calmed for about three seconds, in which all the flight attendants started firmly urging us to our seats. Clapping and shouting orders, it felt like in the movies where time slows down and people hurriedly start to buckle themselves in. I rushed to my seat – which I was beginning to realise was a little farther than I had remembered- and sat myself down as the announcement was coming over the PA system to do so. After that little confidence boost from my fellow passenger, I sought out opportunities to speak to those seated next to me. It had occurred to me that I hadn't listened to any English music since the day before I left Barbados. Now that I had settled back into my seat, I pulled out my laptop and resumed my entry. I don't remember how it started, but I ended up in a half hour conversation with the ladies seated next to me. I don't know where the Chinese came from, but I'm sure that it helped in my attempts to converse with them. We spoke about Barbados, my studies and our families. Like most Chinese with whom I interact, the one to my right told me that my Chinese is very good, though I've only studied it for one year. It would appear to me that they would be thinking that Chinese is somehow hard. I don't know. I give credit to God, notwithstanding, for giving me utterance.

As we reached half way in our flight, some people came to mind, and I started thinking about them. Another set of turbulence hit the plane for about five seconds. There are people who I thought about a lot on this flight. Not because I miss them, but because I would like them to share in this journey of mine. There're some people that you just want to be with, regardless of locale. There are others however, who you specifically want to share in the particular experience happening at that moment, because you know that they would appreciate it greatly. There were, however, some people who I was looking forward to seeing in China. The other scholarship winners and I met at the embassy a couple of weeks before our flights for an introduction to China of sorts. Mathious and I were there. Christopher, Racquel and a few others sat and got to know a little about each other; where we were studying, what majors, and what about China we wanted to explore the most. Unfortunately, Jamar, one of the scholarship winners was not present at the meeting. Because of the time registration for his campus had started, he had to leave Barbados about a week or so early. I guess I would see him when I landed.

For the remainder of that flight, I chatted with the two Chinese ladies on either side of my seat. I went and spent a few minutes with Mathious, and during remaining hours, I slept and watched television. I sat in great anticipation of the flight's landing, and could see the city of Beijing from through my window.

When the plane landed, I thanked the Good Lord for getting me here so safely. It turns out that the flight was a lot shorter than I was led to believe. All that I had braced myself for was finally happening. The dream that I had had for so long was finally coming true. I looked out of my window for the first time since the landing, and noticed a blanket of grey covering the land. I knew what it was, and took my last breath of air before they opened the plane doors. I didn't even have to see when they opened them to know that they were opened, because the almost suffocating smell of the Beijing air filled the plane. For the first time, I encountered what air pollution smelled like. Coming from a Tropical island, the sudden, intrusive smell of metal was a strange one. Fortunately, it was not as bad as I braced myself for, but it still was not easily ignored. Mathious and I disembarked and found each other. He and I made our way to the immigration section and security, and were both amazed at the number of people that were there. I would like to think that I counted 700 people in this line at any given point in time. To recount the details of that long wait to the immigration officer would take too many paragraphs.

Next, I found Mrs Hao. She was one of the people working with me at the Embassy. I thank God for her, because of all the things that she has helped me with from the time they found us, up until the writing of this paragraph. She was already in Beijing by the time I had left Barbados, and was already informed by another colleague of ours when I would be arriving in China. When I came through the arrival hall, I scanned the crowd to see if they had already arrived. Sure enough, there they were. Leaning on the metal rail that separated the arrival area from Baggage claim. After some ecstatic greetings, Mrs. Hao, her husband and son took us from the airport. We first went to sort out my accommodation at the Beijing Language and Culture University, and then took Mathious and me to dinner. Mathious was to take a train from Beijing to Wuhan, but there were no more tickets available. We therefore took him to dinner with us, and when I went back to Campus, he left in the capable hands of Mrs Hao and her family. The way how God is working out everything is continuing to render me speechless.

Finally, I had landed. Finally, I had arrived. The country of my dreams became my new home. When I got to my room, I found my bed, a TV, AC and ample space for my belongings. I also had a roommate who wasn't in the room at the time. Whoever he is, he seemed to have been here for a while, because all of his things were already laid out and organised tidily. When I couldn't think that God would surprise me any further, right on the bed of my roommate lay... an opened Bible...in French! I smiled to myself and thought *I'm going to have such an adventure here.*

SO THIS CHAPTER ENDS, SO MY JOURNEY
BEGINS...

Now that I'm here...

THROUGHOUT THE TIME that I've taken to prepare for this trip, along with telling relatives and friends about my journey to this wondrous land of China, I have heard a lot of rumours and myths about China, none of which phased me. Though I've not allowed them to dissuade me, I kept them in the back of my mind. As I walked along the streets of Beijing, I mentally ticked off the various myths as true or false. For example, let's start with the obvious: **all Chinese people look the same**. This myth was laid to rest when I first started working at the Chinese Embassy. Whenever there were gatherings, I would be able to pick out the ones who I knew, from the others. Moreover, when I got here, I saw all manners of people. I saw short ones, tall ones, cute ones and those who are average looking.

The sky is always clouded with pollution: this one isn't always true. Here in Beijing, the sky is clear and blue, much like where I'm from. However, when the traffic starts to get thick, the grey blanket appears.

The more I walked, and the more of China I experienced, the more of these myths got laid to rest. Chinese people are not as "nasty" as the media has them out to be, and there aren't little orphan children at the side of the street begging for money; at least, not here in Beijing. On the other hand, most of the people I've seen so far look healthy and good. Some of the girls even look *too* good. Their faces seemed so pretty to me. I've taken the time to absorb as much of the culture as I can, and have even taken some pictures to send to those back in Barbados.

The first morning I was here, I dressed early and headed outside for a walk. I wanted to make sure that I get everything sorted out for school and registration. My roommate was kind enough to take me to Student Affairs and Accommodation, and there, I registered myself to my dormitory. I was told by Student Affairs that I would have to wait until all registration starts on August 31st to start registering for classes and such. Right now, I have to pay for registration because I'm not officially a student yet. Thank God, though that rent is only 50 RMB per day. I actually was told that it would be 60 RMB, so that's a small relief.

Akilah was one of 2014's Barbadian scholarship winners to China, and she was studying Environmental Engineering at the University of Science and Technology Beijing by the time I got there. When I was studying at the University of the West Indies in Barbados, Akilah and I took part in a Beginners' Mandarin course together. It was the dream of everyone in the class at the time to go to China, to further our studies. Her campus is about 20 minutes' walk from mine, and I planned to be over there often (one of the reasons being that her Wi-Fi works and I have to wait at least a week for mine to come on). I am glad to have her so close to me at this juncture, even though I thought that I would be good by myself. Though that is true to some extent, she was able to help me with understanding new vocabulary like when the cashier asks if I want a bag. She took me to various restaurants and shopping areas, and I must say that she has been a great help to me in settling in.

Akilah and I passed through a large area called Wudaokou (五道口), and in the first place we went in, I felt someone tap me on my shoulder. When I looked around, I could not believe my eyes! It was Jamar! He was the other scholarship winner from Barbados. He is the one who had to leave before the others because his courses started already. I smiled so brightly as he told me what he was doing, and what he was shopping for. He attends the Tsinghua University, which is also quite close to mine. I was also warned about his University by Akilah. She said that it is so big, that a bicycle is required to move around the Campus. Some other Universities have shuttles and buses for students to move around. Mine is quite huge too, but I think that only a bicycle would do for me. Hopefully, it would not be like the campus I'm accustomed to, where one class is on the east side, and the next class is on the hill. After looking around for a little while longer, we headed inside a mall called U-Centre for something to eat.

Now, food is the number one concern of Westerners when it comes to moving to China. Many a person make fun of the Chinese diet, and even more warn me about the rumours that they have heard from people who heard it from people who heard it from people. It's like that game called "Pass the message". It had reached the point where I got annoyed with people and their silly rumours, and it seemed as though, because they were scared of a little exotic food, that I should unpack all my bags and cancel my flight. Well, I'm glad to say that the only flight I'd be cancelling is the one back to Barbados next year, and I've already unpacked my suitcase.

Before I go on to how Akilah and I ate one afternoon, I must relay how I ate the night that I got here. From the time I was working in Barbados, I was told of Hot Pot 火锅. I believe that we in the Caribbean have something similar, but I believe that's called Pepper Pot. Allow me, therefore, to paint the succulent picture of the food that I ate one Wednesday night. In the centre of the table, there was the burner. The burner would be lit, and a 4-chamber pot was put on it. One had tomato sauce, one had mushroom broth, one vegetables, and one with plain or mushroom water. Then, the ingredients were laid out before us on the table. From seafood to beef, vegetables to mushrooms, there was all manner of ingredients there for the taking. Firstly, there was a bowl in which we had to make our own sauce/dip. I made mine with sesame sauce, spiced beef mini-chunks and chili peppers. The real fun happened back at the table. One would take the ingredients there and place them in the boiling waters, depending on your personal choice. When the water boils again, you'd know that the food was ready to put in your dip, then eaten. For example, the beef was red while on the plate. I would then take the little strips of beef and place them into the boiling water. When the water reaches its boiling point again, the beef would turn to that nice, cooked dark grey colour, and I would take it from the mushroom broth, and dip it into my bowl of sauce. I felt like the little Ratatouille with all the little fireworks popping above my head. I'd used beef, mushrooms, fish, shrimp, noodle, sticky tofu and various vegetables. I ate to my heart's content, and made it my priority to return to that restaurant chain whenever I had the chance (and the wherewithal, of course).

When I was with Akilah, the food wasn't as wondrous, as I went to an Italian restaurant called Saizeriya. The food here was fantastic as it was affordable. The service (as usual) was fantastic, the people were nice, and the efficiency was on point. So far, eating food in China is very cheap because nobody really cooks at home. People always buy food. Maybe it's just the hustle and bustle of city life. People just seem to grab a meal on the go. Maybe in other areas of China, there would be people who don't eat out as much, if at all. But there's also tonnes of food stuff available in the supermarket, in the event that one has that desire to cook. For the time being, I have some cereal, and I would be perhaps eating out until school starts, and the cafeteria opens. It cannot be overstated how cheap food is over here. Where I'm from, buying food on a daily basis is frowned upon, and seen as a waste of money. Here, it's preferred. Since then, also, I had the pleasure of meeting up with Hao Yun, the little girl who I used to tutor English while at the Embassy. She and her mother met me at my gate at school, but not before having the following experience. I was walking around the Campus, trying to get myself acquainted with the grounds, when I heard a voice with a familiar accent behind me. I turned around, and saw an older gentleman walking alongside a younger man. The accent was British, and he was doing all the talking. When he saw that I looked around, he smiled and greeted me.

Man: ...and how are you doing today?

Me: I'm doing well, thanks. Quite relieved to hear English, to be honest.

Man: Well, we're just about to go grab a coffee, would you like to come along with us?

Me: That would be fantastic.

As we walked to the coffee shop, we talked about language and culture. While in the coffee shop itself, we covered a range of topics, and it was the first intellectual conversation I've had with another person since I've here being in China. He and I spoke about the Olympics, Brexit, Trump and Clinton, the Caribbean, the Slave Trade, among other high-minded topics. While there, David (older guy) and Rishi (from Suriname) talked for about three hours. One could only imagine the time it took for all those topics to be discussed intelligently at length. Rishi was seemingly shy, as the conversation was mainly between David and myself. I discovered later that Rishi was leaving his country for the first time. This was his first time travelling, leaving Suriname, and obviously trying to cope with it all. David and I, on the other paw, are seasoned travellers, so the conversation was not as triangular as I would have liked, because I would've really liked to have heard things from Rishi's perspective.

After about three wondrous hours of pure, intellectual conversation, my phone notified me that Hao Yun was outside to meet me. I left the cafe and stood by my gate waiting for them. When they arrived, I was so very happy to have seen yet another one of the Chinese children I met in Barbados. Though Beijing is huge, it really shows that the world itself is still a small world. I am glad for the people that I met, and I appreciate all that they have done for me. Hao Yun, Ma Yan (her mother) and I went to the shopping centre, where we had some more hot pot, after brief deliberation of the many food choices. It was a different theme to the one I had first with Mrs Hao, but I still enjoyed myself. It was quite enjoyable eating with Hao Yun and her mother. After one and a half trays of beef strips, and more than half a tray of mutton, not to mention the various mushrooms and other fillings and sauces, I was full, much to the disappointment of Ma Yan, who kept on encouraging me to eat more. I couldn't imagine how much more she could expect me to eat. I was feeling stuffed, and Hao Yun still wanted ice cream. We went for ice cream, and Ma Yan invited me to her house to play with Hao Yun whenever I have time/ vacation from school. She tremendously appreciates the work I've done with her daughter while in Barbados, and I guess it's only natural that she would want the process to continue. I assured her that when I get my class schedule, I'll see what I can do. After the ice cream, they left and I went back to my school.

I find that now that I'm in the country of my target language, I am able to string together Chinese phrases and sentences much more readily. Talking to Ma Yan on Friday was a lot less taxing than when I was in Barbados, even though I have about the same amount of vocabulary. There were times when we used the phone to translate for us, but, by and large, conversation was uninhibited. I am very happy for that. I look forward to the day when Mandarin is the language of my everyday life, and I can move and operate in the language. After all, that is the reason why I'm up here.

I think I need to spend some time to let my body get adjusted to the food, climate and atmosphere here in Beijing. I find myself being able to go an entire day on only 6 hours of sleep, and sometimes fewer. I find also that my capacity for food is a lot less than when I was in Barbados, because I get full too quickly, and can go an entire day on one serving of food. Looking on the bright side, I take it as an opportunity to save money on food, and to maximise my time spent exploring the campus. I trust that the Lord will come through for me in this regard, and that soon, I will settle in as nicely bodily, as I did emotionally.

One thing, which, though I wouldn't consider it a culture shock, was still slightly traumatising was the toilet situation. Most of you would have heard that **China's toilets are a hole in the ground** over which you must squat in order to "do your business". So, being open minded and eager, I thought to myself *how hard could it be*, and I braced myself. Because I am writing this document to multiple persons, I will spare you all the details of that encounter. However, I was successful –though I showered immediately afterwards. For right now, if it is that I am in a situation where I cannot shower afterwards, I have hunted for and claimed a western toilet in one of the administration buildings not too far from my dormitory. Granted, it is one 'reserved' for disabled persons, and it's the only one in the bathroom, should I be out and about, I will use that one in the event that business need be done. Myth confirmed!

For the sake of the stomachs of those reading this document, I'll go back to David and Rishi. While in Wudaokou, I happened across David again in one of the shops. While managing to contain my excitement to see him, I listened intently as he spoke to me. He told me that he thinks it's best for Rishi to not spend "as much time with the old fogies", and encouraged me to be there for him, as there is only so much that he himself can do. While praying later that evening, the idea came to me that we may be in the same class for the preparatory Chinese lessons. If it is that he would need help with Chinese homework, I can work with him –or let me say that we can work together, so as to "take heed, lest I fall".

For the last time that day, I bumped into David and his wife. We exchanged greetings and smiles, along with the other gentleman that was with them. They remarked at how good it was that I spent more time outside the campus than in. The other gentleman remarked that I'm in the *Honeymoon* stage of foreign student life, in which, he said that the first month is all happiness and excitement; then, in the months that follow, agony and perhaps regret. Whether this sweeping generalisation will apply to me is yet to be known, so I will simply brace myself for whatever comes my way. I have trusted God for everything thus far, and know that He will come through for me, once I yield.

Finally, I got lost for the first time. I was on my way home from Akilah, and I made ONE…WRONG….TURN. I ended up so lost, that not even Akilah knew where I was. Good thing I was walking, and not on the bus. Luckily, her school is so large, that I was always able to keep it in view, even as I walked. It turned out that I was going the opposite direction to where I wanted to be going, and had to turn back. I ended up back in her university where she met me, and walked me to the correct gate from which to return home. I got home after midnight. I am thankful to God for allowing me this experience; not just getting lost and learning new roads, but the entire Chinese experience thus far.

They that wait upon the Lord shall renew their strength; they shall mount up with wings as eagles; they shall run, and not be weary; and they shall walk, and not faint.

–Isaiah 40:31 KJV

There were some people who, upon hearing that I was finally getting my dream come true of going to China, encouraged me greatly to make the most and the best of the experience. Since getting lost, I've shopped, went on bus and train rides and even climbed a mountain. Seeing as most of the people reading this would have taken a bus/train at some point in their life or another, I'll talk more about the mountain climbing experience.

Tian Yun Shan is the home of the famous Glass Bridge, and when Akilah told me that she was thinking of going, I jumped on the bandwagon, and told her to sign me up. On the day of the bus trip, all the participants met at my school, which apparently was a central location. I was quite grateful that it was just outside my gate that they were meeting. I however had to run back to my room to get my book, because I learned on the bus that the trip to the Glass Bridge was two hours long. I grabbed my book, and my tablet, and returned to the bus in time for it to move off. On the way, there were many sights to see. I caught a glimpse of the Bird's Nest, and other Olympic monuments and buildings used in the 2008 Olympics. The other buildings on the way were mostly offices with Chinese characters on the top, much like most other cities I've been to.

When we got to Tian Yun Shan, I raced up the steps, thinking foolishly that the Bridge was "just short dey"[2]. Boy was I surprised to learn that that was just

---

2 Bajan parlance: "just a little bit further away"

the first leg of the hike up the mountain. For the next two and a half hours, Akilah and I hiked, stepped, ran and climbed this incredible mountain of God. When I got to the top and saw how far I'd come, I smiled at the progress. The massive square from which we started was a mere dot in the distance and the only thing daunting about the whole thing was that I had now to climb back down. I lend credit now to my years spent as a cadet, which trained my mind to push past tiredness and brokenness. Akilah, on the other paw, wasn't thus blessed, and so she would say something like "I know I slowing you down, sorry". I did not mind all the time, because it is important to rest, even if you are not feeling tired yet. While climbing a mountain, it is important not to underestimate the importance of rest.

At long last, we reached the Glass Bridge, and paid the entrance fee. They gave us this pair of stocking-like things to put on our shoes, so as not to scratch the glass. There was a landing, where people sat; and there was the actual bridge which people crossed. This was the interesting part. I saw in people a senseless fear. I didn't know what people could be scared of, seeing as they would have spent at least ten minutes on the landing made of the same glass as the bridge. I saw little babies walking effortlessly with their parents, looking through the glass with delight as they walked. A small number of adults, on the other hand, were quite scared, and one was even crying as she held onto the railing for dear life. When my camera panned across to her, she let go of said railing to cover her face. I don't know which she was more scared of, the bridge, or my phone.

Speaking of which, I took the time to take some pictures and videos of my time on the glass bridge. I know that something like that is a once-in-lifetime opportunity, so I made the most of it. When we were coming back down, though I was quite tired, I saw some people participating in a traditional dance, and after watching for a minute, decided to join in the dance with them. The dance itself involved two people on either side of the dancer, stooping and holding the bamboo logs in their hands. So, there would be a log upon which the two bamboo logs were moved, and the two outside people would be holding the logs, and opening them and closing them to a rhythm. The job of the dancer in the middle was to hop and put his foot in the middle, and then take it out before the logs were brought back together to close the gap. Though I enjoyed myself a little, two things made me leave them: I was still very tired, and it was getting close to the meeting time for the bus. Seeing as we were going down a different route, we didn't know how long I would take, and so made our way down the other side of the mountain. Regrettably, there was nothing else exciting or interesting to grab my attention on the way down. We got to the parking lot early, and therefore had to wait on the bus.

When I reached campus, I thought that day was over. I was walking to my dorm when I espied David and his wife at the Hope Café where he took Rishi and myself the day before. My night was only just beginning. I went and sat with them. I "was blessed with more than I could ever ask or think" because David and his wife spoke with me that night, and we had beer, coffee and even waffles. His wife, Mareca treated me to some of her large sandwich, while David let me try some of his duck breast salad. His wife was very interested in the nitty-gritty facts about Barbados.

I delighted in telling her all about Barbados, and answering all her "nitty-gritty" questions. God has blessed me with the ability to paint pictures with my words; and so, four hours later, we were still in deep conversation. "What are the people like?" "What do the retired people do?" "What do the young people in Barbados like to do in their free time?" We spoke about everything: from food, to world history, to Archimedes Principle, to Cadets. I love the fact that they are both intelligent speakers, and that they complement each other's points and speech. They also, because of their knowledge base, make it easy, as I don't have to explain most of the concepts which I bring to the table. When the coffee shop was closing up, we left and I went back to my room to finally shower and get into bed. Barbados is flat. So flat and small that it is possible to see the ocean from almost anywhere on the island. Not many Barbadians can say they climbed a mountain. I'm glad I did.

He looks down on the earth and it shakes; He touches the mountains and they start to smoulder. I will sing to the Lord as long as I live; I will sing praise to my God as long as I exist!

– Psalm 104:32-33

REGISTRATION

When the trumpet of the Lord shall
sound, and time shall be no more,
And the morning breaks,
eternal, bright and fair;
When the saved of earth shall
gather over on the other shore,

And the roll is called up yonder, I'll be there.

James M. Black

On the afternoon of Monday, the 22nd of August, 2016 I was taken up in the clouds (1 Thessalonians 4:17). No, not in the rapture; on Air Canada flight #AC 1967 to Toronto. But, just like it is described in the Holy Scriptures, I could not just be caught up without having my name on the list. When you book a flight, you do so mainly in private, and your name is written in the Pilot's book of passengers. Just like salvation. You surrender your life to the Lord in private, in your heart. Your name is written down in the Book of Life, and very few people know about it. However, when it comes time for the roll to be called, all who are on the same trip as you are *~caught up together in the clouds~*.

When I arrived at my destination (Beijing Language and Culture University) there was a roll with names on it. Like any University, the names which were on this roll are only those who have enrolled. So, before registration day, I lay in rest in my dormitory, and awaited the proverbial trump to sound. When the day of registration had fully come, I left and was escorted to the Administration building. *~After these things, I looked and saw a multitude no man could number from every nation, tribe and tongue.~* I stood there, and heard people calling out in various languages, and students hustling and bumping about to get themselves, and their documents sorted out; joining various lines and filling out various forms. *~Many books were opened~*.

At every station, there was one document which I had to present, and that was my admission notice. As its name suggests, it is the document which shows that I had applied in private to the University, and had been accepted. In short, I registered at all the various stations which Scholarship Students had to go, and got all the necessary materials. It was a long and tedious process, which required an eye for detail, and a godly amount of patience. When done, however, I sought to help out those who were not getting through as quickly as I was. Among those new pals I met were Sarvarjon Khayitov from Uzbekistan, Walter Fergusson from the Bahamas, Rishi Kesharie and Kishal Hindori from Suriname and Rudolfs Oto Selga from Latvia. When the Chinese call this place the "mini United Nations", there can be no doubt what they mean.

When I was finished with the registration process, I joined the Association for International Understanding. With the other members, we scheduled shopping trips for our dorms, organised activities for new students; and took some pictures. One of the other students and I went to stick signs on the road, pointing the way to various important locations on campus, such as the gym, library and administration building. The climax of my time in Beijing so far happened on the day after registration.

Thursday morning, on the first day of September, I got up at 4:30am, and started walking about the corridors. I noticed that there was a nice, dark red cloud which hovered above Beijing, long before the sunrise. As China is 12 hours ahead of Barbados, I took the time to talk to some of the people that I left in Barbados. I showered at 6, and headed over to Rudolfs' dorm. From there, we spent the rest of the day together. We had breakfast, toured the campus; and I even showed him where the one Western toilet is that I know. We chatted, and got to know more about each other, and each other's countries. I took him to activate his Bank Visa Debit card after breakfast, when Rishi joined us in the bank. During the afternoon, Rudolfs and I were walking outside, when we saw a man selling and repairing bicycles. We had asked for the price, and found it so unbelievable, that we started converting the currency over and over in our heads to make sure that we weren't being tricked. The price was so good, that we bought the bikes immediately, and started riding around the campus. We rode for the remainder of the evening. I still smile to myself whenever I think of the joy that was had between us that day. It was just seeming too good to be true. So good, that we got Rishi to buy a bike too. He didn't seem as excited to have one as Rudolfs and I, but we were still happy for him. We know that the campus seemed tremendously huge at first, and bikes would be as great an investment as it was a convenience. We were walking Rishi's new bike back to our dorms. We were going to go to Happiness Mart (yep, that's the real name. I didn't make that up), but something caught my eye. The Muslim Restaurant. Needless to say I suggested that we put Happiness on the back burner and try the Muslim food. I had the Tree Ear mushroom with shredded roast meat, and Cong Hua bread. The remainder of the evening was enjoyed with drinks and friendship.

Looking back, this journey so far has been a tremendous experience. In an impromptu interview I had with the Association of International Understanding, I told them that it seems that every day, there's something new and exciting to be learned and experienced about BLCU, Beijing, and China on a whole. When it's not the food, it's the shopping; when it's not the shopping, it's the new and friendly people that you come across. When it was not the people, it was the amazing fact that one day soon, every person on this campus will be united by the Chinese Language. Sarvarjon and I can hardly communicate now, and my roommate and I don't talk at all; but there's coming a day when Chinese unifies us, and will enable us to clear that language barrier that so easily gets in our way. I saw a girl reading the Chinese version of Lord of the Rings. I was wearing my replica of the Ring, and showed her. The look on her face was that of pure glee. Though we couldn't communicate, the only thing I regret about that encounter was that I didn't get her number. But I am sure that we will meet again.

My new bike is coming in very handy, as it is a great convenience to travel around the campus. I had to buy a bell for it, because, as you can imagine, there are so many people on the road at school, and half of them are riding bikes and scooters –with the occasional car. I said aloud that I have to thank God for my new bike. As I knelt on the pavement, Rudolfs got slightly confused as to why I would need to thank God for something that I bought. *Ah, young grasshoppah! You know not of the Providence of God! You shall soon learn.* God has me in his life –well, let me say that God has us in each other's lives, because had not for Rudolfs, I would have never bought the bike. Look how God is going to use this simple bicycle to bring Salvation to a young man. Ya gotta love God, eh?

From here, we will close off registration, have orientations, tours, shopping trips, and the placement test.

I look forward to seeing (and documenting) what God will do in the coming months.

BLESSINGS!

And so, it starts

AT THE POINT of me writing this paragraph, it is the day before classes start. It has been a long and confusing process which has led many a student frantic. To put the entire circumstance in order chronologically would take up as much time as it would to write this entire document (however long it might be). Therefore, I have decided to just come up with a title that was short, and somewhat tickling: leaving the reader begging for more. The title brings with it some expectations of an ordeal in which much stress was had, many people were confused, and much hair pulled. Needless to say, all of the above happened each day of this registration process, all of which adds up to your typical university experience.

One student was pulling out her hair because she hadn't got her scholarship stipend as yet. From the way she was acting, it would seem as though her house was on fire, and she needed the money to call the magician, who'd then cast something like a Flameo Reverso or some other ridiculous spell on it before it was totally razed to the ground. She was really looking like a sheep without a shepherd, and I encouraged the friend that was by her to give her some of the water he was having, because she was really making a scene.

Only because I mentioned it in the previous post will I expound upon it now, but I really don't wish to recall the horror of the placement test. As its name suggests, the placement test is one which indicates to the school which class a particular student is to be placed. For one who has done some Chinese language before, they would place that person in a class suitable for their particular language proficiency. That way, one who only knows how to count, would not be placed in the class with someone who can speak about renewable energy. The placement test is divided into two: the oral, and the written. The oral test was in the morning, and it was fairly okay. The teachers were all nice, and encouraged conversation, and a comfortable environment –not too intimidating. When I came out, the other students commented and compared, and it turns out that when you respond to their initial question, the proficiency with which you answer will influence the level at which they ask you the next question/task. That way, hardly any of us got the same questions.

The written test, on the other paw, was the horror. I would not be surprised if I get placed in the baby class, learning numbers because of that test. The first section was all right. The speakers played scenarios, and we had to choose which of the 4 sentences fit the question given. About fifty questions later, I was ready to surrender. I had to keep remembering that it wasn't a test, merely a sieve to see which student belonged where, so I needn't worry about not being able to answer the ninety questions which followed question number fifty. For those of you still scratching your heads, know that each section got more arduous than the one before. We went from simple multiple-choice questions to paragraph long documents about which we needed to answer questions. I left and went outside, still eager to know into which class I would find myself.

MY FIRST CLASS

On the morning of the 7th September, I was to have my first class, and my schedule for the semester. I was told to get to the notice board for 8 o'clock, and so at 7:45 am, I found myself in front of the notice board looking for my name and classroom. When I found it (Room 407) I came in and sat down. I was the only person in the classroom, because I was still rather early for the 8:30am start. While there, a girl walked in. She greeted me and said that she was the only one in her classroom. Well, being a charmer, I invited her inside to have a seat until she has more people in her classroom. Her hair was in braids, and her skin was dark brown like mine, so I asked her from where she hailed. She's an Antiguan. When I said that I was from Kazakhstan –kidding, Barbados we both rejoiced at having found another Caribbean colleague. As we chatted a bit more, and as time went by, a friend from Bangladesh came in and greeted me. It took me a while to place what he was saying to me, but I soon got it the gist of what he was trying to tell me.

Soon, class had started. There were about 12 of us, and the majority of us had some semblance of Chinese proficiency. From the way in which my classmates were talking to the lecturer, I would rather count myself as the least of these. The teacher came in and began the roll call. He then started introducing the semester to us in detail. He spoke to us only in Chinese, and this proved rather difficult for me to understand. To make matters more interesting, the other students in the class were asking questions and answering him in Chinese as well, and I was looking around for someone else who was as lost as I. Humility is key for me in this classroom, for I feel now that I have been placed in a very large pond with large fishes.

After the first hour, we had a 5-minute break, in which the teacher spoke with the students who chose to stay inside. He asked me again for my name, and then asked about my country. As I am the only one from Barbados on campus, I expect many similar reactions to his. He asked about its climate, and I told him that every day was hot. I also expressed that I hadn't been understanding all that was said in the classroom, so he took out a book. After appraising my oral Chinese skills, he inquired about my character reading. Opening the text book at random, he pointed at a sentence and asked me to read it. I read about 8 out of 10 characters successfully, and this was satisfactory enough for him.

On the other hand, the teacher had expressed to us the things that are not satisfactory for class. Class is from around 8 o'clock to noon; 1:30 pm to 3:00 and 7 pm – 8:30 pm on Tuesdays and Thursdays. The last class from 7 pm are in addition to the other two allotted times, making it 34 hours of class per week. Lateness, therefore is not encouraged. Being late a certain number of times results in various penalties, depending on the severity of lateness, and the number of times late. Being late for three classes is equivalent to one full day of absence. Even being late by 15 minutes is frowned upon, and has penalties –though obviously not as severe as being an hour late. Conversely, there are awards at the end of the semester for earliness and activeness in class. Out of a possible 100 points:

☑   *10% - homework*

☑   *10% - attendance*

☑   *10% - class performance*

☑   *30% - three monthly tests*

☑   *40% - final test*

I'm sure that I would be completely lost, were it not for the PowerPoint Presentation which was mostly in English. In fact, I got most of the above information from reading it. I kept thinking, and asking myself if I truly was in the correct classroom; but I kept in mind that my name was on the roll call, and this was the class which was next to my name. This must be the right class. When that class was over, the teacher said that there was no more class for the remainder of the day – which I found rather strange. All my friends had classes after that, and mine was the only one which didn't. I asked, and asked. I even sent a text to the teacher for clarification. He said that there was no class in the afternoon for that day, and that we begin again the next day at 8:30 am. Even as

I wrote this paragraph, I kept thinking and wondering about it.

When I had stepped outside of the classroom, I saw a familiar face, and began telling him about the class I just had. According to one of the comments made by one of my classmates, some of the people in my class are so proficient because they failed the year before. While speaking to this unnamed acquaintance, he asked me how many hours I have a week in class. I told him, and he said that he's going to be absent at least 20 times in this semester. This nonchalant comment placed me in bewilderment, as I searched my mind for a possible reason why anyone would waste so much valuable class time. It was only much later in the year that I found out that some students were skipping classes because they were out at clubs the night before, making money. After coming back to their dorms in the wee hours of the morning, they would then be too tired to make their 8:30 classes.

As for those who are doing over their preliminary year, I don't see how they could have failed, seeing as everything is so geared for passing. Though the pass mark is 60%, it is not impossible to achieve, especially as there is not that much emphasis on the final test. If I work hard during the semester, I would be able to do well, even if I mess up on the exam day. I was virtually horrified to see that some of them seemed to be care-free about failing, and others had attitudes towards school work which left a great deal to be desired. I guess that is university life everywhere for you, but my attitude has to be different, as being here is what I want, and this is what I have been given. I will not let down myself, or the God who brought me here.

Back in my room, my roommate found it strange that he came in and found me. So began another one of our attempted conversations. It's always a headache whenever we try to communicate, and this time he was trying to express to me that I wasn't in the right class (same thought I was having all day, thanks) and I was trying to tell him that the teacher said I was okay to stay there. At the end of most of our conversations, I leave feeling that he never really understood what I was telling him. He was also trying to tell me something about the AC, but the only things I understood were "sick", "cold" and "temperature". I long for the day when we will be able to understand each other better, it would prove a great convenience.

When I think of the situation in which I find myself, and I think of my roommate being here, and from Africa (The Congo), I can't help but bring to mind a letter that I saw, written in 1712 by a man named Willie Lynch. The letter was intelligently written, and was entitled "the Makings of a Slave". This is one of those –what I like to call "armpit topics", because they're hairy, ticklish topics that most people like to avoid touching. In Lynch's letter to his fellow slave owners, he purported that you must separate slaves from similar backgrounds and tribes. He goes on to say. *"Crossbreeding completed, for further severance from their original beginning, WE MUST COMPLETELY ANNIHILATE THE MOTHER TONGUE of both the new nigger and the new mule, and institute a new language that involves the new life's work of both.*" (Lynch). I'll be honest here and say that I found it difficult to read more of Lynch's letter, due to its graphic and accurate description of how black people were treated. What hurts more, is that most of what I read is still being played out in what I see in a lot of black people today; especially since Lynch predicted that after using these methods, the black populace would love the white people, and would be their slaves for 300 years at the very least. I'll give the reader a moment to add 1712+300…if you're as sad as I am, you'd want me to go on to the point of this paragraph as much as I would like to get there, myself.

He (my roommate) and I fit the perfect bill when it comes to the separation of black people, and the annihilation of mother tongues in the 18th century: he can't speak his dialect to me, and I can't speak English (or Bajan) to him. What's fortunate though, is that I see my roommate studying the Bible daily, and praying regularly and unashamèdly. I will assert here that I believe my roommate is a believer in Christ, the Risen Lord; and that, language barrier or not, we are united in the Blood of the Lamb of God in a way that is more solid than any other connection that I have elsewhere. Our forefathers may have been enslaved, but he and I have been set free by the liberty that Christ brings through His Death and Resurrection. We may not be able to understand each other in this world, but I look forward to understanding him perfectly in the New Earth to come. Good! I managed to end this paragraph on a positive and hopeful note.

BIG ROCK HOMEWORK

There is no need for any explanation of the above topic, as it relates to the first set of classes, I've had thus far at BLCU. After a bit of uneasy sleep, I rose early in the morning to learn the lesson that those extra dumplings with the spicy sauce was not as good an idea as I had previously thought. As the Bajans would say, "wuh sweeten goat mout"[3]. My classes were to start at 8:30 like the day before; but this was the real thing now. That other session was just an introduction to the course, and the outline. We started the class on time, and I was slightly surprised to see a different teacher to the one on the schedule. She came in and introduced herself. Ms Cheng came in and began talking at the same speed as the previous teacher we had, Mr Zhao. However, this time, I found that my brain adjusted quicker, and I was able to grasp what she was saying; as well as reply with a certain level of accuracy. I remember the words of my Spanish

---

3   "wuh sweeten goat mout' does burn 'e tail" = Things that appear nice at first can have dire
    consequences.

teacher, when he said that sometimes you hardly notice that your brain has made the switch from one language to the other. While in Panamá, a young woman told me that I shouldn't think about the language, but think in the language. That way, one wouldn't have to stop to translate into English, but speak and think solely in the target language. That being said, I didn't notice when it happened, but it happened. I was able to string together, and understand most of what the teachers [and some students] were saying.

Mrs Cheng came in to us, and we did a review of the characters, and their various types. This was very insightful, as by it, I was able to understand more of the structure of the characters, and how they are written. I found that when I look at them closely, I see the relationships described by the teacher, and thus was able to succeed in the exercise given.

After a small break, we had Mr Zhao again for Comprehensive Chinese. This time, we used the books that we were supposed to be given. Thank God for the Scholarship, because all my books are free. *I shall care them well.* The book is called CHINESE IN TEN DAYS, and I really would like to be speaking like a native in ten days 'fuh tru'[4]. There's really no encapsulating my enthusiasm into words. I am grateful to God for bringing me here, and for the love and passion for language that He's given me.

Commit your works to the Lord; and your plans will be established. The one who deals wisely in a matter will find success, and blessed is the one who trusts in the Lord.

– Proverbs 16:3, 20

Now, more to the point of this section. After my third class for the day, I double checked that there was no evening class, and headed to Rudolfs' room, where I completed my homework. It took a while to do, and it also took a toll on my wrist, as I had to concentrate on the strokes' length, precision and order. After writing my first hundred and fifty characters, I took a small break, and then got on to the paragraphs of characters which was for the second section of the homework. I still have much to practice, and so will get to that as soon as is possible. Up next, I should have more class, and the opening ceremony to look forward to.

---

4 seriously

The opening ceremony wasn't as spectacular as I would have expected. I find this surprising, as Chinese are known (at least in the West) for overdoing it at opening ceremonies. It was merely an orientation into which the new students were roped. It involved a rundown of the rules on class attendance and punctuality, and shared experiences from previous students graduated last year. I paid very close attention to everything that was being said, as my teacher had told my classmates and I –very few of which came- that the orientation was very important, and had a lot of useful information which we could all use. Given the level of participation and attitude of most of my classmates, it was not surprising at all that very few of us came. I, two Bangladeshis (maybe three), an Indonesian and a Southern Sudanese came, if memory serves me correctly. There were many other students from the other classes, so I could have miscounted; but when the register for each class was called, there could be no mistaking that many of my classmates were absent. After the orientation, two former students got up and were positioned to answer any questions which we may have had. One of them got slightly derailed when a guy from my class raised his hand after giggling with his chums and asked if she was seeing anyone. It was at that point that I was very disappointed in not only him, but my fellow men. It was amazing to me how one could go out of their way just to make corrupt the pure motives of others. [Yes, this shows, for the second time, that not all the students are there to study.] I would not blame the poor girl if she had since classed all men as thirsty dogs with no respect for women; not to mention time and place. *C'mon man!*

FIRST SHOPPING EXPERIENCE

Since that orientation, it was the weekend and I had decided to go shopping for clothes with Akilah. I thank the Lord often for her because she has been nothing but helpful to me since I got here. We have been talking about China for years, and it is good that we two are here now. She took me on a series of train rides, and we arrived at this clothing market opposite Beijing Zoo. For those of you readers expecting to read of me riding on a lion's back or dragged along gracefully on a two-seater watercraft by six swans, that's in the upcoming document. No, I didn't go to the zoo, nor did I get to see anything close to it. We headed straight for the clothing market.

From the moment I stepped off the escalator, my eyes lit up as the first thing I saw were suits. The first thing to come to my head was the fact that the Ambassador of Barbados to China had invited all the Barbadians studying in China to attend a dinner reception for the 50th Anniversary of Barbados' Independence. I figured what the hey, and went up to the store and started looking around. I say store, but I really mean cramped cubicle, reminiscent of those typical of markets. The shops were all completely stuffed with clothes, and with no room to store the extras, boxes lined the floor. So cramped were these stores, that one could find oneself tripping over a box, or even having to sit on one to try on shoes. The lady came to me and started putting jackets on me. She then tried the shirts on my back and shoulders and snatched two neckties from the rack to add to them. Before I knew what was happening, I was walking out of there with a full suit. She gave me a great deal. She gave me the shirt, and two ties together for a reduced price. I think she also took off some more from the jacket, but I can't be too sure. I know for a fact, that it was the most affordable suit I ever bought, or even saw the price for. For those of you thinking in US Dollars, I spent a grand total of US$82.50. That's BBD $165.00. I was very happy for my new suit. However, as that was still 550 元, I was still quite concerned about my budget; and Akilah and I finished off the shopping experience looking for a dress for her for the same event.

Having emerged from the clothing market, we got ourselves some Japanese food, and headed back to our campuses. On the hour-long bus ride, there was this guy who was always texting Akilah, in whom she had no interest. I therefore took the phone and sent him messages for her, describing the fun she was having with me, so as to 'scare him off', but he was very persistent. His level of thirst was too high, and he kept texting her ad nauseum.

Just before my stop, I heard a familiar sound. It was the sound of a tune that I first heard many years ago. Before I could catch myself, I was speaking Spanish to myself as this sound grew more and more familiar. When I looked around, I saw a guy bopping his head to the sounds of Daddy Yankee's *Ella Me Levantó*. I leaned forward and peered through the crowd to make eye contact with the guy; and as many of you readers would have guessed, a Spanish conversation struck up. He's a Venezuelan student, studying Finance at Master's level. After further talk about our countries, he mentioned that he knew a Barbadian studying here, and mentioned the name of one of Akilah's friends from her campus. *It's a small world after all.*

The next few days, I'd be honest, were the toughest I'd had in Beijing since school started. When I first started the class, as I had mentioned before, there was a certain level of lostness which I felt, to the point where I went and asked the teacher if I were placed in the correct class for my proficiency. Even though the teacher had assured me that I was in the right place, I still went ahead feeling quite down and discouraged. I appealed to the Lord to ease my nerves, and to calm me. I was not understanding the majority of what my lecturers were saying, I was not remembering the characters, and their stroke order; and when I *did* remember them, I wrote them too slowly. In one class, the teacher gave us a test to see our writing speed. Out of a class of 12, I placed 11th, with a recorded time of 10 characters a minute. I wasn't very pleased with myself, and I thought that I should be doing a lot better. So worried was I, that I spoke to the teacher again, this time regarding the marks for class performance. I was concerned that if this kept up, my marks for class performance would leave a great deal to be desired. The level of shame I would feel should I have to repeat this year would be immense, as the University has serious consequences for persons who do not pass the CSC (China Scholarship Council) Examinations at the end of the year. Upon asking the teacher, he (Mr Zhao) assured me that one: I have nothing to worry about; my Chinese is good enough, and will continue to get better as the weeks' progress; and two: the marks for class performance have everything to do with one's attitude in class and work ethic, and nothing to do with the marks I get in little exercises given. *That's a relief!*

As is His custom, God began sending people to me who all were telling me things which were particularly encouraging, even though I didn't share with many people what I was feeling. The teacher who gave us the test for speed (Mrs. Cheng) was also, unbeknownst to us, testing for accuracy of character writing, and stroke order. She gave us back our results one morning, after scrutinising our mistakes **heavily**. For the paragraph which we had to write about our family, she wrote a number of sentences on the chalkboard which were all incorrect. I was wondering if this was just another exercise, until the Nepali guy in front of me put his hand on his mouth, looked back at me and said "that second sentence is mine". Then, I discovered that the twenty odd sentences on the board were the mistakes that others made in the paragraph we were to write (which really felt like an essay). I searched the board, and noticed with a sigh of relief that none of the sentences were mine, which I interpreted to mean that I made no grammatical mistakes grave enough to warrant public humiliation. Just then, the projector whirred to life, and the screen came down with, to my great surprise, the marks of everyone in the class.

However, instead of the names of the persons in the class, there were numbers. Judging from the number of people who are called before me for roll call on mornings, I estimated that my position was between 6th and 10th. Out of those 5 slots, there were two zeros. I knew that I couldn't be that bad, that I would get a zero, but I wasn't too sure either. I waited for the teacher to hand out the assignments. When she got to my desk, I put my hands over my face and she smiled brightly at me. She placed my work on my desk, turned to the class and said "Stefan's characters are very beautiful" in Chinese. I could not believe my ears. *This woman setting me up ta get beat!* I thought to myself. And if my ears were deceiving me, I turned the page to see the same words written in red ink on the bottom of the page. I looked higher up, and saw the mark I got for that test: 95%. My eyes began to well with water as I realised that all that worrying wasn't necessary. The teacher then went to the front of the class and began scolding the other guys for boasting of their ability, yet not performing when the time came to 'put pen to paper', as it were. After just praising my work, and scolding that of others I thought to myself, *this woman really want me get beat fuh tru'*.

After class, I was to report to the east gate of the campus for the school's bus to take us to the hospital. Those whose medical examinations were taken more than 6 months ago were to report there to get them checked. The doctors at the hospital would perform the various tests, and will confirm the results. They shall then send the results back to my school for my scholarship requirements. The process took a matter of minutes, and was quite fun. I guess it was fun to me because I'd never experienced a hospital in that way before. There was a lot of rooms, and every room had a different kind of doctor. You'd go into the one for sight, for example, and he would take a scan of the barcode linked to your name, test your eyes; and then place his stamp on the form next to his room number. Then, you'd go out, and head to the next room. Knowing that I wouldn't be able to make the next class, I sent a message to the teacher, letting him know about the hospital situation. He responded, and put the homework in the group chat that we have for the class. However, it had to be a lot of homework, because the next two days were the Thursday and Friday of the Mid-Autumn festival 中秋快乐.

CHARACTERS ASIDE

While on the bus to the hospital, I overheard two students in the seat behind me talking about their experience thus far learning Chinese. The only thing I heard before plugging my ears was when the Pakistani said "I hate Chinese characters." Now, I understand that they are difficult to write, and slightly more difficult to read. The characters; however, are the very essence of the Chinese language, and the language is the very essence of the Chinese culture, which, in turn, is the very essence of the Chinese people. It is very unlike English, in that the language and the culture are inseparable. Any language that has been around for as many millennia as Chinese, and in the same place, will have welded itself to the people, culture and customs of those who speak it. Then, for anyone learning it now, 4500 years later, will have to embrace said culture in order to get a clearer grasp of the language, and how the Chinese operate. For example, it is so culturally inappropriate to ask an older person their age, that it is actually taught as being grammatically incorrect. This is due to the tremendous respect that the Chinese place on the elderly. Without an understanding of this, one would just ask someone their age, without giving respect. Therefore, it is grammatically incorrect because it is culturally incorrect.

Mrs. Cheng in class explained to us the uses and difference between "others" and "the other". One of the sentences (mentioned earlier) that she was correcting gave the haughty impression that the writer was looking down on everyone else, when he was just talking about another person. There are characters which look extremely similar to other characters; and to mix them up would prove catastrophic to any sentence. You readers may have to take a closer look, or perhaps zoom in, but I shall put an example here of three characters which look similar. Firstly, there's 我 (wǒ). This is the character for I/me. It has what looks like a line in the middle, connecting two other lines together: one straight, and one like a merging lane on the highway.

The other one is 找 (zhǎo). This one has the same right side as the first, but the left side is different, and the line connecting them is broken. This is the word for look/find.

The last one (that I know about so far) is 钱. This is the character for money/change. Similar to the first two, but with an added line. The left side is also different, as it carries the radical for metal, telling the reader that the nature of the character he's reading has something to do with metal: in this case, coins. Therefore, it is quite possible, given the meaning of these three characters here, to have them all in the same sentence, and make perfect sense: 我找钱给你。(I find change give you) Well, not exactly "perfect" sense, but you'd get the hang of it.

What I also like about Chinese is that there is so much that you can express in such few words, much unlike English, which has many (seemingly useless) ways to say the same thing. It can be argued that English would be able to survive with 25% of the words removed from its lexicon. Whereas English words look nothing like what they mean, Chinese, at least Mandarin, has characters which explain certain and specific ideas; and when another similar idea need be expressed, simply take a modifying character from somewhere else, and stick it on to make a new word. People would already know the two characters independently, and wouldn't have to bother learning a whole new word (like my status if you just burst out in the Aladdin song). For example, the word for "hand" in Chinese is 手. It is written to resemble a hand (neat, huh). The word for machine is 机, and this can be used for most machines, coffee machine 咖啡机, printer 打印机, airplane 飞机, photocopier 复印机, etc. So, when you put the characters for hand and machine together, you get the Chinese word for that machine that's always in your hand –cell phone 手机. So, for a language learner like myself, it's easy at times to even guess how to say something by combining parts and characters to describe what you want to express.

One example of this was when I was working in the Chinese Embassy back in Barbados. One of my colleagues had asked me to call Mr Zhu. Now, the thing about that was that there were two men there by that name, so I asked in Chinese if they meant the Counsellor or the food+cook+man. At that time, I was like a blind batsman swinging in the dark, trying to guess the Chinese word for chef. Granted it was nowhere close to the word for chef, the person to whom I was speaking understood me to be describing the one who prepares the food, and saw nothing wrong with my sentence.

More on radicals, I took the liberty of explaining to a colleague at the Embassy why it is that certain English words are the way they were, when asked about words of water. My meaning is thus: when people were speaking English, the land in which they lived didn't have certain things, and only when the language moved to places which had those things, did English pick up certain words. However, in Chinese, the radicals indicate the nature of the word. So, the word for water is 水, and when a character has something to do with water, the radical was changed to the three dots（氵）on the left side of certain characters like 海边 (beach) 游泳 (swim) 江 (river), etc. Most, if not all characters to do with water have the character for water in it（氵）and every word in English to do with water, as even seen from the above examples, have no indication whatsoever from their spelling or pronunciation, and anyone learning English would have to know the words. You'd either know, or you don't know, and if you don't know, you'd be as lost as a polar bear in the woods.

Enough of my rambling. I've just looked down and noticed that I wrote almost half the average thesis. I have not even been here a month yet, and have done more than people who have been here for much longer. I conclude by saying that I am grateful to God for allowing me this opportunity to write to you people who take the time (or even have the time) to read these somewhat lengthy documentaries. I'm thinking about compiling them and publishing one long document, maybe of my first year in Beijing. Until then, I'll keep your interest piqued. Up next, we have the mid-autumn celebrations with the Liu family, and my first outing with a Chinese girl. That should keep your eyes peeled.

TILL THEN, KEEP HOLY!

Getting in the swing of things

"As a hawk flieth not high with one wing, even so a man reacheth not excellence with one tongue."

– Roger Ascham

ENTER MYSTERY GIRL

WHEN I WAS studying Chinese in a beginners' course in my final year of university, my classmates and I were curious as to the Social Media used in China, seeing as Facebook and most Google-centric applications/sites are blocked. The lecturer directed us to **QQ International**. This app was like WhatsApp, Skype; Facebook all in one. I immediately joined, and heavily encouraged the others in my class to do so with me. Unlike Facebook and the others, it is possible to just look for random friends from a description, and build a friendship from there. One of the ways I would make friends, is that I would enter the details of the kind of group I would be interested in joining. Once accepted, I would start speaking in the group about myself and my country. As it is strange for them to hear someone of my…persuasion, who hadn't come from Africa or America, people took an interest and messaged me privately. We would then get to chatting, and build the friendship. It was in this wise that I met someone named "Bunny from China". We were in the same group of friends, and like many others, she sent me a private message. Luckily, I had some pictures of Barbados' beaches saved on file, so that I could send them when the curiosity arose about my country. I would also use Rihanna as a reference, and would sometimes add that she went to school with me for extra points.

Over the next two years, Bunny and I chatted often; and for long periods.

Unfortunately, because of the time difference, I would always be going to sleep in the middle of her day, and vice versa. As the computer at work left a great deal to be desired, I would not be able most of the time to freely access QQi, and so, our conversation dwindled slightly. However, whenever I would log back onto QQi, I could rest assured that those who treasured my conversation the most would be there to greet me, namely she and a few others. When it was coming time for me to travel to China, I notified all the QQ friends I had close contact with (or *with whom* I had close contact) and I told them when I was coming. As Providence would have it, Bunny lived the closest to BLCU, and she was my age. The others varied in distance and years younger than I; therefore, of all the meet-up plans I would have thought of, hers was the most convenient.

The trip to Bunny's hometown was quite fast and convenient, yet I had to pay close attention to the numbers and destinations of the various trains and gates in order not to miss any of my trains or transfers. Firstly, I had to walk to Wudaokou Station by 6 am. I took the Xizhimen bound railway to the subway station. I then took the subway train to the intercity train station where I took the intercity train from Beijing South to Langfang. *That was probably the most concise description of any trip, as it was over an hour in total.* As the train came to a stop, I got a text message telling me to follow the people. It was Bunny giving me directions to where she would be, and where I should meet her. As I was walking, I saw the light coming from the exit, and I was getting my passport and ticket ready, when I heard a squeal of delight coming from the door: it was her, and she was jumping and waving and shouting my Chinese name.

After an exchange of greeting, I tried to loosen myself up, and converse with the young lass. I see why she would choose to call herself "Bunny" as she was hopping and skipping with excitement after having finally met me. We both expressed that this is the first time that we've met someone in person who we met online. I was also quite relieved that this wasn't all a very well planned prank. We talked and laughed for a bit as we exited the train station, and she escorted me outside. When outside, she announced "我的车！" which means "my car!" When we got to the corner and turned, she pointed me to a little scooter parked on the side of the building. The scooter was patterned in pink camouflage and had a little basket to the front. We both laughed hysterically, as she unlocked it. We embarked and I sat at the back as she zoomed merrily from the train station to a place where we had breakfast. I say "merrily" because she burst out in song on many occasion, and was bopping her head from side to side. As we rode, she would describe her hometown as we were passing, and would sometimes ask me some questions in Chinese.

What I immediately noticed about Langfang was that there were hardly any English writings or signs anywhere. Bunny said that it's because it is not as international as Beijing which would be more welcoming to foreigners. As

Langfang isn't as welcoming to foreigners as Beijing, one would well imagine the number of foreigners there. The other thing I noticed was that I was the only person of my…persuasion there. For those of you who have read my JOURNEY TO URBANA report, you would have seen me use my coined term 'solo-negro syndrome' which is the discomfort one feels when one is the only person of African descent in any given place. I thank the Lord that this does not happen to me, because I was most likely the only person there that was black. The people there certainly were not accustomed, because they started staring and giving more than one glance at me. Some took pictures, even. The children to me were the most fascinating. They sometimes would stand and stare for a while before going to their parents to draw me to their attention. On the road it was funnier. Other people riding on scooters drifted into the road as they looked over their shoulders at me. I would smile and wave like the His Excellency that I am, and they would smile back. Bunny told me that she felt like a superstar by my side, because they looked at her after having examined me. It is as if they wondered 'what manner of creature is this?' and 'what crazy person brought him here?'

At breakfast, we had boiled egg in soy sauce, deep-fried breadsticks, and warm soy milk. This to me was a very strange combination, but I enjoyed it nonetheless. From then, she took me to her former university, where she let me ride her scooter. There, we lay on the grass and talked about our countries. There were no clouds; instead, there was a translucent sheet of grey over the atmosphere from the pollution. That, however, didn't stop us from having a fantastic time there, walking and talking. We zoomed to the shopping centre, where we did some shopping, and had some fruit. Lunch was the most enjoyable, as she promised me the best restaurant she knows. From the sights and smells of the food, I could understand why it was her favourite too. What makes it even more enjoyable was that even though there was more food than the table could hold, the bill came to less than BDS $40.00. We had dumplings (two portions), she had a seafood platter with mushrooms, I had a mushroom platter with roast pork and clear noodles, and we still had another platter to share between us. I find myself getting into the hang of using chopsticks with my food, though I haven't totally forgotten how to use a fork.

While I was with Bunny, my phone had rung. In the mall, I checked to see who it was that called me. To my delight, it was Mr Liu who worked with me at the Embassy. He was inviting me to dinner with his relatives, and those of his wife. When I told Bunny of this, it was still mid-afternoon, and she happily changed the time of my ticket so I could meet them. *She's so nice!* We spent the remainder of that afternoon riding around on her scooter, singing and laughing. Afterwards, she took me merrily back to the train station, where I had about 4 minutes to check in and get in line for the train.

The train station was filled with people. *Obviously. It is China!* However, there was not a sound to be heard. Coming from a country where the conversation betwixt two souls could be heard for miles, being in a quiet yet crowded place seemed really strange. There was no shouting; but everyone stood in a perfectly straight line behind their number, and waited quietly for the train to arrive. On my ticket was the number 6, so when the train came, I would stand in the #6 line, and get into that particular car. I followed suit, and lined up behind everybody else, got in, and we left.

DINNER WITH THE LIUS

When I got back to campus, I barely had enough time to put down my bag before the phone rang. It was Mr Liu. He was outside and ready to take me to meet his family at a traditional Chinese restaurant in the WanLiu shopping centre. We arrived at this very large shopping complex, the top floor of which was the restaurant. I pretty much enjoyed myself there too because of the food and the company. At the table were Mr Liu and his wife and son, his wife's cousin and his sister. I believe there would have been more people, but I think they couldn't make it. Since I had plenty food for lunch that same day, I decided that the next day would be fruits at the very most, especially after eating a good set of food with the Liu's. After dinner, they dropped me off at home, and gave me a very large box of moon cakes. Moon cakes are the traditional gifts to give to family and friends at this Mid-Autumn time. I thanked them very much, and thanked the Lord for having them in my life.

"The Lord has been good to me these last few weeks." Saying that would maybe give someone the impression that the goodness of God to a person is conditional, or that sometimes He's good, and sometimes He isn't. Honestly, there is no way to rightly say what I would like. The Lord has been good to me in showing me the way to Salvation through His Word. Even today, I was singing the song "I Know Whom I Believèd". I was thinking that He is good, regardless of whether I'm experiencing wondrous things, or dying from cholera. What is a more accurate thing to say in this instance is that God is good. He has seen it fit during this time to allow me to enjoy good things and lovely blessings that, while good and lovely, are miniscule and infinitesimal compared to the *~blessings all mine with ten thousand besides.~* The passage of Scripture which I have been using as a reference as of late comes from the book of Proverbs, chapter 26. It says, "Commit your works to the Lord and your plans will be established." (vs. 3) I am glad that the Lord has brought me here, given me a place to stay, food, clothes, an education; not to mention medical insurance and money, all at no charge to me. He has also given me intangible blessings like friendship.

One of my favourite things about Jesus which I read in the Scriptures was that He chose the twelve to be with Him, first of all; then to send them forth and preach. He only sent them to preach when He was ascending [Mark 3:14; Acts 1:2]. The lesson I take from this Example was that Jesus, the Incarnate Son of God [John 3:16], the Living Word [John 1:14], the Bread of Life [John 6:35], the Creator of all the lives and breathes…needed friends. It's almost humbling to conceive. Think of it. He only sent the disciples out when he was taken up into the clouds, which means that as long as you are on this earth, literally, you are going to need friends. Jesus needed them, He chose them well, and He didn't discriminate against their background, but used whatever they had for their own betterment and His Kingdom's furtherance.

> "I know not how the Spirit moves,
> convincing men of sin, revealing Jesus
> through the Word, creating faith within."
>
> – D.W. Whittle

SWINGS GO BACK AND FORTH…LIKE ME THIS MONTH.

More along the lines of 'getting in the swing of things', I have been keeping abreast of my homework. I am accustomed to the stresses of living in BLCU in terms of the long lines, the administrative mishaps, just to name a few. It's tough enough studying Chinese –arguably the world's toughest language to learn- without the worrying thoughts of whether your visa will be granted or not. One example. I was given my scholarship money for the first month on August 30th. This amount is to last me for the month of September. Therefore, I budgeted for that amount, and that number of days. Meanwhile, I had to get the visa organised as well. When I was first registering, they told me that once I had got my medical examination done in my country, I was good to go. What they didn't tell me was that it had to be done within the last six months. This seemed to be quite the set-up, because, in order to get the scholarship, I had to get the medical done before March of this year, for that was the deadline. Therefore, I did mine in February. Seeing as they waited till mid-September to start the visa application process, my medical examination records were long expired. I therefore had to go to the hospital to get it done over. This I had to pay a few hundred RMB for. Then I had to wait for the medical records to come back from the hospital to go apply for the visa (residence permit). All this time, it is getting closer and closer to the expiration date of my visa. The first time I went to the visa office, I waited 2 and a half hours to be told that I was missing a paper with a stamp which I never heard about, and walked to the other end of the school to retrieve it, to find out the hard way that it was closed. This time however, I only stayed in the line for 2 hours. When I got there, I had to pay another couple hundred dollars for the application process. This doesn't include the hundred + dollars which I had to pay to stay on campus when I landed (because school hadn't started yet). All the while, I'm buying food because to cook would cost a couple hundred dollars more, because I would have to buy the appliances and the pots, pans and all the ingredients myself.

When I was finished with all the administrative hassle (hopefully, I'm done now and there's nothing more I have to do that I wasn't told about) I was so tight on funds that I had to use some of the emergency money that I left Barbados with and change it into RMB so that I wouldn't starve. I still had to buy notebooks, stationery, Wi-Fi and drinking water. I had even cut my daily expenditure by 40%, because I had calculated that I would spend only half my allowance, but because of all these charges, only a small amount was left. I thank the Lord, however, that I have friends like Savarjon (Uzbekistan) who gives me snacks whenever he sees me, and Dave (UK) who always invites me for a coffee, which often turns into a full dinner. Trusting in the Lord is becoming a habit of mine. There's rarely a chance I have to not trust in Him. Daily, I pray and tell Him that there's nothing I can do. I tell Him that I have no choice but to trust Him, because everything is over my head.

HERE'S TO QUARTER CENTURY: A CHANGE IN MIND SET

Now, the thing that used to always bother me about being born in September, especially in Primary School, was that my birthday would always come just in the beginning of the term when we were getting into the swing of things. In the days when one used to get 'birthday lashes', a more suitable birthday would have been during the summer holidays. However, this was my place, and so I thank God for every birthday I've had so far. Funny enough, one Sunday,in Barbados it was my birthday, and as I was climbing the steps to the church building, I stopped in my tracks and thought to myself these birthdays coming a little too quickly. That was my fourteenth birthday. Almost another fourteen birthdays later, I have long since given up worrying about the pace at which my future was coming to me. After all, everyone was getting the same 60 seconds/min, and it was better to think about what I could do in that time, than to worry about how much time I have left as a child, adolescent, young adult, etc. Even when it came to studying, I had to leave my old attitude behind, and trudge on in the academic life. When we're young, we like to sit down and plan out our lives, and say things like "I want to finish university by age 22" and "I want to be married by 25, and get my house and car and kids and doctorate and picket fence…" and we go down this fantasy road, where everything goes according to plan, and there are no mishaps. Then, life happens. You have to repeat a year at school or you fail a major requirement. Maybe you break an arm or fracture a wrist, or something that sets you back a short year or two. Those are just the minor setbacks. The big ones are those that come and hit the hardest: a change in study, a natural disaster, chronic illness, a heartbreak, a death in the family, getting laid off; or even eviction. These things, the adults fail to warn us about, while we're growing up, because I guess they don't want to crush our dreams. I am the kind of person that would not attempt a thing if it looks like I would fail it. If I pass someone attempting something, I would watch; but I wouldn't attempt it if that person looks more capable than me or the task seems beyond my ability. If the odds are in my favour, as in if the task looks like I would get it in two or three tries, then perhaps I would be more optimistic.

Maybe it is for this reason that I wasn't told much about life, because I wouldn't want to go on. The aforementioned setbacks that get into the plans of any random individual were too discouraging to take on life. At least, that was the discouraging thought I had as a child. Anyhow, enough of that…

The mind set on academics is the one which I had to overcome and change in order to be where I am today. As many of my readers would know, I have already got my first degree in Linguistics with Spanish. In Barbados, the next question is always "are you going to get a Master's?" Granted, none of the people who have Masters have asked me this question, because they know how difficult it is to study for one, and they know that jobs which would cater to that high an education are really hard to come by. There seems to be a kind of trap where the young are kindly pressured into getting tertiary education, while all those without get all the jobs. Three to five years later, the educated ones emerge from University with Bachelors and Masters, and head to the working world. They are then told things like "you're overqualified for this position" or "we can't afford to pay you for the degree that you have". You may be even as lucky as me and be told "you're too intelligent for the job, and it would be an insult for me to give you BDS $4,500.00 a month". Meanwhile, all the people who didn't pursue tertiary education are the ones working, the ones with money, and most importantly, the ones with the working experience. Poor me went and studied, rather than worked, and after University, I had no working experience, to go to a world where you needed experience to get work; yet needing work to get the experience. The mind set from all this is that education is that which prepares you for life. So, someone would get educated so that they would be able to readily face the world. Therefore, the more education you have, the more ready you are to face it. I will leave it up to your very capable minds to figure out if this mind set is problematic or not, based on the information given above. My mind set changed when I realised that I couldn't do the Masters in International Relations that I wanted. Amid all the different views and voices out there, I heard one or two speak differently from the above mind set. Therefore, I thought that education does not prepare you for life, education is life.

While I was in the process of readjusting to my new mind set, I had written a friend of mine, telling her of my ordeal. I will put a snippet of the email here:

I had wanted to do a Master's Degree in Chinese Language, but there was no such offer at any University. Any University that offered a Master's degree required HSK 5 or higher to apply. Seeing as I would be able to scrape a HSK 2 if I really apply myself with all the knowledge I have acquired, it would be literally impossible for me to attempt a Master's Degree in the field that I would be able to do. Even if I tried to do a Master's in Applied Linguistics, my research proposal and references all point to Chinese Language. Seeing as I already handed in the remaining application materials, I will have to do another Bachelor's but in Chinese language.

*Disappointed? Nah. I am doing what I want to do (learn Chinese) and I am going where I want to go (China). Above all else, Annie, my colleague reminded me that this is free. I am being paid for to go where I want and study what I want. Do I care that it is another Bachelor's? Yes, slightly. I actually went online and asked Google what was so wrong with having two Bachelors. I was growing really gloomy and depressed. I began to question, and hold my head in dismay. But God used my colleague to remind me that this is free and the Lord God uses whomsoever with whatsoever. I'm reminded that Moses was used by God, and his education came in handy with leading the people. The apostle Paul was able to share the Gospel on his way to prison because he spoke in the dialect of the people. This to me, J***, is God's plan in action. Everything that has happened from the day I took Spanish at CXC till now (I could go back even further) has been used by God's interpenetrating hand for the accomplishment of His work.*

Now on to the actual birthday. Yea, I noticed that it was quite abrupt, but I was doing a lot of rambling. The day started like any other day, and I had actually forgotten that it was coming up. Everything happened just like any other day. However, I came into the classroom in the morning class, and when the teacher put my paper on my desk, it was the results from the last exercise we had done, and on it was written "Happy Birthday" in Chinese, along with some other encouraging words. In the listening class, the teacher asked us as an exercise when we arrived in Beijing. He then told us quickly when he arrived in Beijing (quickly to test our listening) and I noticed he said he was born in 九月 which means September. The following Chinese discourse ensued:

Me: You're born in September? Me too!!!

Teacher: I'm the 10th, when are you?

Me: I'm TODAY!

Teacher: TODAY???

Me: Yes, today. I'm 25 today!!!

*Teacher: Ah, congratulations, Stefan. *to the other students* Today is Stefan's birthday. Which means you all can relax, and he will answer the next set of questions for you. Okay?*

Students: AGREED!!!

After lunch was the much-dreaded test that everyone was preparing for. When I came into the classroom, I was taken completely aback to see that someone had written happy birthday to me across the entire surface of the chalkboard. It stood there for the rest of the night, even during the exam. I was very happy to see it written.

The test itself was simple enough, much to the relief of many a worried student. It comprised some multiple choice, some character testing where we had to put characters in the correct order to make a grammatically correct sentence; and an essay of sorts. I say "of sorts" because it was supposed to be 60 words or more. However, your friendly neighbourhood Stefan interpreted the question to ask for 60 characters, as opposed to words, which, isn't exactly the same thing. For example, I can say 牛, which means "cow", or I can say 自行车, which means bike. So, you can imagine my horror when I heard my mark, and that it was 86%, especially when I have been averaging 90+ in the little class tests to come in a big one, and score in the 80s bracket. When I had inquired as to the reason behind my mark, the teacher explained to me that marks were taken off for writing fewer words than required. It hurt my poor heart to calculate the score I would have got, had I written just about 2 or 3 more lines in my paragraph.

Looking at the paragraph itself, all of my characters were written well, and, unlike those of one of my classmates, only one of my characters had a red mark in it, while his had as much red ink as black.

This was to give you readers a glimpse into the student life in Asia. As I'm sure I now have a long way to go, I'll be sure to bring you guys along with me. As they say in China, "the journey of a thousand miles starts with a single step", and one of the many steps I had to take when I got here was finding out where I can fellowship; and that… is another paragraph.

"I started out to win this race, to serve the Lord and to look upon His face. But the way's been long and the road's been rough, but there's one thing for sure– I've got my mind made up."

– The McKameys (1984)

"PART DE CHRISTIANS IS?"[5]

When I was at the Urbana Student Missions Conference in St. Louis, Missouri in December 2015, I went to all the seminars which dealt with China and Chinese culture, and Chinese Christians. I learned a lot, and made a few contacts. One of the contacts which I will mention is Dr Kevin Xiyi Yao. He did a seminar on 'Sharing the Gospel in a Confucian Context', and it was after his presentation that I managed to snatch one of his business cards that I may email him as soon as I got the chance. He gave me some tips on living in Beijing as a Christian, and was able to direct me to a Christian fellowship. When I got here, I began to tip-toe around the question, and really wasn't expecting to join any fellowship in the first year of BLCU. I would have wanted to get my Chinese Preparatory Studies out of the way before I think about joining Chinese Christians. However, when I was on my way from Wudaokou Station after my day out with Bunny, behold, I espied two people sitting on a bench by the bus stop reading a strange looking book. I knew that there are only two books on earth whose pages are divided into two columns: Bibles and dictionaries. When

5 Bajan parlance: where are the Christians?

I stopped them and inquired about the book they were reading, we ended up in a nice conversation, albeit choppy due to language barriers. I, though grateful for their words and telephone number, somehow knew that I may not see them again. However, when I relayed the experience to someone else –a friend of mine, actually- she directed me to the Beijing International Christian Fellowship (BICF). This branch of the fellowship was actually just outside the North Gate of my campus, and would only be 5 minutes ride from my dormitory. So close was it, that I decided to finish all my homework on Saturday, and spend all my Sunday with the church folk the next day.

One Sunday morning, I got up and got ready. From the onset, I felt as though I was supposed to go to church that day, and that the Lord was making ways for me to go there. First off, I had set my alarm for 6:45 am the night before. When I got up that Sunday, I noticed that it was 6:43 am. When I went to then turn off the alarm, I noticed that I didn't set it to alarm for the weekend. It was still set to alarm only on weekdays; but it was as though I was awakened just before it was to alarm to show who really is responsible for waking me up on mornings. *[yes]* In Barbados, we sometimes say "I want to thank God for waking me up this morning" so we can get out of actually thinking about something to give God thanks for. That day, however, I was reminded that God has total control over every aspect of my life, because I have bowed and yielded it to Him. I am His, and he could do whatever He likes with me. It would be a scary thought to those who don't know God, but to the Believer, to have God in control is a comfort. God showed me His Fatherly side that day by waking me up at the time I had personally wanted to get up. I am glad, though I cannot relay the extent of my gladness here, and must therefore get back to my story of getting to church.

When I got to the conference centre in which the service was to be held, I was dismayed to see a wedding – of all things, going on in the conference centre. I showed the picture of the church schedule to a random guy, and he pointed to the building next door, and said something in Chinese to me. I followed his directions and went up the stairs to the room where the church was moved to. As it turns out, the government allows the church to meet there in the conference centre, but if there's something "more important" that happens on a Sunday, the church session will be moved to a "back-burner location" (my words) and the greater event will take pre-eminence. I attended the Mandarin service, and I was very glad to be there. There really is a grand feeling that one gets when one is in a community of believers *~from every nation, tribe and tongue~*. During the Mandarin service, I was playing catch up with the Chinese Characters on the screen. I had to look up the character, so I could find out which book of the bible it was in English, so I could find it to read along on my tablet. They asked for the new comers to stand and introduce themselves. When I did that, I felt warm inside. I've introduced myself in Chinese before, that wasn't the issue.

What made me feel extra good was that I was introducing myself in Chinese…to Chinese Christians. That's something you don't see every day.

During the song service, I was fortunate to have the Pinyin underneath the characters on the screen, so I could sing along. I, however could not hold back the tears when they started singing "Oceans" in Chinese. It was like Urbana '15 all over again. The entire service was in all Chinese, but I could pick out a few words to know that the sermon was theologically solid. He preached on God giving each man according to their deeds, and encouraged those in the Lord to good works. When it came to the English service, I figured that there was some sort of common theme, as the sermon there was focused on the good works of the Christian. I was very glad for the preaching. It was good to be in a place where I could nod in agreement with what is being said on the platform. Though I do not intend to burden that church with the weight of me jumping onto their bandwagon, there shall come a time in the near future when I may lend my talents there. There is always something going on with BICF, and the ministries there are ever-bubbling with enthusiasm and participation from all in attendance. There even was a seminar held after church for all those new international students, and families in the congregation are signing up to host students in their homes for dinner. I look forward to seeing what the Good Lord has in store for me in that Church.

"I don't know about tomorrow, it may
bring me poverty; but the One who
feeds the sparrow is the One who
stands by me.
And the path that is my portion
May be through the flame or flood;
But His presence goes before me;
And I'm covered with His blood. Many
things about tomorrow I don't seem
to understand; but I know who hold
tomorrow, and I know who holds my
hand."

- Alison Krauss

I never would have thought...

CHAPTER 6

"Pure and undefiled religion before God the Father is this: to care for orphans and widows in their misfortune and to keep oneself unstained by the world."

- James 1:27

THE APOSTLE JAMES describes this religion as being pure and undefiled. He makes no allusion to jumping, lifting hands or speaking in tongues, but kindness and compassion to those who are most afflicted. In fact, this verse comes directly after the one about bridling one's tongue. However, that is not the focus of either James' discourse, or mine. I draw your attention to the verb phrase immediately after the colon: "to care for orphans and widows in their misfortune". Unfortunately, this has been something which I have never done in all my years of professing Christianity. I regret to say that I had never visited an orphanage. Widows, I have visited, but as much as I claim to love children, I had never been to see any of them. I would talk to other Christians about it, and they all agreed that one day we should go to an orphanage; while others just brushed off the idea as too much commitment, and never went. Others still thought that I was taking the Bible too seriously, while they themselves claim to be Christian. This is one thing that I didn't want to continue. I wanted that when I stood before God on the last day that I would be able to answer Him, should He ask if I was just a theoretical Christian (just knowing the facts) or a practical one (doing the Word, rather than just hearing).

Therefore, it was with great delight that I scrolled through the group chat of a certain set of people and espied the words "Orphanage visit", and I stopped scrolling. The Christians at BICF were planning a visit to the Living Tree Orphanage, and any interested persons were invited to come along. Of course, Stefan Lorde, being anxious to fulfil the Scripture in James 1, grabbed the opportunity to find out all about this visit, and to sign up as quickly as possible. Even though the visit was the day after I found out about it, I decided to put all feelings of tiredness aside, and head to bed early.

The meeting place for the visitors was quite a fair distance from my campus, and so I had to leave at 5 am. It was not a problem for me, as I tend to be quite determined when it comes to getting somewhere on time. I took a few trains to get to the meeting point, which was a KFC outside the train station from which I disembarked. I got there at 6:30 am, because I didn't know how long it would take me to get there; and so, I felt it better to get there early -as early as possible.

After half an hour of singing on the pavement, the KFC finally opened, and I went in and got myself a coffee and a little breakfast sandwich. When my watched said 7:26am, I went outside to meet up with Deborah Trefzger (the woman we were to meet at 7:30). Debbie, as she preferred to be called was a very passionate and energetic woman. I don't want to use the word *old* to describe her, but a Bajan would say *she ain't two mornings*. God saw it fit to take her voice twelve years ago, and so I have to lean very close to her in order to hear her speak. She is a member of the BICF I went to once before, and she had been visiting the orphanages once a month for the last five years. When we got onto the bus, we got to talking; and it seemed as though she drew my life story out of me. There are some things which you would not usually share with the average person. However, when asked, there are certain questions which you cannot answer honestly without sharing that one story which you wish never happened. She asked about my family background, and I ended up sharing about my parents' divorce. We all have those skeletons in our closets which we wish never existed, but she had such a warm and loving countenance, that I felt completely free –compelled even, to share those otherwise hidden details of my short life. When she spoke, she spoke as one having much experience in Christian living. I nodded in agreement at most of the things she said, and others really took me back to some of the experiences I have had with God. She spoke about prayer, specifically praying according to the Word. She gave the example of a man she knew who admitted to taking long amounts of time to focus on prayer, until he started praying according to Scripture. Should a verse say something like "love is patient, love is kind", this man in question would not only acknowledge God as such, but pray that God make him to be patient and kind to others.

As she spoke, my mind raced back to when such a habit had been revealed to me a while back. Hearing my story, she was very touched, and told me that it seems that I have been through a great deal. She also called me humble (and I must admit that I had difficulty accepting that description. I think, therefore, that the humble one doesn't proclaim himself humble, but allows others to exalt you) and said that it seemed also that God had use for me in Barbados before allowing me to come to China. While I was telling my story, there were some points that really amazed me. Looking back, God has really done some things in my life which have shaped me into the person I am today. When the Bible says that He works all things into my good, for His purposes, we need not take it lightly. Sometimes we can spend our entire lives never knowing the purpose behind certain occurrences which happened to us, but we need to thank and trust that God knows what He's doing in our lives, and submit to Him.

While along the way to the orphanage, Debbie started talking to me about the children there, as well as a brief history of how the orphanage came to be. As it happens, the owners of the orphanage are two unmarried Christian Chinese women. It was always emphasised that they were unmarried, and I never bothered my heart to ask or even wonder why it was that they never married, or why it was always mentioned. Next topic of discussion was the children specifically. There was something very special about the children that I will release later in the document, but knowing that about them really prepared me for what I was about to see.

We got off the city bus, just opposite to the community in which the foster home was. It was approaching ten o'clock, and Debbie and I, along with the others crossed the road. While outside, she briefed us again, and prayed. When I got to the door and saw the first kid, two things happened to me. Initially, I felt a wave of sadness and heart-brokenness at what I saw which felt knock my spirit back a little. Immediately after that, I felt as though my spirit hit something on its way back, like a wall. So, it felt like what I saw knocked me back, but also, as though something strong was supporting me.

After coming to grips with the spiritual battle going on, I stepped inside and immediately fell silent. All the preparing in the world could not prepare me for this: all the children suffer from cerebral palsy. Debbie had told me about their condition before. While we were on the bus, she had mentioned it as a sort of 'warning' to prepare me for what was to come. I could put the words together and figure out what the condition entailed somewhat, but I had never encountered it before. I certainly had never seen anyone with the disease before. Seeing the first few children as I entered, watching them lie there, knowing that they were incapable of moving normally, was heart-wrenching. Sobering also was the fact that there was nothing in the universe that made me different from them. There was nothing I could do to have prevented myself from having the same condition.

It was indescribable. I never would have thought that my first orphanage visit would be this traumatic. I don't think that I have ever interacted with a child with palsy before. All my previous thoughts and expectations of running around and laughing with little kiddies in the orphanage went up in smoke as I looked upon every child. None of them could stand, far less run around with me. There were about 20 children there at the foster home, two of which were in wheelchairs. They were also the only two that could speak. One of the two spoke as if his mouth had water in it. I was told that the children who are worse affected are upstairs, so I steeled myself and ventured up to see them. The noise of the grunts and howls of these children met me as I ascended, and I braced myself for what I was about to see.

As I ascended the stairs, one child grabbed my attention. He was being held by a volunteer, and looked like he was about 6 years old. I sat there and spoke with her as she held him. She then offered to put him in my lap, and I acquiesced. When she put him in my arms, he immediately tensed up and started to arch himself into a 'C' form…backwards. His head seemed to automatically bend over backwards, and his scrawny legs seemed to bend back to touch his head. As I held him in my arms, this unnatural movement squeezed my knees together and I was beginning to feel helpless because I did not know what was happening, nor did I know what to do. He never made a sound, but his tongue stuck out and his hands and arms clasped firmly at his sides. I placed my hand on his hard chest and felt his ribcage protrude as he arched his small frame backwards in my lap. As my heart raced, the volunteer took him from me, and I gladly obliged. "You're being too soft on him," she said. With that, she took him from me and firmly positioned him on her lap. "This one is stubborn," she said, "and he senses that someone strange is in the room." This was not obvious, because, though his eyes were open, they seemed rather oblivious to his surroundings. The most shocking thing about him was his age…he was 11.

He called a child, had him stand among them, and said, "I tell you the truth, unless you turn around and become like little children, you will never enter the kingdom of heaven! Whoever then humbles himself like this little child is the greatest in the kingdom of heaven. And whoever welcomes a child like this in my name welcomes me.

– Matthew 18:1-5

The next child that I saw was more unable to move than the previous. He couldn't move anything above his waist. I was sitting next to a child across the room from him whose breathing reminded me of some of the mythical creatures which I have seen on television in my youth. Though he was wide awake, his breathing with inhibited by large amounts of mucus, and he sounded as though he was snoring with a huge cold. His frame was also very small, so I didn't assume his age; and his skeleton seemed grossly deformed. His big, bulging eyes seemed to search the room, though he appeared to know that I was there. After spending some time with him, I looked over and saw two of the girls who came with me singing to a child in a crib. One of them remarked that he smiled at them singing, and I went over to have a look when they moved.

This last child was a boy also. I made my way over to him, and his eyes locked into mine immediately. Like the others, his frame was overly small, to the point where the bones in his legs were about the circumference of the average curling iron. He looked up at me and smiled. His small, fragile body lay snuggly in the crib in which he was placed. His countenance warmed my heart as he tried desperately to control his own body.

I took my hand, and held it close to his. A simple gesture which I believed would be reciprocated. He started to bubble with some emotion that I could only interpret as excitement. He started writhing and wriggling in his crib, spitting and grunting all the while. His little hand started waving back and forth as if he were trying to swat a fly or something. I was completely taken aback, and I didn't know what to do. I foolishly thought that he would take my hand if he wanted to – I guess I was still conditioned to think of him as "normal", and had yet to change my thinking. After a few seconds of holding my hand there and trying to understand what he was doing, the thought hit me to just grab his hand and see what would happen. I did, and what happened next amazed me.

When I took the little boy's hand, he stopped grunting and wriggling, and grinned all his teeth at me. *Was he…smiling?* I never would have thought that all I had to do was to take his hand in mine. I was at a loss as to whether he wanted to hold my hand or just to move it. Now I knew. I felt his tiny grip on my fingers as I rubbed my thumb along the back of his hand. He calmed completely down and gazed up at me. I took out my phone to take a picture with him, and his eyes followed it. *Seems as if these are just like any other kids - fussy over cell phones.* We took a few pictures and I asked one of the people that came with me to take a picture of him and me. She obliged, and I took the time to rub the back of his hand against my face. *Surely, he's never felt [a] beard like mine before.* When I did, he grinned and started to get really excited. I moved it, and he waved my hand around for a bit before pushing for me to touch my face again. I laughed and smiled all over myself as this process repeated about 4 times. I learned from this that he *was indeed* trying to move, but his brain isn't able to control his body like mine is.

I said goodbye to him, and turned to leave the room when I saw the girl who was holding my phone. Her face was dripping with tears as she was watching the two of us interact. I could not for the life of me understand why she was looking so sad, when I and the little child were so happy. Anyhow, I left her there, and went outside with the others. There, we rolled the children who were in wheelchairs outside, and formed a circle with the other persons who came to visit, to introduce ourselves, and talk about Jesus. We sang a few songs, played a few instruments, and chatted a long while. While the others remained outside chatting, I snuck back inside to pay my friends another visit. I went and said goodbye to them individually to each of them before leaving the building for good.

As we walked away from the building and the community, I reflected on what I learned that day. I got first-hand exposure to what cerebral palsy looks like, and how it limits the life of a child. I remain ever grateful to God for the childhood with which I was blessed, and I thank God for all the little children that are being taken care of by those at the foster home. In China, it is said that some parents, when they realise that something is "wrong" with their child, they put them in a garbage bag, and toss them in the trash. Sometimes, it is only because the Providence of God allowed for one or two garbage collectors to see the bag moving strangely, that some of these children are saved and brought to foster homes like Living Tree. Even on the bus back to the train station, I sat in thought, as my body ached with the thought of having a child with cerebral palsy. My thoughts also went to the mercy of God towards children with brain disorders, retardation, early childhood deaths, and stillborn babies. I never would have thought that palsy could be so devastating; I never would have thought that God would use children like these to teach people like me how He truly operates. I never would have thought that my day would turn out like this… [I would have liked to see you do more with the 'spiritual battle' part of the story. What else did you think/feel while you were at the orphanage and was there any kind of debriefing on the ride back? I think you started something really interesting and then just left it. Maybe we'll get back to it later, but I'm left wanting some closure in this chapter.]

"…When did we see you sick or in prison and visit you?' And the King will answer them, 'I tell you the truth, just as you did it for one of the least of these brothers or sisters of mine, you did it for me.'

– Matthew 25:39-40

A Change of Scenery

Through all the changing scenes of life,
in trouble and in joy, the praises of
my God shall still my heart and tongue
employ.

THE BLESSING OF TEACHING

ONE OF THE main things foreigners come to China to do is teach; especially English. I, as a student, thought it would be a great way to add a few more dollars to my minuscule bank balance. Moreover, it is said that Chinese pay top dollar to have their kids taught in the *lingua franca* of the world. I thought that I could start small by teaching one or two kids, and then work my way up to being a Linguistics professor. It would be a dream come true. I love language, I love talking and I love watching people's faces light up with new knowledge. That being said —well, *written*, I figured to myself that it was a moderate enough ambition. I began to seek the Lord about it, to see what He would do about it. I am taken back to the 4th chapter, GETTING IN THE SWING OF THINGS "Trusting in the Lord is becoming a habit of mine. There's rarely a chance I have to not trust in Him, as there's always some challenge that comes up, that would be a little too much for me to handle. Daily, I pray and tell Him that there's nothing I can do. I tell Him that I have no choice but to trust Him, because everything is over my head." So, it came about that one day whilst at church that I happened across a woman who spoke to me. After a while, we exchanged contact information and went our way to the service. Usually, Bible study and lunch follow the service, and we went; speaking all the while. It was only when I got home that evening that I got a message from her, recommending someone to me. She showed me a screenshot image of the conversation between them, and they were asking for a foreign English teacher. She gave them my name. The next thing I know, I'm talking to the principal of a kindergarten by the name of Cici. During that very conversation, Cici invited me to come to her school to have an interview that following Friday. To say that I was utterly astonished would be an understatement of astronomical proportions. I immediately obliged, and that Friday evening, I left class and headed for Kid Castle.

At Kid Castle, I sat and talked with Cici. She asked me some questions about my teaching experience, and whether I liked children. She had explained to me with much seriousness that there were some teachers she had to let go, because they were seeing this as merely a means of getting money. Therefore, she wanted to be clear that I actually loved children. I had to fight the urge to not tell her all about Kunal and my goddaughter Dalena, just so we can focus on the interview at hand. Then, something happened that I was neither expecting, nor was ready for...she brought in two children and sat them down in the room and told me to teach them the letter C. Though my heart pleaded, and I insisted that my experience with teaching children that young is negligible at best, she smiled and told me to just give it a try.

It was then that it hit me. Everything that I have been doing, I've been doing for the last ten years, at least. My meaning is this: there are no skills or talents which I have been doing for the last decade that are completely new to me. Everything school related, work related, even language related, I've been either very accustomed to, or not that far from, that it wouldn't come across as strange for me. Working at the Embassy was a new experience for me, yes; but it dealt with administrative work and checking the application forms and reporting to superior officers, all of which I was well accustomed to from my tenure in the Barbados Cadet Corps.

Now that I am standing in front of these two curious faces looking up at me, completely unprepared, I'm faced with the reason why old dogs can't be taught new tricks. I held over with three large pictures in my hand, of cake, chocolate and candy, and tried my very best to teach these two children the letter "C". When I was finished, Cici and I spoke some more. I don't remember that about which we were speaking (*or should it be* 'I don't remember what we were speaking about'), because my mind had gone far from there. I became very despondent. I thought to myself, *do I really love children as much as I say I do? Can I do this? Why weren't they learning? Was it something I said? Were they scared of me?* Am I a poor teacher? I began to think that I wasn't good enough for this job, but Cici assured me that if I work hard enough that I would be a good teacher, and that I would even get a raise from Kid Castle. That however wasn't enough to stop me from worrying. I had to seek the Lord for help. I encouraged myself in the Lord saying that the experience that Moses had as a Prince in Egypt didn't prepare him fully for the task ahead of him. God had to prepare him in the wilderness of Midian too; and so, if God has given me this job to train me for greater things, then He will be the one to train me for it. At least, this was my understanding.

THE BLESSING OF SHARING.

One of the many things which I have grown to live by —or at least *try* to, is that no matter how small something may seem; thank God for it, and tell others about it. While at UWI, I remember saying that it would be robbing God for Him to do something for you, and for you to not give Him glory by telling others. That being said, here comes Small Group.

While here in Beijing, the International Christian Fellowship here had invited me to their Small Groups. Luckily, there was one right on my campus that met on Thursdays. At first, I didn't want to involve myself any more than mere church attendance, because I didn't want to launch myself into too many commitments too early. Having suffered many a disappointment at the mediocre and lukewarm level of 'passion' displayed in some churches to which I am accustomed, I had even planned to stay away from Christian gatherings for the first year of my tenure. God, apparently was not having it, and I was roped into a small group. I went to my first small group session. I sat down and focussed on not speaking. What I **did not** want was to speak, and people to think that I am endowed with so much knowledge of God, and then I end up being put in some position and upon some pedestal. Humility is something with which I have wrestled in the past, and I know how tough a battle it could be at times. My head grows so very quickly that sometimes, I simply deny compliments, so as to ricochet them away from my ego, lest my head swell with pride and the sides of my head knock on the door posts on my way out.

HUMILITY ASIDE

Coming to China was something that I always wanted to do. I would often be found sitting and reading things and books and articles with relation to Chinese language, people, history and culture. Often times, I would bring up random facts about China, and their language in conversation simply because I find it tremendously fascinating. About the language, I had sought to learn as much of the cultural aspects of is, as well as the traditional idioms and proverbs used in Chinese. When I arrived here and started speaking to Chinese people in their language, they would often remark on how "good" my Chinese speaking skills are.

They would ask me how long I was here in Beijing, and be flabbergasted that I was only here a few months. They would say "Your Chinese is so great!" I would get so many remarks about how great I am, that I would think that I were in a Joel Osteen congregation.

The fight against self-exaltation is raging here, especially when I consider that the skills given to me are above-average. I was talking to a teacher in Chinese in the hallway one day, when another teacher passed by and with a smile, remarked about how proficient my spoken Chinese is. She also said that my Chinese sounds the same as that of the teacher with whom I was previously speaking. Another teacher, while we were on a bus, leaned over to my class teacher and began tossing ideas back and forth as to how my Chinese proficiency could be "so good". Yet another teacher, while on the train, as I walked by them, whispered ever so loudly to my class teacher asking him how I could speak Chinese so well. All of this happens, and I can almost feel my head pulsate with the pride which would be knocking at the door of my mind. The battle against pride rages, and so far, the Good Lord has been helping me to conquer the pride as it arises. Also, constantly reminding myself that it is only by the Grace of the Good Lord that I can speak as well as I do; and as I remind myself, I also pray and thank Him for allowing me to be where I am. One conquers pride by realising that it is not YOU who lives, but Christ who lives in you!

Back to the blessing of sharing, I was in Small Group when I was approached afterwards by a young man from Nigeria. He asked me the question of how to get a job. Of course, I know nothing of China, I know nothing of how to apply for work, but I know God. I told him: "Talk to people during the day, and talk to God during the night". I explained to him that this talking is the working on the faith that you've placed in God. I told him that when I'm out, and the subject of teaching or working would come up, I would mention my skills and I would mention how long I was here, and I would mention my interests. At night, I would then go home and pray to God to grant me favour with those to whom I had spoken throughout the day. It's like a man who plants seeds during the day. He knows not how they grow, but he does His part and does not expect grain to fall from the sky. So is my attitude towards God. The African brother thanked me for sharing my experience, and I thanked God for the opportunity to so do.

IN LEARNING, YOU WILL TEACH…

"It is only when you learn while teaching
that you discover that knowledge does
not come from you."

- Anonymous

After about two training sessions with Kid Castle, Cici had told me of a branch in the Haidian District which would be close enough to my school for me to work at. She knows that Kid Castle HQ is quite far from my campus (90 minutes by subway) and thought that this one would be quite convenient for me to go to, to teach the kids there. I happily obliged, and believed it to be the Lord that orchestrated this, as it was a mere 20 minutes' walk from campus. I was truly thankful to the Lord for this, and continue to thank Him for it to this day. One Friday, I met one of the teachers at the subway station where we walked to the school nearby (not really a school in the common sense, but a set of rooms in a building, set up like classrooms for little kiddies). We arrived in the classroom, and the fresh pang of uselessness and hopelessness hit me in my chest. Then, I was asked the question that really set me a trembling: "so, have you prepared?" *Prepared?* I didn't know what class I was teaching; I didn't know who I was teaching, and what. I didn't know anything, and didn't know how or what to prepare. Though the name of the teacher who was helping me at the time slips me, her encouragement and patience never left, and she allowed me time to prepare a class for these three children who were coming to be taught in a half-hour's time.

That time preparing could not move any slower. I was sitting in the office there like a polar bear in the woods –simply lost. I pulled aside the book that was next to me, and tried copying the format that was there. I had to teach them the first three letters of the English alphabet. For the next hour and a half of teaching, the seconds moved like minutes and the minutes moved like days. I tried everything I could think of. Things worked well for the first 40 minutes, and then they got restless. They couldn't sit still; they were not paying attention; they were not retaining the information presented to them. My mind began to race, and I started to worry. I knew for a fact that if the parents were to see this incredible failure, they would withdraw their children from Kid Castle, and I would be asked to kindly withdraw my services. While teaching, it got to the point where I was frustrated with the fact that I had more time than lesson; and I was running out of ideas. I was teaching the letter 'C', and one of the little girls was screaming something at me. I was so annoyed that did not pay attention to what she was saying. It was only when a woman dashed in the classroom, snatched the girl up, and whisked her off to the bathroom that it hit me: the poor girl wanted to *niao niao*. I remembered, and I felt so bad that I had little children held hostage and not even letting them go to the bathroom for more than an hour and a half. *Stefan, you monster!*

During the break, I admitted to the teacher who helped me that I was out of ideas, and that I didn't know what to do for the latter part of the class. I didn't know what to do, and I was praying for the Grace needed to not worry myself half to death. That latter part of the lesson was mostly a blur. I remember the other teacher sitting them down for a while, and reading them a story. I wanted to get the whole night over and done with. As the rest of it was a blur, the next memory I can excavate was me walking home from the centre. All the while pondering these things in my heart like Mary.

MEETING WITH THE AMBASSADOR

From the time we had landed in Beijing, one of the things which the remainder of the contingent had agreed was imperative was a visit to the **Barbados Embassy in China**. Though I am not one to be at all the proverbial cock-fights and dog shows[6], I decided to get up and go. Sometimes, in my life, there are things that I don't feel the need to do, and places I don't feel the need to go. I have experienced this on more than one occasion in the past. Most of the time, I simply go to whatever activity it is, because it would be for the greater good if I go. Should I at any time decide (and say) that I will not go to any particular event, the question of "why not?" will surely follow, like grace and mercy. Then, to try to explain why one wouldn't want to go, not because there's anything about the event itself, but I…just don't want to go, would prove rather irritating. I do not think there is a simpler way of explaining it. Anyhow, all this aside, I decided that it would be best to get acquainted with the Embassy here first, let them get familiar with me now that I'm still a small fry. Were I a bigger fish, and had more substance, maybe I wouldn't be too bothered with diplomatic covering and the like. However, as I am still quite a small fish, it is a calculated benefit that I go meet the ambassador.

Dr Chelston Brathwaite is a charm. A man with a magnetic disposition and a commanding voice like that of Mufasa met me as his six-and-a-half-foot stature strutted smartly into the room. His smartly clad figure and confident smile brought

---

6   Bajan parlance: every event to be attended

with it a warmth and welcome that a thousand trumpets couldn't conjure up in all their blasting musicality. We shook hands and sat down. As the conversation ensued, he, Chris, Daniesha (two other Barbadian students) and I spoke in depth about the flourishing economy of China, the apparent "tumbling collapse of the culture and society" of Barbados, and its economic repercussions, and the benefit that the bilateral relationship brings to both countries. I sat in awe at the knowledge this man had, and the experience that flavoured the conversation he put forward. When Job was complaining about his troubles, the Lord asked "who is this that darkens council with words without knowledge?" It is as though the Good Lord is saying that when a person without knowledge speaks, all council is darkened, and it would be better for that person not to speak, for even a fool is considered wise when his mouth is fastened shut.For me, whenever I'm in a situation which triggers my passion about anything, I proceed to forget all around me and focus on what is going on in that particular circumstance. In most Bible studies, I have to pull myself back a few times, so as to make space for others to speak. When he and I were discussing (because, by then, I had dominated the conversation) about the things which plague the Barbadian populace, I found myself being more and more educated. Things which I thought I knew about the culture and economy of Barbados were taught to me afresh, and I humbled myself under this teaching, like any good young man, as *only a fool hates correction*[7]. After a few more minutes of splendid conversation, His Excellency escorted us upstairs where we continued our discourse. He treated us to some sandwiches, pizza bites and other finger-foods which we gobbled up with much haste and enthusiasm. We even took some with us in our bags back to our schools when we left. When the conversation (which was, in my opinion, much too short) came to its smooth landing, I took my goodies, and left the embassy, but not without meeting the lovely wife of His Excellency. With some final words of encouragement, we bid the Ambassador adieu and headed for home.

En route à la train station, Chris expressed to me that he was quite impressed with "my little speeches". A confused Stefan looked around and inquired as to what he could possibly be talking about, as I had no idea. He said that when I spoke to the Ambassador, I mentioned things like "giving back to the Linguistics arena" among others which now escape my memory. As a young Christian fighting against pride daily, I downplay what I was said as "not that impressive" and moved on in conversation. We boarded the train, and I paid Chris' dorm a visit before heading back to my school (he had a meeting there, and figured having a travel buddy to talk to wouldn't be so bad.)

---

7 Proverbs 12:1

DINING WITH LUKE AND JANE

One Sunday when I was at the English service, a couple went on stage during the announcements and performed a skit in which the husband played an international student interested in bonding with Christians over dinner during the month of October. What grabbed my attention was the he acted out the perfect embodiment of being international. Not that he had a dozen passports and didn't pay any taxes. Then, I don't think I would be able to mention his name so freely. No, I mean that in that one announcement, he spoke about four other languages, addressing different language speakers in the audience. To me, speaking so many languages that well was the epitome of being international. He asked "are there any English-speaking families here interested in hosting a few students for dinner?" He then asked a paraphrased version of the question in Spanish, French and Swahili, with Igbo getting special mention. I felt my admiration leap from my heart and head for this mysterious man on the stage. I was immensely enthralled by his linguistic prowess. In his presence, though I can carry myself in basic conversation in four languages, and can greet people in 6 others, I felt like a child who just learned how to say "da da". The purpose of that exercise was for the church to organise which family will host which set of international students, and they would register and so on. Turns out, praise God, that the lovely couple on the stage was my host family for that dinner.

After weeks of messages sent and received; after days of calling and confirmations, I finally met my hosts, and knocked upon their door. I was at their house with Dan, Esther, some African young ladies (who came a little later) and we were met with pleasant smiles from Luke, his wife Jane, Ezra, Lily, Amy and Isaac their children. The children greeted me with such warmth that I immediately felt at home and started talking with them, discussing with them and just enjoying myself with these four little angels. Around the time when the sisters from Africa came, I made my way to the kitchen to see if I could lend a hand to Jane who was in the process of preparing the evening's meals. When I got in, she hit me with a question which unlocked that one prohibition that stops you from unloading your whole life story on a person. She was stirring a frying pan when she looked at me, and with a welcoming smile, she said "so, Stefan, is it? Tell me about your family". That was it for me. It was almost like the experience I had on the bus with Debbie, on the way to the orphanage. I unloaded all I remembered about them from my Granny's grandmother being snatched from her evening meal and tossed onto the slave ship (yes, that's how it happened) to me now being in China. Though she was busy, Jane was completely soaked in my story. She was giving the usual "uh huh's" and "mm-hmm's" evident in day-to-day conversation, but there was an interest in how she received what I was saying. Sometimes, there would be times when she'd look up at me for a second or two, as if to spare that ounce of spare energy and attention on what I was saying. When we finally left the kitchen, I felt that Jane, from how she responded to me was perfectly capable, if she wanted, to recite all that I said verbatim.

During dinner, I learned that Dan, who was with us at the beginning, and who I had met on my first visit to the English service had recently married the Chinese woman he met seven months prior. Stefan Lorde said "…oh", and that is all he expressed (and will express) concerning. I also learned that Luke, albeit of the lighter persuasion, was raised in Africa, though the specific country escapes the grasp of my otherwise dependable memory. He was chatting with the African sisters in Swahili/Igbo and I had to wipe the dribble ("drool" for you non-Barbadian readers) from the bottom of my mouth as I sat in awe. Swahili is one of those languages which I would like to learn in the future. In fact, I wouldn't mind learning Chinese, Arabic and Swahili at the same time, though that would be dreadfully unwise. Speaking to people in their own language is something which "goes to the hearts" of people, to quote Nelson Mandela, and it is something which I endeavour to continue doing until the day that I breathe my last.

As if the night couldn't get any better, the children were taken to bed, but not before giving us a show. Luke put on the music with its Spanish and Swahili lyrics, and put Lily on a chair to stand. There, she proceeded to dance her heart out, twisting her little body to the beat of the music, while the others were in the background like backup dancers. It was a truly splendid and heart-warming sight to behold. I had to snap myself back into reality, however, because I was close to picturing myself with my own family, serving the church with our home. What followed were more heart-to-heart conversations which, looking back, appear to be the focus of the dinner: to get the students to feel comfortable in this strange land.

FOOD ASIDE

The last thing that was on the menu for the night was a very special dish from Africa. This dish was Ugali, and it was made from corn meal. The way it was done was similar to that of cou-cou back in Barbados, though it didn't have the okra and the salt fish and such (good luck getting salt fish in Beijing). From what I've heard, this meal which we enjoy in Barbados is a direct descendent of this Ugali which I've seen these Africans enjoying. I called it "The Great Grandfather of Cou-Cou", and it's quite possible that the Africans brought the recipe with them when they were dragged off to the horrid life of slavery. They now are gone, but the Ugali remains; and it lives on in the houses of many Barbadians to this day, as they serve and enjoy cou-cou with their families.

The main difference was in the eating. The manner in which they ate it was so strange, but still so intriguing that I found myself partaking in this post-dinner activity. The pinched off a piece of the cornmeal and water mixture which was semi-solid and proceeded to roll it in their hands until it was firm. They then took their thumb and pressed a dent in the now spherical mixture, and used it as a spoon to scoop up the sauce in the bowl provided. This method of eating was really new to me: a colonised Afro-Caribbean young man, only accustomed to eating with utensils; but it created a curiosity within me, that thirsted after Africa and all her cultural intricacies and complexities. As I have some years here, I may find myself en route to South Africa soon, to see what life in the 'Motherland' is like.

WHAT'S IN *YOUR* CORNER?

In a country where Christianity isn't allowed to flourish as freely as in other countries, the saved ones in China have to find creative ways to spread the Gospel of Christ. Seeing as most of the Christians are English speaking (as far as my limited experience and knowledge go), and seeing as there is a great need for English teachers here in China, the Church has begun teaching Chinese the Gospel of Christ, under the guise of an English learning platform. This I found to be a marvellous way to preach the gospel. The **English Corner** is said platform, and it focuses on the teaching and practice of English and I was invited by the one who runs this particular one nearby our campus. This humble English Corner happens on Saturday mornings, and is held in a very convenient location, not too far from this campus, and those surrounding. We sit down, we introduce ourselves, and we discuss various topics which are quite simple to English speakers. I was even asked to help lead a session one evening, on the topic of Success. It went quite well, and I learned a lesson in objectivity and patience from hearing the views of others. Usually, after English Corner, we stay and chat with the people that come, because sometimes, people just don't want to let go and wait for another week before coming to the next session. There is a Chinese restaurant on the opposite side of the road from English Corner (as we're in China, we'll just call it a restaurant) where we'd usually have lunch.

While there one afternoon, I was in conversation with a Chinese Christian. I believe he was a recent convert (and it is amazing how much these people grow spiritually in such a short time) and I was talking to him about the story of Noah. With my God-given imagination, I painted the scenery for him, of the situation of what was going on in Noah's day, from my limited knowledge of geography and biblical history. He had some questions about God which he asked, and after praying in my heart, God granted me the wisdom to answer them in accordance with His intended purpose. He was amazed, and I was humbled and edified to have shared. I left with my mind on my intended purpose on coming to China. I love the Bible, and I love talking about the Bible. I remember seeing a video on FB where this underground church receiving Bibles in Chinese for the first time. Their gratitude was overwhelming, and it was quite emotional to watch. To read with them, to understand with them, and to help teach them what the Good Lord has explained to me and made me understand…in Chinese, would be the apex of my life here in China. When I was in Barbados, I would chat with persons about the Bible often, and would also lead study groups and sometimes even preach. I am humbled that the God of Heaven would use a simple kid like me to do His work, but I believe that I can use more of my talents here in China to teach the Bible here in Chinese. I thank God for what He has allowed me to do thus far, and I look forward to His unfolding plan in the near future.

WABBIT BWAINS

While working at the Chinese Embassy, I had met the family of a man by the name of Chen Guanqiao, or Jack, for those too embarrassed to attempt pronouncing his name. He has a son by the name of Niu Niu, or Noah. When we were in Barbados, Noah would often come into my office. I would help him read, or watch him draw. His mother, who sat behind me in the office, would often encourage him to speak English to me for practice. Sometimes, I would supervise him and Hao Yun when their parents were off to meetings. When I was in my second year at the Embassy, their tenure was up, and they left Barbados. Jack had assured me that should I need any help in Beijing, he'd be more than happy to assist. Now that I'm here, I was privileged to be invited to dinner with Jack and his family at a restaurant near their home. What I particularly liked about this restaurant was that it was Sichuan cuisine 四川菜 (Sichuan Cai) and I was told that the food from there is the spicier, and from then it was a desire of mine to try that food. There was a signature dish from that restaurant which I was urged to try… you've guessed it, rabbit heads. Yep, your boy, Stefan was sitting down at a restaurant when someone placed a bowl of plastic gloves next to me. The gloves were to eat the rabbit with, and when they brought the meal, I understood why.

Two plates, two heads per plate. Jack and I were waiting on his family to arrive, and was allowed to have a little appetiser before his wife and son arrived. I donned the glove and grabbed the first head and proceeded to maneuver it in my hands and mouth. When I was yet trying to get more out of the little meal, I concentrated on the image I had in my head of a rabbit skull, and used that image to work my way around my appetiser. I was getting accustomed to my little meal when I was struck with the question. Like Isaac with Abraham on the mountain, my question was framed with two observations, and a main interrogative: I ate the eyes, the tongue…but where is the brain of the rabbit? I used two thumbs behind the jaw and spread apart the remaining bones. The skull completely dismantled in my hands, and there it was. I leaned to Jack and asked if I had to eat the brains too. Without looking up from devouring his rabbit brains, he said "you must! It's the best part!" With that, I made a go for it. I wouldn't say that I agree with it being the best part, but the meal on a whole was quite delicious, and I'm glad I went. Of course, there were other meals, which I thoroughly enjoyed, and I took part in all the eatings and drinkings provided, until my stomach was full. When dinner was over, they escorted me to the subway station where I took my ride home.

A CHANGE OF SCENERY

When I first landed at BLCU, and even before I came, I had always prayed for a roommate. I prayed and asked God for a roommate that was German, or at least one with a language that I didn't know, so I could learn from him. I even went so far as to pray that he had a sister who I could be introduced to, and later marry. When I got to my room, and found my roommate, I was immensely disappointed. Of course, there were the initial pleasantries of "good morning" and such, but after that first hello he didn't talk to me. He never sought to find out my name, where I was from, how old I was, nothing of the sort. We never had any form of conversation, and there were even times when I would try to contact him, and be totally ignored. It seemed as though he made every effort to ignore my very existence. He would walk by me without making any eye contact, and seemed to be in his own world; not wanting to be disturbed by the likes of me. I went to my Jesus many a time for him in prayer. I prayed for myself. I prayed for the patience to deal with him. Because he never spoke to me, I could never get an understanding of what's going on in his head. Therefore, I couldn't tell whether my phone conversations were annoying him, whether my music was too loud, I couldn't know anything, and it made living with him rather uncomfortable. Only when he would leave the room would I feel the proverbial weight being lifted off my shoulders that I kept hearing about in church. I could honestly say that living with him was a burden.

As if living with him wasn't enough, it turns out he was quite a difficult and inconsiderate person altogether. I managed to overhear a conversation he was having on the phone one evening. In fact, I'm being modest. He was talking so loudly, that I thought the person was outside down the hall, rather than on the phone. From my limited knowledge of Chinese, I understood that he was inviting himself by this girl's dorm. Long story short, the girl was busy doing a lot of homework, but he kept calling her back every half hour or so to find out what time he could come over. Because the phone was also on loudspeaker, I could hear her responses just as clearly as I could hear his. I was minimally relieved that it was not me that he had a problem with, and that he was just pushy and inconsiderate by nature. Funny enough, when he would get forward[8], he would proceed to bathe himself and his jacket in cologne, and leave. It is at this juncture that I would like to emphasise with what he bathed himself. He would seldom bathe himself, and when he did, the baths took less time that it would to read this paragraph. Moreover, his towel was green in colour, but brown due to much use and little washing. He also kept it atop his suitcase which was located above his wardrobe. If that didn't disturb you more than the rabbit brains, his diet was 90% milk and bread…plain bread and plain milk every day, three times a day. I think this poor diet was the contributing factor to his awful body odour, coupled with his blue moon showers.

Did he ever eat anything else besides bread and milk? Oh yes. He would cook in the room (which is forbidden, by the way) and his cooking smelled just as welcoming as he did. The raw fish which was left over was kept *uncovered* in the fridge. So, all the bread, water and fruits which I kept there smelled and tasted like raw fish. Not only that, but the cooked fish was kept in the computer table. I had complained once, twice to the dorm staff downstairs for him and his breaking of the school rules. I would have liked for him to be immediately expelled from the campus forthwith, but I didn't think that it would happen. I was at least hoping for a suspension from the room, but because I don't know what he would do, I didn't know whether he would attack me in the night (that actually already happened to a student here), I was a little weary about how I complained about him.

All the while, I was praying to the Good Lord and telling Him all about what has been going on. I asked him whether I should move. I asked Him for a change of heart towards my roommate, who, by the way reads his Bible and prays every day. I had also sought council from my earthly father as well, and after explaining a little, he gave me one word, "move!" With that, I went and inquired as to the procedure to move. I was told that a room should open up in a few days, and I should wait before I start packing. After 2 days, I went and

---

8   Bajan parlance: the attention a girl pays to a guy who likes/pursues her

asked again, and was told to come the following week. The following week, like clockwork, I was in front of them, inquiring about the room's availability. She gave me a room number and told me that I can move as soon as I can. While in the room that morning, I waited around for my roommate to leave for the shower before I started packing. My idea was that if I could get ready and leave before he got back that would be perfect, as I wouldn't have to face any questions or confrontations.

He left. I started packing. I made haste so I could finish before he got back. I was about 90% completed and moved when he came back in. Like all the times he came in before, he walked straight passed me and continued what he was doing. I should have expected that he would be quick, because he usually doesn't take long in the shower (not that length of time equals quality, but there's only so much quality you can achieve in such little time). He came in and I looked at him for any reaction. As expected, he displayed none, and didn't even look in my direction as I heaved suitcases around. When I was done, I walked out and moved all my things to my new room. All the while, I was praying to God that I wasn't making a mistake. In the West, we say "out of the frying pan and into the fire", and I would have hated for that to be my situation. I got to my new room and knocked. After hearing a little shuffling about inside, the door opened and was greeted by a taller, sleepier young man. He rubbed his eyes as though he just woke up (it was about 10 in the morning) and I told him that I was to move into this room and he said "okay, cool. Come in and do your thing, man. I'll shift my stuff". *Wow*, I thought. *That was more conversation in 2 minutes with him than I had in two months with the previous roommate.* When I looked into the new room, it smelled so clean. It had been a while since I had entered a clean smelling room. Sometimes, I would be on my way to my room and sigh heavily because I didn't want to face that room. I didn't want to have to open the door and see him. I didn't want to open the door and be met with the awful smell of someone who hasn't graced the showers with his presence. I wanted to move. I had to move; and I had to move quickly. I had all my things in the new room, and I went back to get my water dispenser. I ran into my old roommate on the way in, and he passed me (as usual) as though I were not even there, and went about his business. I was glad that there was no confrontation nor any negative *vibe* or whatever. I got to my new room after moving everything, and I was amazed to see that the entire left side of the room was cleared away and prepared for me. My new roommate was fast asleep and I came in and sat down on my new bed, finding it to be more comfortable than the older one. As I sat there examining my new room, I received a new message on my phone. *Strange. No one in Barbados is up at this time, and no one else in Beijing would message me at this hour.* I looked and behold, it was a message from my old roommate, saying "你为什么要换房间？" (Why is it that you wanted to change rooms?)

I'm going to give the reader a few seconds to find any sense in this question. He had never messaged me before, he had never spoken to me before, yet when I move out, he'd want to know why? I'm of the view that he sees nothing wrong or weird about his lifestyle, and therefore, for me to explain would confuse him even more. For this reason (and the fact that he can't be serious), I have decided to leave that question until a time came where I can answer without any hard feelings. That day has not yet come.

HALLOWEEN SACRIFICE

In the previous chapters of this long…uhh, exposition I had spoken about opportunities to teach at Kid Castle. I had got an opportunity to solidify the trust of the parents there. One Saturday in October, I had taken the time to go to the Kid Castle for training. An hour and a half after leaving home, I finally arrived there to be told that there was no training that day. Instead, they will be having a Halloween party and asked if I would mind staying. I thought to myself. I thought of all the documents I read about the Christian perspective on Halloween. I spent a few seconds in prayer asking the Good Lord for His perspective, and for the Godly choice to prevail. I thought then to myself that God has given me this job, and He would be more interested in my excelling at it, than if I were standing in a room with little kids dressed like witches. I thought, moreover, that there was this was more about the kids and their parents than it was about my peripheral views on public holidays.

So, I stayed for the little party. The party was actually an organised class for the kids to learn English words related to the festival. Words like 'ghost' and 'skeleton' were used along with pictures of these, in order to get the children to learn them. The teachers (this time, myself included) also did some interactive things to entertain the children and their parents. This involved singing and a dance. I was asked if I can do a song. I thought for a while about a song that would be slow enough for them to pick out the English words familiar to them, but yet sweet enough that they would enjoy it. I chose 'Sacrifice - Elton John' and hit play on the music. As the intro played, I could feel the expectant eyes piercing my black flesh, and curious mouths opening as I swayed with the first few bars of the music. I opened my mouth and began the first line "It's a human sign when things go wrong…" There was a resounding awe that waved across the audience as I imitated the voice of Sir Elton John. The mike failed me during the first verse, and I put it down while still serenading the audience. I also used that as an opportunity to get closer to the audience. I adopted my body language and mannerisms into my song and sang *to* the audience rather than just singing for the audience. It got the children very excited when I would stroll toward one of them during the song and sing a line or two to that one specific child. I would then walk to the other end of the room and do the same thing to another child. The smiles shone brightly like…no, not a diamond, but as brightly as a smile of a child would shine. I think I would rather have the smile of my own child than that of the brightest diamond, and that came out in how I sang to these lovely children. At that time, it was no longer about the Christian view of Halloween; but about loving children as Christ said they should be loved.

I must admit that this note is getting quite long, and I thank my wonderful and committed readers for putting up with my meanderings. I shall therefore cut here and continue later in another document. Up next on Bajan in Beijing:

> » Two too's and a two

> » Long-Distance Class trip

> » "Believe and be baptised."

I HOPE YOU LOOK FORWARD TO READING IT, AS MUCH AS I LOOKED FORWARD TO WRITING IT.

Far away and back again

"Language is the blood of the soul into which thoughts run, and out of which they grow."

– Anonymous

GREETINGS TO YOU. As promised, I had told you belovèd readers that I would start this document with the continuation of what was happening before, and then we could move on from there…I think. I am writing this paragraph while sitting in the new room that the Good Lord has blessed me with. I sit here in thanks at how much He has blessed me over the last few months of my life. It was as though I were under a waterfall, but standing on the side. The good gifts and blessings are like the water coming down and spraying, and I know that it is from above. I use the analogy of water because it seems as though the good and positive experiences just keep coming. Just when I thought I would be used to being blessed, more seemed to come. However, the more I look, the more I see that I have yet to be moved into the centre of the waterfall's impact, to feel the full weight of its crushing magnitude. I say 'be moved' and not 'move' for reasons not so obvious to some of my readers. As a Christian, I am of the firm belief that God, by His hand is able to move me in and out of circumstances as He sees fit. That being said, it would be wise to wait until He is ready to move me, rather than jump into what I think He may have for me. That way, if it is that I wasn't ready for the full force of the waterfall, I would not be overwhelmed and crushed by its impact. God will move me into the fullness of which He has prepared me when He sees it fit. Like when Proverbs says that a man may make his own plans, but the Lord is the one who determines his steps. Though I'm in China, and my "plans" are pretty much established at this point, the things that

I experience; the blessings that are bestowed on me are still determined by the Lord. He is still orchestrating what happens when, and the intensity of trials that I have to endure as well.

TWO TOO'S AND A TWO

For those of us who have any knowledge of the seasons, you'd know that *winter was coming.* My aerodynamic sneakers are very breathable, and they were taking in every ounce of wind that was reaching 10 degrees centigrade. For those of you whose only experience of cold is in passing the freezers in the supermarket and feeling that very slight feeling of discomfort lasting for just a few seconds. The sensation of the cold gripping your entire body is foreign to you. I felt it though, and thought it best to think about where to find warm clothes and shoes. However, I found that the more I put it off, the quicker time seemed to fly. Soon, it was impossible to ride my bike or walk without having that feeling of numbness surround my toes. I think it was me being too cheap that led to putting off buying winter clothes. November was approaching, and so were the blistering cold winds. I had consulted Akilah with the intent of ordering a pair of boots which I think would be most appropriate for the changing temperatures. I had looked at the tag in my sneakers, and used the size there. I saw that it was a 42, so, I logically thought that it would be best to get one that size. I was told that by the end of that week, I would have my new boots.

Two days turned into two weeks and I still hadn't seen any sign of the shoes. I had begun to think that they got lost in the mail, and set out to desperately buy another pair of the same shoe. I had started to worry as two weeks turned into three. As opportunities to go and shop with someone who actually knows where to go seemed more and more out of reach, I began to wonder if I would ever get my shoes. Finally, they arrived. I had got a message saying that they had arrived, and that I should come get them. In a hasty attempt, I rode over to the nearby school where I would see her and get my long-awaited boots. When I got there, she told me that both pairs of boots had arrived at the same time. I didn't care at the time, because I would at least have one pair to wear, and my toes would be finally protected from the cold to come. As we sat and watched a few videos, I took the first boot out of the box. From the time I held it in my hands, I knew that something was wrong. I played it off as minor, but this was not easily ignored. The shoes were too small. They were too small, took too long to get here, and now, to my dismay, they were two pairs. Fortunately, the more Mandarin I learn, and the more of these Chinese apps I explore, the more I am able to navigate and see the status of my packages. I am more and more able to exchange and even return any unwanted items, and even send items to other people. This is good, as I will be less dependent on Akilah.

What am I to do with these shoes now? As they were new, I didn't think it was a good idea to throw them away. I didn't know anyone who had that size. I learned later that Debbie was going back to the orphanage. I arranged to give them to her at church the next Sunday. I had hoped that if I couldn't enjoy them, someone else should.

LONG-DISTANCE TRIP

Now, this is the thing which I along with a lot of students had been looking forward to: the long distance trip. We were going to the south part of China to visit Hangzhou 杭州, Suzhou 苏州 and Shanghai 上海. For some, it was a chance to explore the language and culture of China, and experience life outside of Beijing. For others, it was a chance to get away from class and engage in a few days of sex, alcohol and violence (more about that later) or 打情骂俏 (Dǎqíng màqiào) in Mandarin. For those of you readers who know me, you wouldn't take that long to figure out which category I belong to. We gathered at the Eastern Gate of the school, and left on buses at around 3 pm. After arriving at the Beijing Station, our teacher checked and rechecked our passports and tickets. I stood with him most of the time, because I think I was already getting tired of the behaviour of some of my classmates. I was eternally grateful for the opportunity to go on this trip. I glanced down at my ticket and noticed the price. I was even more grateful that this ticket was paid for in full, and handed to me for free, and all I had to do was accept it and endure the journey. *Hmmm, sounds a little familiar.*

In the train station, we waited a long while before boarding the train. I used that time to talk to the teacher, practising my spoken Chinese, and learning more idioms to sound more native-like. While others were competing to see who could flip a bottle of water and land it upright, I was translating a well-known English idiom into Chinese for my teacher to get a laugh. I said "小东西娱乐小脑子" (Small things amuse small minds). The desired result was attained as my teacher held his head and laughed aloud. When seven o'clock came, we boarded the train and headed for Hangzhou.

ON THE TRAIN

There are many different kinds of trains in China, and depending on your budget, you can get from Beijing to Shanghai in five hours, or fifteen. For us students, we would get to Hangzhou in thirteen hours. I was delighted that I would be in the same cabin as the teacher I've been talking to the whole time. He and I speak often, and I am glad that I was able to chat with him during the trip and practise my Chinese. The cabin consisted of six beds, three on each side.

As night quickly approached, I found myself talking with Larona from South Africa, and Carmel from the US, originally from Haiti. As usual, I was talking the most, and completely consuming their attention with talk about language and the philosophy of language. While I was yet speaking, and as people came and went from our cabin, a Spanish girl from Equatorial Guinea came in and we spoke in Spanish, much to the amazement of Carmel and Larona who were still there. The minutes turned to hours, and it was almost time for lights out. At that time, it was only myself, my teacher, Carmel and Larona who remained. Carmel had yet to go to his bed, and the other three occupants in my cabin were already asleep. As we were talking, my teacher (here and after known as Mr Zhao) asked me what it was that the other two were saying. I was slightly taken aback. With a smile, I took a breath and began translating into Chinese that which my two new found friends and I were talking about. They sat there with mouths ajar, and when I was finished, I found even myself surprised that Mr Zhao had understood what I had told him, and even got the gist of the conversation had among us. Even the jokes and little pockets of laughter, I had translated for him.

Carmel then turned to Larona and remarked on how well my Chinese was. He then got rather overwhelmed that I was only three levels above him in our College, and he thought that the level of Chinese with which I spoke was too far above his, and too unattainable: out of his reach. I assured him that my Chinese is not that far from his and that we are on the same level. Though I don't remember verbatim what Zhao had said, I remember it being reassuring to Carmel. The fight against pride rages on in my heart, and daily, my ego must be pummelled into subjection, for our God hates the proud.

PRIDE ASIDE

Think of it, there are many verses which speak about pride, and many examples of people whose ego got too inflated for God's liking, and He burst their little bubble. The Bible says "God sees the proud afar off." (Psalms 138:6) Other than His eyes being omnipresent, it is as though that verse is particularly fixing the crosshairs of God on those whose heads have grown too big. Secondly, the Word goes on to say that He resisteth the proud. James not only reiterates what David was saying a few centuries earlier, he further emphasises the amount of hatred God places on those who are proud, to the extent of not only seeing them from afar, but resisting them. Like a burning furnace, the absolute holiness of God is too potent for the proud and self-righteous to come close. God Himself came to this world. He stepped into time and creation, and unlike what we would expect from any King, his profession was that of a carpenter. If Jesus didn't see equality with God the Father as something to keep a grip on; but let it all go to be a Galilean carpenter, I believe that there's reason for God to not really fancy those who, though they are nothing, puff up their hearts too high. In Proverbs 6:16, there is listed, the things which God hates. Seven things which God the Father, the Righteous Judge and Lawgiver of the whole world, hates above all else and sees as abominations. The first such thing…is a proud look.

*Christ came to this world, and He humbled himself. He took the form of a man, served people, washed the feet of those who he **knew** would betray him the day after, and all this while wielding the power to wipe out the planet, and all of creation. The star that led the wise men to Bethlehem was created and set in motion by the same babe that lay in the manger bawling for his mother. It stands to reason that anyone who wishes to be like Jesus, must, **must**, MUST humble themselves and fight against pride. It is not easy when you have something that you can actually boast about.*

HANGZHOU 杭州

In the morning, I rose to the sweet sounds of the train rhythmically gliding along the tracks. It was a very relaxing sound, which I knew would soon be cut short, as the morning brought with it Hangzhou, and all its marvellous adventures. There was a small number of people bustling about as they got ready to disembark the train.

From there, we met our tour guide, Danny. His spoken English was as good as any Chinese, with its few hiccups here and there. He was a really joyful soul, full of vigour, and always ready to help and answer whatever questions we may have. We got to our buses and I sat next to my friend from Bangladesh, Shagor. **"Chaiyya Chaiyya"** (English: [walk] in shade) is an Indian song from the 1998 Bollywood film *Dil Se..*, and it was also the soundtrack for the 2006 movie Inside Man. Though the song was in a language spoken mostly in India, Shagor and I sang it for our entertainment as the wheels on the bus went 'round and 'round. The audio from my iPod was low, but we still were able to hear it as the bus drove on, and I had the lyrics on the screen for my reference. Out of the places I've been on this trip, the ones most dear to me and most memorable would be noted. At the tea plantation, I could see that a lot of my peers were not as interested in the history and culture of the place, and didn't pay that much attention to the tour guide. I guess that there will always be those people in the world; and so, not many brain cells were wasted worrying about them. The tea, LongJing tea was the tea that only Emperors used to drink, and there was a very interesting story behind the harvesting of this tea.

The Emperor wanted tea from Hangzhou. However, as he was the Emperor, only the best tea would be accepted for his service. His officials noticed that the leaves were crushed upon picking, and were not fit for his Majesty's goblet. There had to be a way to get the leaves picked without bruising them. The Emperor then ordered that the fourteen-year-old girls of the village would use their lips to pick the leaves necessary for his cup. Stefan Lorde wondered, *why fourteen, of all ages?* It was then said that at that age, their lips are not too hard from… (The Emperor didn't want to risk using girls who were older, for reasons we'd have to think about long and hard) and they were young enough to understand still, the service for which they were called. For the roasting of the leaves after picking, he used the boys around the same age to roast the leaves with their bare hands. The leaves were put into a large steel bowl over a fire. After a little oil was placed in the bowl, the leaves would go in, and the boys used their hands to stir and toss the leaves to perfection. This ensured the highest quality of tea for the Emperor. When I saw the display on how beneficial this tea is for the health of the buyer, (I was gonna say "drinker", but that may have an intoxicating connotation) I bought myself a bottle of tea leaves. Fortunately, tea leaves aren't picked in the same way as they did all those centuries ago, nor are they roasted in the same manner. I would not feel comfortable purchasing a product that I knew was produced by child labour.

From this point, we went to the most famous West Lake. It was one of those cultural heritage sites where you'd want to take a nice uninterrupted stroll with a sweetheart. As I had no such company, rather busloads of classmates, I walked alone for most of the tour. From there, there was a short tour of the Buddhist village. A little shorter than this paragraph, this tour took us up a hill and back down, despite the fact that there were plenty of things to see, and many roads to explore. There were carvings of Buddha, and many other natural sites like caves and waterfalls. We barely got enough time to go in and out of one cave when the time was up, and we had to leave. I had thought and pondered in my heart as to the reason a trip so well organised would have so many hiccups and potholes. I wondered why it was that so many things were cut short, and had to be hurried on. I know that if I write this description the way how it actually went, you the readers would think that something is up, and maybe perhaps blame the lack of excitement on the skill of the writer. It is not, however the fault of the writer, as I am using my thoughts and feelings to document what I was experiencing. I then came up with a conclusion: I had noticed that when the tour guide was speaking, there were a few students who thought it funny to mock his English, and stop him from time to time to ask him questions which were both silly, and unrelated to the tour. This wasted five minutes here, and five minutes there. After two hours, only half of a tour would have been completed, and we would have to move on swiftly to the next one, and I would feel cheated out of a tour.

The next few hours went by quickly. From Hangzhou, we went to Wuzhen in Suzhou. This is a water village, and the inside looks a lot Venice. The more we toured, and the more we ate, the more I was grateful for the opportunity to be here, and to explore the ins and outs of China, and its various provinces. Every time we stopped, we got into a different restaurant, and ate the typical food of that province – all paid for by the school on our behalf. I had taken a picture of my food, and put it on social media. One of my Chinese friends commented on the picture and could tell where I was by just looking at the food on my plate.

SHANGHAI 上海

This was the place everyone was waiting for. The big city of Shanghai. To me, it was just another part of the tour. Yes, I was most grateful for this free tour of China, but I appreciated all the provinces equally. Though others complained daily and hourly about everything that could be complained about, it didn't take much to impress me and make me grateful. I say "others", but it was only one guy in particular who was complaining about everything. What was frustrating was that he wasn't just complaining about things that were wrong. He was just complaining. For example, he was look at the food and then exclaim "look at this food, ugh!" Even others who were misbehaving on the trip found him annoying. If I let myself be consumed by the thoughts and annoyances of all those who complain, I would in no way be grateful for the things which I have here in China, especially this trip.

Anyhow, back to Shanghai. Shanghai is the financial capital of China, whereas Beijing is the cultaral capital . There's the iconic skyline of the Bund (外滩) which, really is available online wherever you go. But, there's none online with me in it, so I took a few pictures. There was also a huge monument called the Monument to the People's Heroes, dedicated to commemorate revolutionary martyrs. I believe that there was also supposed to be a boat ride going somewhere that was to be part of our tour. However, because some of the students took so long to corral, that ended up not being a part of our tour.

By the afternoon of the final day, I was ready to leave and go back to my home in Beijing. I had missed Beijing. I don't know why I preferred Beijing over Shanghai (or any other province for that matter). Maybe it was a case of love at first sight. Maybe because it was the part of China that I was most accustomed to.

Whatever the reason, I gathered what was left of my self-control and went into the Shanghai Museum. I don't believe that the taking of pictures was allowed in the museum, but I very much appreciated the artifacts that were on display. I also appreciated that in the painting section, the displays lit up as I was walking towards them and then grew dim after a few minutes of my absence. It reminded me of a Psalm that speaks of God's word being a "light to my feet and a light to my path" (Psalm 119:105).

I could not get back to the bus quickly enough. Though I had enjoyed and appreciated the exhibits in the museum, I was feeling as though the number of like-minded individuals grew thinner and thinner. Because of the level of immaturity which I was enduring for the trip for the most part, I felt more urgency to return home. Enough negative feelings, now. Let's brush off and move on.

HE DID WHAT?

"Pardon one offense, and you encourage
the commission of many"

- Publilius Syrus

On the train back to Beijing, I was excited to know that we were returning on the speed train. Instead of 13 hours, we would be there in 5. When I was on the train en route to Hangzhou, a high speed train passed us like if we were stationary. Now, I was excited to see what it would be like to be in such a vehicle. Some of the teachers were telling their students that they were required to do their homework on the train. I had whispered and asked my teacher Mr Zhao if we were to do ours too. He shook his head and responded that we should hand in ours the following week. Now, it is here on the train ride back that we found out about the things which transpired beneath the surface. I found out about the drunken fights, the drugs and sex which were indulged in by so many of my comrades. Truth be told, I lost a large amount of respect for some people, even those for whom I thought I had none in the first place. My respect for Mr Zhao, on the other hand just kept getting higher and higher. For him to have kept his cool for this entire trip while managing our class had me really impressed and pleased.

I promise you, ladies and gentlemen, that there is more positive news to come in this trip. There really is. But before I get to that, there is a reason I entitled this message in such a manner.

There was a young man. This young classmate of mine is often late of class, usually disruptive and his grades and proficiency in Chinese leave a great deal to be desired in every aspect –along with having the maturity of a teaspoon and the attitude of a cactus. He had been caught cheating on every test which we had so far for the semester, and he is a pathological liar. He was in the train drinking alcohol (one of the rules I was talking about earlier) and the teachers got wind of it and approached him. As I sat there reading my book *More Drops - George Verwer*, I was overhearing the loud conversation which was being had between this boy and my belovèd class teacher. The volume level rose and rose as the teacher was asking him what was in the cup. He insisted that it was water. After guzzling down the remaining bit, he was adamant that the substance in the cup was water. Though the smell of alcohol was "knocking ya down"[9], to quote Barbadian parlance, the kid continued to lie to the teacher's face. Even from behind my book, I could feel the tension building. It rose and rose, until my Kenyan sister Susan gently moved the book from my face and whispered oh so surreptitiously, "he panched 'im". In comes the title of this paragraph. "Wait, hold on," was my reply as I wanted to be 100% clear on what was going on. "Who punched whom?"

It turns out, ladies and gentlemen of the jury, that all of the annoyances and frustrations that were caused by this terrible student from time immemorial finally reached its breaking point, and the teacher crushed the Styrofoam cup into the face of the unsuspecting vagabond with his fist. Stefan Lorde was sorely disappointed. *Why? That student had it coming.* It would be as though somebody hit the back of your car and you turn around and punch them. It dirties your hands in the sight of the law.

MY OPINION ASIDE

Were I in any way an influential figure in the scheme of things, that difficult student would not even have reached this far in the trip. The students were told not to smoke in the train. This high speed train is called high speed for a reason; and when it stopped in Nanjing, some of the students wanted to step off the train to smoke. If I were in charge, I would not have opened my eyes, because they were already told to remain on the train until they got back to Beijing. Should any of them attempt to get off the train, and be left in Nanjing, it would not have been anyone's fault but their own. We, as a class were given the rules once a week, three weeks before the trip. The rules were clear, and the penalties were just as clearly outlined.

9 Extremely strong (fragrance)

I had told my classmate Susan my opinion, and she told me that I was being too harsh, that any school run by me would be very strict. My view is that if the rules are clearly outlined, and are broken, especially in a sense of rebellion, there should be no sense of leniency. Time wise, if he were left in Nanjing as I would have liked, he wouldn't be in a situation where he finally broke my otherwise well-mannered teacher. This is the same teacher, the company of whom I enjoyed for the majority of the trip: a pleasant man, always willing to help, ever willing to answer any questions. I would be so daring as to say that my Chinese is 100 times better because of him, and he has earned a high place on my ladder of respect. He had caused my teacher so much stress, that even before that incident, I passed Mr Zhao sleeping on the train, and his face was so changed from the pleasant smiling and warm disposition to a contorted and frustrated look of disdain. This trip was taking its toll on him, and I was feeling glad that it would soon be over.

SOME GOOD, AS PROMISED.

One of the smarter students in the class Shagor and myself went to inquire if the train served coffee. At least, with a dose of coffee, we would be able to make it until the train stopped. When we passed the teachers, we asked, and as they pointed in the way to the service area, their warm smiles were so encouraging that even if your Chinese was not too good, you'd still feel on top of the world. Now, we went to the bar, and asked. The waitress said that one serving of coffee was 28 RMB. I thought that my Chinese was a bit off and she really meant 2.80, but sure enough, as I asked her to repeat, she confirmed that the price of the coffee was ten times that of coffee anywhere that I had seen. I thanked her and returned to my seat. Upon passing the teachers, Mr Zhao saw that my hands were empty and asked if they had any coffee. I utilised my acting skills to put on a show of an angry customer. I spoke loudly and clearly, expressing my gross displeasure of the eye-stabbing price of a simple coffee. Using my hands and body language, I carried on, and I even surprised myself with how fluently my sentences flowed. The teachers were all entertained, and even the other Chinese passengers were getting a kick out of my performance.

Mr Zhao: "But, Stefan, this is the high speed train. You can't expect the price to be the same as other places."

Me: "I understand that Sir, but high speed shouldn't mean high priced.

It's a simple coffee"

To be able to make puns and jokes at the same time in a language as tough to understand as Chinese made the teachers and those in earshot, including Shagor laugh joyfully. I was glad that I was able to bring them such joy, and practise my spoken Chinese at the same time. I left them laughing and went back to my seat. As I was walking, I overheard one of the teachers as he leaned to Mr Zhao, asking him how it is that my spoken Chinese got so good. Ha, the fight rages on against pride and arrogance. I learned a word which I want to use, but I can't find a context fitting enough. I've already used *surreptitiously* and am anxious to use this word. Aha! I'll say this: These things, the things which I say about myself and the things people say to and about me and my Chinese proficiency are not for *self-aggrandisement*, as it may seem to some. That's why I point most often to the battle against pride immediately afterwards.

At long last, we were getting closer to Beijing. I spent a few minutes talking to Larona who was in my cabin from before. The list of topics covered was endless, and afterwards he told me that he picked up so much from me. Surprised, I tried to downplay the importance of what I was saying, but he insisted. We chatted away until the train reached the destination, then we separated into our respective classes and headed for home.

LIFE BEGINS AT 50

No, this paragraph isn't about me, for I was still half that age at the writing of this paragraph. For those of you don't who know, this year (2016) marks 50 years of independence for Barbados. When I was at the Barbados Embassy a few paragraphs ago (different chapter altogether, actually) the Ambassador and I spoke at length about the things which would be considered as "problems" for the populace and economy of Barbados. He is of the view that with the students that come out from Barbados, there would come with them the attitudinal and practical means that would prove advantageous for the turning around of the country. This would then birth anew the country of Barbados. Now, at the Kempinski Hotel (at least, for now, I believe that's how it is spelled) the Embassy of Barbados had arranged a reception dinner, and all the students in Beijing were invited. I was most pleased to see Mathious and a few others who flew in from other parts of China, and we all sat and reminisced on the times and food back in Barbados.

During the reception, the Ambassador Dr Chelston Brathwaite gave a speech outlining the advances which Barbados has made in its relations with China, since its establishment in 1977. He also remarked on how a continued trust with the Chinese would benefit both countries involved. After his well-written and well-articulated speech, we had the buffet. The Embassy had flown in a top

Barbadian chef, and he had done some food that made our lives flash before our eyes. Not that it was inedible, but that the taste and flavour reminded us all of Barbados. So, we sat at the table and recounted stories of our times and experiences. At the end of the reception, there was some meeting and greeting, some pictures and some catching up.

A TASTE OF THE MOTHERLAND

> "No life can escape being blown about
> by the winds of change and chance; and
> though you never know all the steps, you
> must learn to join the dance. You must
> learn to join the dance."
>
> – Jethro, from Prince of Egypt

While I was on my way to Barbados' independence celebrations, I was met by Susan, the same Kenyan classmate that sat with me on the way back from Shanghai. She complimented me on my attire, inquired as to where I was going 'looking so smart', I told her about the event. She then said that Kenya was celebrating their independence as well. I expressed my interest in coming and celebrating with them. She was very happy and said that she'll add my name to the list of expected persons, and until the event, kept me posted as to the time and place.

When the time had fully come, I had got dressed in similarly smart attire and headed to meet Susan, my friend. I had prayed for her before we met up because she was having some problems which had her and her family really stressed, and I just wanted her mind to be at peace for her sake, because she has exams coming up too. I am writing this paragraph while sitting in my chair the morning after the event, and smiling to myself at the amount of fun that was had.

We left campus by taxi because the subway was overpopulated at this time of night. For those of you readers who have any idea of how the subways get in the most populated country in the world, you can appreciate why we would hail a taxi. Luckily, as soon as Susan's other friend arrived, a taxi was waiting for us, and so we got in and left. Fortunately for us, the celebration was at the same location as Barbados' Independence celebration, namely the Kempinski Hotel, so we had no trouble explaining to the driver where exactly we wanted to go. When we arrived, we could hear the music from downstairs, and just followed our ears till we found the others.

Kenyans everywhere! It had been so long since I've seen so many black people in one location. It felt so refreshing and nice. I felt at home. For the first time since landing in China, Chinese were the minority, coming in at about a dozen. The other couple hundred were people of my persuasion, black. They were all dressed in formal suits and elegant dresses, and they were standing and talking. One of the things which struck me about the room was that there were only cocktail tables, and no place to sit. When we arrived, we barely had time to put down our bags when a friend of Susan's greeted her in the line for food, and invited us to go in front of him. Kenyan food is delicious. Their style of beef and rice was exquisite, and their fish was so soft and melted in my mouth with exotic flavour. The double chocolate mousse was palatable and sweet, deserving of the name. The mid-level elegant music in the background was soft enough to accommodate conversation, yet loud enough to grip your entire body and sway you like a boat on the pier.

After the majority of people had eaten, I got the reason for why there were no dining tables. The DJ hit the play button, and the party began. The people started to dance in their places, as I looked on. However, the music, though unfamiliar: the beat and rhythm grabbed hold of my body and I found my legs and knees unable to keep still. I knew that it wasn't the red wine, but the music. My foot started tapping. As I looked on, the MC said, "Join the line", and I saw in the middle of the room that there was a conga line of about five people, dancing and moving through the crowd. I reached for my phone and by the time I got the camera running, there were twenty people in the line, then thirty. The line grew and snaked through the crowd. When it passed by me, I saw a familiar face of a guy from church (yes, believe it. I always see people I know) and he pointed in front of him and I joined the line with glee. As I tried my best to dance along with my brothers and sisters, the feeling of people watching you disappeared, and the sense of belonging, and the sense of family took its place. I no longer felt like I was on the outside looking in. I felt welcomed; I was with family.

I didn't know that I could dance for so long. There seemed to be no end to it. We shook our bodies and moved our feet for hours, with many little circles forming and doing their thing, with a person going in the middle to dance, cheered on by those surrounding. I'm sure that if you told me that I would be dancing with the Africans, I would tell you to go home. However, there I was doing the knee bender and the shoulder shaker. Dancing with Africans, there is no right and wrong move. You simply leave your pride and inhibitions at the door and loosen your limbs. There's music and wine to help with the loosening. Men in suits, women in dresses; suddenly all that came to naught, and these elegantly diplomatic officials transformed into the Africans we see on TV with the dancing and the hollering and the smiling and the laughing. One of the dancers even came up to me afterwards and commented on how good I was dancing. Apparently, all you need to dance is a grateful heart and a smiling face; enjoy yourself and all will be well. There were one or two people, though (who weren't Kenyan) who, though they were having fun, no amount of music or wine could make up for their lack of rhythm. But as stiff as they were, the only weird people in the room were those who weren't dancing.

Many officials and army personnel were also there, and I introduced myself to them, and offered my hearty congratulations to Kenya for their 53rd anniversary of Independence on behalf of Barbados and the rest of the Caribbean. One top general (I don't know his official rank) asked me if I had ever been to Africa. I told him that my family hasn't touched African soil in four hundred years. He smiled and said to me that I have to visit Africa. I agreed, and continued floating about the room. By midnight, the majority of the people there had left. There was one Chinese guy that was having the world of fun, dancing his heart out. I think he was one of those who stayed a little later. Later, however the majority of people had left and some of us took the opportunity to grab some of the leftover food in boxes; and Susan, her friend and I headed back for home.

BELIEVE AND BE BAPTISED

Now when they heard this, they were acutely distressed and said to Peter and the rest of the apostles, "What should we do, brothers?" Peter said to them, "Repent, and each one of you be baptized in the name of Jesus Christ for the forgiveness of your sins, and you will receive the gift of the Holy Spirit. For the promise is for you and your children, and for all who are far away, as many as the Lord our God will call to himself."

–Acts 2:37-39

One day, I was at church. Now, Church in Beijing is not like church in Barbados. However, anyone who believes the Bible to be the Word of God will do and believe certain things. I could go on and on about the differences between the two church cultures. For example, in Barbados, there's a lot of clapping and dancing and playing of the tambourine. In the Chinese congregation, there were no such expressions. We mostly sung hymns, and stood still. The Chinese congregation met in the great hall of the Xijiao hotel, because there wasn't anything else going on that would warrant that space. Should there be anything else going on that the hotel would deem important, then the church would be moved to a much smaller space. This is alright (to a certain extent) for the Chinese congregation, but when the English service starts, there would be so many people, that some would sometimes resort to sitting on the ground and standing at the back for lack of space.

While sitting in the great hall one Sunday, I couldn't help but notice that though I wasn't understanding a majority of the sermon (the more I go, the more I understand, don't worry) I noticed that the pastor had concluded a little earlier than was accustomed. Also, he was saying something else, and "while he yet spake", two or three people dragged a tub onto the stage behind him and about ten people got up and ran out one of the doors with plastic bags. I did not see what they contained, but I then discovered that the people who ran, did so to get changed to be baptised on stage. They went on stage one by one, and the pastor baptised them all. There was a certain feeling that came upon me as I watched these young people get baptised. I usually am quite happy to watch people get baptised, but this time was special. It was quite remarkable to see the same thing that I saw and knew from before, being transposed into a different context. I felt like the Psalmist David as he asked in Psalm 139:7-10 "Where can I go to escape your spirit? Where can I flee to escape your presence? If I were to ascend to heaven, you would be there. If I were to sprawl out in Sheol, there you would be. If I were to fly away on the wings of the dawn, and settle down on the other side of the sea, even there your hand would guide me, your right hand would grab hold of me." I felt the overwhelming internationality of God, and His omnipresent Word. I could feel His Spirit of conviction move through the congregation as these people outwardly showed their commitment to Jesus. I thank God.

Contrary to the practices in China, when people are to be baptised, everyone would pack picnic baskets and blankets and dress with hats and jeans. We'd then drive or charter a bus or large van to the place where all Christians are baptised: the beach! For those who are in the bus, there's lots of singing playing of the tambourine on the way. Sometimes, there're a few tuna sandwiches that are snuck out and passed among the younger persons. When we get to the beach, we have the church service on the sand with more singing and prayer. The one who is performing the ceremony then takes the candidates into the water, where they are baptised. Of course, shouts and cheers await them when they emerge from the water. After some more singing and prayer, the congregation spends the remainder of the day at the beach playing, swimming and eating whatever sandwiches are left. There's a lot more food where that came from.

CLASS TRIP PRESENTATION

I came to China. I have been blessed of God to have experienced so many things with so many kinds of people. Writing these chapters is honestly becoming more and more difficult for a very happy reason. When I experience something like climbing the Great Wall, walking along the Glass Bridge, or visiting children for Christmas Eve at the Children's Hospital, I feel an overwhelming urge to tell the world about it. However, after I return to my room, and get ready for school the next day, there is not much time to write anything. Seeing as I have school all day, time is becoming less and less accessible. Moreover, I became very sick for about two and a half weeks because of the pollution. Either that, or I got sick, and the pollution made it worse. This sickness, whatever it is, affected my grades, class performance and overall mood, but I praise God now that it's over…for the most part. Before I get into what that sickness was like, I'll first share a bit on the presentation for the class long-distance trip to Hangzhou and Shanghai.

Three persons from each class were asked to create a PowerPoint Presentation on the Long-Distance trip; and I was one of the students chosen to represent our class. I am not surprised that I was chosen for this task; but pleased that I wasn't being graded for the presentation. The entire college was split into two groups (C1-C9 and C10-C15). I am in C11; and I think that C8 and C9 had switched because C8's proficiency was higher than that of C9. Anyhow, I had gone up to the front of the auditorium and tried to present my part of the presentation, when the computer proved too old to support the format of the presentation. In doing so, the application ruined the presentation, and nothing that I had prepared showed on the screen. In Chinese, the phrase 哭笑不得 (kūxiàobùdé) means 'I didn't know whether to laugh or cry', and that was the way I was feeling at the front of the auditorium with all the students looking at me, and all the teachers pointing their phones at me with their cameras recording us as I stood there speaking through the microphone. It was funny. I started saying things like "I can't believe this" and "this machine is as old as my grandfather" *in Chinese* and this was rendering the teachers teary-eyed with laughter. I even used one of the old Chinese proverbs 塞翁失馬 (sāiwēngshīmǎ) which speaks to having a positive outlook on negative circumstances. I could not help but smile, and neither could the Chinese in the room. In the end, I had to do the presentation from memory and forget all the photos and animations in the presentation.

However, when I was done, the MC who was a teacher from the college, took the microphone after the applause and said to the rest of the college that "even though C15 is the class with the highest proficiency, none has the pronunciation of this student from C11". She went on to say that "if the rest of you work really hard, hopefully by the end of the school year, your speaking proficiency should be as good as Chinese people, or *his*". I was most taken aback. I could not believe that she said that in front of the entire college; *and here I was killing my pride, now I'm likely to be killed by my own classmates.*

CHRIST GETS 10 KUAI

This one of the most memorable moments in my Chinese life. I was coming from the supermarket, and I was on my way back to the campus when I came across an old lady. This old lady was sitting on the ground, and was struggling to get up from sitting. This was the same old lady that I had passed on my way to Kid Castle (which I had to leave, by the way) that very morning. I remembered Matthew 25, and I knew that God will see what I will do next. Upon seeing this woman, my heart was moved with compassion, and though I didn't get to her in time to help her stand, I was still able to put some money in the little tot which she had shaking for alms. As I was coming from the supermarket, I had some extra money that I could spare to give to this old woman. I gave her and continued walking. It was when I was walking, that I noticed that there were still a few more bills in my wallet that I missed. I turned around and walked back to the woman, and made sure to empty the wallet in the tot which she had and told her "I have no more to give you". The woman, seeing that I not only turned back, but gave my last, clasped my hands and bowed herself low to me. The amount of emotion I felt in that moment was overwhelming. Jesus was right when He said that it is more blessed to give than to receive (Acts 20:35). She bowed herself multiple times, and she seemed to be crying as she did so. There was a catch in her voice as she thanked me profusely which indicated a lot of emotion. For a woman to bend her back to bow to me, after taking about ten seconds to get up from the ground, *just* to express her gratitude for what could be described as a small amount of money, but with a large amount of love, struck me. I had to leave her quickly before I started crying too. I left her rejoicing. I remembered the line from the old hymn we used to sing in school "saying 'what ye do for others, ye are doing unto Me'". I remembered also the passage of Scripture in Hebrews 13:2 regarding entertaining angels unawares and showing hospitality to strangers. This being understood, I smiled to myself knowing that it could have been Christ to whom I gave money. Kindness from Christ is my portion, and I share that portion with others.

This document is the supposed second half of the previous chapter **A Change of Scenery**. I have had many wondrous experiences besides these which the blessed Lord has allowed me to have.

This is the disciple who testifies about these things and has written these things, and we know that his testimony is true. There are many other things that Jesus did. If every one of them were written down, I suppose the whole world would not have room for the books that would be written

- John 21:24

Like pulling teeth

"Whosoever therefore shall humble himself as this little child, the same is greatest in the Kingdom of heaven, and whoso shall receive one such little child in my name receiveth me. But whoso shall offend one such little child which believeth in me, it were better for him that a millstone were hanged about his neck, and that he were drowned in the depth of the sea."

- Jesus Christ

SOMETIMES, living abroad can become really discouraging. The life you live is completely run and managed by you. You are responsible for the organisation of your time, money, studies and travel. If one is not careful, then poverty will descend upon them like a thief in the night. I have stood and witnessed the financial downfall of many classmates and schoolmates of mine due to the squandering of funds on women and beer. I feel myself rather old when I think that it would be better to do without that extra meal, and save the money for later. Moreover, the level of pollution here in Beijing sometimes gets to the point where sickness and disease follow you like grace and mercy. Recently, in the last few weeks of 2016, I would say that I was struck with a plague of proportions beyond my imaginings.

I was sitting in the cafeteria one particularly polluted evening, talking to some friends of mine. All was going well, albeit a rather dry conversation, when all of a sudden, I felt a sensation as though something pricked me at the back of my throat. It seemed big, and somehow, I seemed to know what it meant. I was getting sick. Ironically, I had left them and went to visit a sick friend of mine.

When I arrived at his apartment, he offered me some soup. I accepted on the grounds that I believed that it would get *rid* of this thing in the early before any further viral or bacterial infection could take place. I had bought a few oranges, and had taken them for him to help with *his* sickness. He offered to share the orange (yes, he is a Christian) and we sat and talked. I pretty much enjoyed our conversation as always, but there was some study that I had to be doing, and I didn't want to take up too much of his time. So, I returned home and attempted to sleep. I woke the next morning with a sore throat, and nasal congestion. I went to class, did my work, and treated this like it was just another little cold. Where I'm from, treating the cold is as simple as spending a long Saturday at the beach with some oranges, and you're ready to hit the road by the following Monday. With that in mind, I continued to work, study and operate as though this cold wouldn't be any different. I was never so wrong.

TEN SYMPTOMS SAVE ONE

After dosing myself with green tea and fruits, the nasal congestion and sore throat left, and a cough and headache took their place. As to whether the headache came first, or the cough, is uncertain; but it would be noted that the headache was exacerbated by the excess coughing. The nasal congestion was cleared; or at least, it had gone down to my chest (hence the cough) so when dust came in, instead of mucus catching and expunging it, my body had to rely on good, old-fashioned sneezing to be rid of it. What I thought would take a few days to get over was taking more than a week, and I had examinations coming up for which I needed to revise. What's worse, is that as a result of blowing my nose constantly for over a week and a half, my ear popped; and though it did not hurt, it still left me turning my head to the right, so I could hear what the teacher was saying. All I could hear from my right ear was a nice high-pitched ringing of my temporary deafness.

Though I had examinations for which to study, taking medicine, or just having a tired body from doing the same things as usual *and* fighting off whatever this thing was, would have me asleep before ten each night. At night, no matter how long I sleep, I would still get up feeling as though death had answered the question "Where is thy sting?" In class, I would be falling asleep, though I was early, and participated when I could; but after class, I would head back home and fall asleep. One night, I fell asleep around eight pm. After a short time, I felt really cold. Though it was winter time, and my room's heater leaves a great deal to be desired, it was colder than normal. My roommate hadn't donned any more clothes, so I knew that fever had stepped in. I was trembling and could not sleep for a long time. If memory serves me correctly, fever was the only symptom which occurred on its own; all the others came in pairs. By then, I had just finished taking the Chinese medicine which got rid of the previous two symptoms. By now, if you're reading this, and aren't confused, there's a good chance that you're not paying attention. I myself was even getting confused as to which symptom came when. Some of these weren't even symptoms at all; just side effects of medicine, or a result of some other thing. Though I have absolutely no medical training at all (I learned to do CPR when I was a small child, but I'm sure that I've totally forgotten all that by now) I noticed that on the days when I took the Chinese medicine for the flu-like symptoms, something strange would happen.

One morning, my phone alarmed. Usually it doesn't startle me, but on that day it jumped me out of my sleep, but when I jumped up, I couldn't open my eyes. *What is going on here?* I was fumbling and fidgeting trying to find my blaring phone to shut it off. As I could not see, I frantically moved my hands about the bed until I found it. When I managed to shut it off I stumbled to the door and began peeling whatever secretion it was that calcified, sealing my eyelids. By the time I had got to the door, I had got rid of most of it, and was able to see myself in the small mirror hung on my roommate's wardrobe. At the sight of my face, I hastily headed to the shower to warm myself and make my face presentable for class. *That took some work.* In the afternoon, when the others had left for lunch, I had remained in the classroom. The fever had returned, and I was wearing my down jacket in the well heated classroom. Mr Zhao, who you'd remember from Chapter 7 *Far Away And Back Again*, had inquired as to my well-being, as he noticed my lowered participation. He then asked if I had eaten. Not only had I lost my appetite, but just walking to the bathroom from class felt like a trek across the Arctic. He deduced that I had a fever and left the classroom. He returned with a bag of KFC and a bottle of dissolvable aspirin to take. When he entered the classroom, I looked and beheld the bags which he presented to me. I was completely bowled over by this level of kindness. I was struck dumb and almost trembled as I took the food from him.

Every time a symptom came up, I would take something like fruits, tea, Chinese medicine, or Western medicine, and it would work…for that particular symptom. Then another one would take its place, and knock me back down again. Yet, it was all one big sickness. After about two and a half weeks, I finally felt better, and resumed my studies as per usual. I thank the Lord for bringing me back to health, and trust for His continued hand on my body.

As this is the first time writing for the New Year 2017, and I thank you for all your support over the last seven chapters of my life in China, even as far as taking the time to read all my meanderings. As mentioned earlier, discouragement is something which takes hold of me from time to time, and I need your prayers. I was even discouraged to stop writing altogether. It was as though the thought was "you don't need to write anymore, give yourself a break. Nobody reads what you say anyway." I admit that sometimes, many days – perhaps weeks would go by, and not a word is written. Then, I would get an email from a friend here, a Facebook message from another friend there, and one by one, the messages of encouragement would keep pouring in. One friend told me forget about the "Happy New Year" and get to sending more of my writings. I found that tremendously encouraging, and this particular paragraph is for them. Thank you.

WHATEVER YOU DO…

Some people partake in feasts, some hold parties. Some go to church for the only time in the year. Others take time off from work and remain at home with their families, or even fly across continents to be with them. What about me? What did Stefan do for Christmas – his first Christmas in Beijing. Well, I wouldn't say that I had a feast, nor did I see any of my family members. My first Christmas in China was spent…in the hospital. I wasn't the one who was ailing, though. By then, my cold had gone, and only a few coughs remained. No, I had been invited to go to the Peking 3 Children's Hospital in Beijing with a friend of mine from the Fellowship. Of course, remembering the Children from Living Tree Orphanage, I immediately cleared whatever I had to do, and met up with the group which was going. From the train station, we met up with another team which had gathered to wait on us at the train station where we got off. From there, we had walked a few minutes to the hospital and split up into two groups, as the numbers were quite large. One of the leaders of the team was a large white male, so he brought along a Santa Clause outfit to wear.

The head nurse was extremely happy to see us, and showed us where we could sit and sing Christmas songs. Those children who were able to come outside were brought out, and upon seeing Santa, they hurried and sat on the ground with the nurses as we sang English and Chinese versions of some well-known carols. While we had their attention, some of us had little booklets with the Gospel of John in Chinese to discreetly hand out to some of the parents and nurses who were there. There were also little pamphlets with the true meaning of Christmas, which we gave out as well. Maybe if we had gone in saying that we come to share how you sinners need saving or will spend eternity in Hell, we probably wouldn't have got through the front door. However, with the God-given creativity granted some of us, Christmas cards were made (more than 80), toys and other gifts were bought, and instruments were played to bring joy and smiles to the little children who are sick and suffering in the hospital, those patients who are recovering from various surgeries, and parents who are worried over the health and wellbeing of their beloved children.

There was a large area where we sat and played and sang with the children, but my heart was not satisfied. I hadn't yet touched the hands of any of them, nor had the opportunity to speak to any one of them vis-à-vis. I overheard a woman asking a nearby nurse if there were still more children in the wards who couldn't come out. Hearing what the nurse said, I grabbed a few pair of tiny socks and started scouting the remaining wards. I went into the first ward and saw a mother who looked rather drained, and a small child on the hospital bed. I came in, and lowered myself to get close to him. After greeting him, I reached from behind my back and produced a Christmas card. When the boy saw it, he dropped the one that he had already and grabbed the one in my hand with great enthusiasm. *This one has STARS!* He was so very thrilled that I gave him this new card; and the mother could just stand there looking on, smiling. In the midst of his excitement, I produced a pair of socks and handed it to him. He took them and though his mouth was covered with a mask, I could see his eyes open with delight as he took the socks from me and started examining them. He showed his mother. He then looked at me and in his tiny Chinese voice, said "谢谢你给我这件圣诞礼物" (thank you very much for giving me these Christmas gifts). I smiled, took a picture with him, and left him rejoicing, tossing the socks up like a man in a pile of money.

Leaving his room, I ran back outside and grabbed more cards and more socks. I was overwhelmed by the tremendously positive effect that a pair of socks could have on one person. I remember when I was in Barbados, I had a drawer that couldn't close because it was so full of socks and other clothes. An entire chest of drawers was in my room, filled with clothes. At my father's place in the same country, I had another set of clothes. I was blessed with many things. Clothes is one of those things, and I am grateful to God.

THANKSGIVING ASIDE

Christians are to be thankful. Sure, things don't always go our way, but we are to be cognizant of the ever-powerful hand of the One who holds the sun in place, and gave His Son for our salvation. I encourage the Christians reading this to take into consideration the magnitude of the sacrifice of the Lamb of God. When we understand that we are the ones deserving of death and separation from God for all of eternity, we would then have a slightly deeper understanding of the Cross. There are many scriptures supporting this, but this is an aside on Thanksgiving. The reason I had mentioned the Salvation aspect is that my attitude is that if the only good thing God gave me was His Salvation, He would still be most deserving of my thanks. Paul, the apostle and bond-servant of our Lord and Master Jesus Christ had put it much better than I. When I search the Scriptures, and see the many times that thankfulness is *mentioned, I think more and more that this is something that should be characteristic of the person who professes Christ. Colossians 3:17 says that ~Whatever you do in word or deed, do all in the name of the Lord Jesus, giving thanks to God and the Father by Him.~ Ephesians 5:20 affirms this by saying that we should be ~giving thanks always for all things unto God and the Father in the name of our Lord Jesus Christ.~ 1 Thessalonians 5:18 says ~In everything give thanks; for this is the will of God in Christ Jesus concerning you.~ If I had a US $1 for every time I hear discussions about "God's will for your life", without mention of thanksgiving, I would be able to book a flight from here to Moscow every week for the next 200 years.*

As the exaggeration is a bit much, so too is the amount of discussion on the topic of God's will for a person and their life. I even know a young lady who was told by a man on a pulpit that it was God's will for her to go into a particular field of work. As she plunged herself into this field of work, she discovered quickly that it was something that she did not like. She found out further that no matter how hard she tried, and no matter how much she studied, she did nothing but fail. She consequently became miserable, and spent many nights crying herself to sleep because of the regret which she felt for following a man's words blindly, without consulting God first. She had now wasted years of her life in what could be deemed as a wild goose chase. Now, I am not saying that this is the case for everyone, nor am I using this poor girl's story as a control for all those seeking employment or a field of study. What I am saying dogmatically is that there is the verse in Thessalonians which says that the will of God for our lives in Christ Jesus, is not that we become doctors, lawyers or even prophets; but that we give thanks in all circumstances, along with the other attributes listed in verses 12-23 in the same chapter 5. It means that no matter the situation, the Christian is always to be thankful. Our thankfulness does not depend on happenstance, because we do not feel very happy when our mother is diagnosed with cancer, or when an earthquake kills thousands. However, the hard thing to do is to be thankful to God amidst the tears, amidst the heartaches and amidst the calamity. As the bride of Christ, we are to be thankful to Him for richer; for poorer, in sickness and in health, as long as we shall live.

A STITCH IN TIME

> "As you go through life, you'll see there is
> so much that we don't understand; and
> the only thing we know is things don't
> always go the way we'd planned."
>
> – Simba, The Lion King

Most of the people who would be reading this would know the age-old saying that a stitch in time saves nine. The idea that prevention is better than cure is one that has been adhered to by some, and ignored by many. I could go into all the details about people who have refused to take preventative measures, and ended up paying a costly price later on. One day, I had looked into my mouth and seen a small hole in the bottom-right molar at the back. I had prayed that it was merely a dent, and told the Lord that I would go to the dentist to have it checked out. The dentist took one look at my mouth and exclaimed. He advised that it was crucial that I get the tooth extracted as soon as possible. However, I couldn't get it done there, I had to go to the larger public hospital for the operation. I was beginning to get discouraged, and did like David and encouraged myself in the Lord. I went to the hospital and made the appointment. The dentist at the school's hospital had told me that I have to get there early, and I found out when I got there what he meant. The hospital opened at seven o'clock for appointments, but when I got there, albeit on the dot, I found that half of Beijing was there as well, with similar and vastly different problems to mine.

There were over forty persons in the line ahead of me, and there were 15 lines. I'm glad that I had brought a book with me to help pass the time. My appointment was made for the afternoon, and I still had enough time to get back to campus, pack my bag, and head to class on time. I left at lunch for the hospital, assuming that I would be able to accurately squeeze the operation into the time slot between lunch and class, so that I would be able to minimise the amount of time spent away from class. Class time is very important to me, as I had zero absences for the semester: something which even the teachers admit is not a very easy thing to keep up. I thank the Lord that my dormitory is practically next door to the teaching building.

As there were people who needed more complicated surgeries than my little extraction, I had to wait a really long time before I could see the dentist. Finally, when I got there, I had to get my mouth X-rayed to verify my suspicions. The doctor quenched any other hopes I had of avoiding the procedure by affirming what the first dentist said, though the two of them were miles apart. I took his advice, and agreed to the operation. Having had this done already, I knew that the risks I would be taking by having it pulled paled in comparison to the dangers of leaving it, and letting the pin-sized hole develop into one too large to manage. I was given the anaesthetic injection, and I was soon numb in my tongue and gum. Soon afterwards, I began to feel pressure on the area where the tooth in question was. Though I was not able to understand what the doctor was telling the assistant, nor was I able to see because of something they placed over my face, I laid there and started to pray…for other people. I thought of people who I knew were going through tough situations, and prayed for them. I thought of my good friends who are not saved, and I prayed for them. I thanked God for them, and prayed for their salvation. As I prayed, I felt the doctor pulling and heaving my rather large tooth. My tooth was giving him hell to extract. I know that it was because its root was really big, just like the one above it that was pulled a few years back. I also knew that as this one was the bottom one, in the jaw, it was close to the nerves and some pretty big blood vessels. As to the extent of my biological studies, I stand under correction and do not speak on this matter with much authority. What the doctor did tell me was that it was a risky procedure and I could get hurt from it. I felt a chill run down my spine as the thought seized my mind of something hitting an important nerve, and causing paralysis . I took a deep breath and continued praying for others –even the doctor.

Suddenly, after changing positions three or four times to no avail, the doctor said something to the assistant. The assistant then began to hit my tooth with some manner of hammer! It felt as though they had a chisel of some sort and they hit it in about four sets of three hits. I was stunned. *These people seriously pounding my tooth with hammer and chisel?* I tried to hold myself together and continued to pray. I knew that they were just trying to dislodge it some more, but I know that when the anaesthetic wore off, this is going to have me in some serious pain.

After some more pounding, I felt some more pushing and pulling; and then, I felt a string. *A string? They're going to tie it to the door and slam it to yank out my tooth?* Fortunately, the tooth was already out, and the dentist was just stitching the gaping hole left by it. It was over, and he allowed me to sit up in the chair. He spoke and told me in his best English what he had done, and that I needed to get back to him in a week to remove the stitching. He also prescribed some pain killers for me which I was to take twice daily, along with telling me to take some time off from class. Luckily, it was a Thursday, so I would not be missing that much class. Moreover, I could present my receipt and note to the student affairs office, and have my absences cancelled on account of doctor's orders. When I had got my first tooth extraction, I was still able to go to class, and there was not much pain involved; I couldn't speak, but I was still at class, and doing my work.

Riding on this experience, I actually thought that I would be able to make class the very next day. I was wrong. That very night, the anaesthetic wore off and the pain hit me like an 8-ball was thrown at my mouth. The pain rocked me, and took me by great surprise. With trembling hands, I reached for the painkillers and took them; but the pain continued for another 2-3 hours before subsiding a little –like a golf ball hitting me instead of an 8-ball. Later that night, I tried lying down, but I could not find a position comfortable enough that would cause the least pain. They all caused some manner of discomfort, and I didn't want for any of my sleeping positions to dislodge any of the other teeth. Closing my mouth, I felt some of my teeth colliding instead of fitting together like they would usually; and it was difficult to deal with as I tried not to fear my mouth's position staying this way. I would get to sleep after a few hours of trying, and get up early in the morning, because the pain would return with full force. This continued for a few days, but I was able to make it to class the following Monday.

HAPPY NEW YEAR

Immediately following Christmas, we had…more class. Class was to continue until the middle of January, as Chinese do not celebrate the New Year like Westerners do. The dates are different as they gauge from the Lunar Calendar. The New Year here in China is from January 18th this year. Next year, the date would be different. People around this time travel back to their hometowns to spend the time with their families and loved ones. However, as Beijing is the capital, very few people who live here originated from here. Ergo, around this time, Beijing becomes a ghost town. Luckily, my friend Bunny from when I was "Getting in the Swing of things" had forewarned me about this situation, and invited me to come over to her province, which was nearby Beijing. Until that time, however, I still had some more class to attend, and my final exams were also coming up. As it was the New Year, the school (well, my College) had still put on a small party for the students. It was organised in such a way that the different classes were paired with another of similar Chinese proficiency. My class, C11 was paired with C12, and we were given a small amount of money to purchase snacks and drinks for the party. When the party got started various students went up to perform skits, songs and play various games. My class teacher had told me that I was expected to sing. Though at the time he told me, my throat was still very much affected by the cold, I chose a song I thought sounded cool and sang it for the class. Shagor accompanied me on guitar, and I started the song. Despite much practice, I still forgot a few of the words, but the crowd's eyes were still fastened on me, to the point where I had to close mine. Because I knew what the song was about (entitled "一千个伤心的理由" "a Thousand Reasons to be Sad") I sang with the passion of someone who was in the situation described within the lyrics. When I was finished, there was a second of silence before the crowd erupted in applause. My spirit was taken aback at their response, as I made my way back to my seat. I thanked them for their kind words whenever they came afterwards telling me of "how well" I sang. I even kept to myself for a while to let the hype die off, but as that was the last performance, it was a little harder to avoid the compliments. Anyhow, thank God for a wonderful party.

What better way to celebrate the New Year than to have exams? Finals were quickly approaching, and we had to prepare. Moreover, the classes were designed in such a way that the final sessions were all review. So, when I went into the exam room, a lot of the information was still fresh in my mind, and I was able to do well on the exams. Because of my attitude in class, punctuality and homework performance, my final transcript showed distinctions all across the board with remarks of excellence from my class teacher. Also, I did fairly well overall in my examinations and scores, bringing my total performance to way above satisfactory level. I thank God for allowing me the privilege of studying Chinese and even the grace to do well.

PUTTING TWO AND TOO TOGETHER

Now that exams were over, I had more opportunity to leave campus and do other activities. English Corner was seeing more of me as well, and I was even bringing a friend of mine along with me. One particular Saturday afternoon, I was having lunch with the other participants at the restaurant across the street from where English Corner is held. Debbie, the loving lady that takes us to the orphanage, suddenly became very excited as if she had just remembered something. She stops the chatter that everyone else was having at the time and called everyone's attention. With excitement in her voice, she pointed to me and announced "they loved the boots". It took me a while to process what she was saying, until one or two of the others lit up and agreed with her. It then hit me. *My boots!* The boots which I had bought that were too small and two pairs, I had decided to donate them to the orphanage. That was in October of 2016, as I thought that if I was trying to buy boots to protect my feet from the oncoming cold winds, that the orphans would appreciate them too. I took both pairs and sent them to the orphanage. Debbie and the others that went said that the kids that got them came rolled out in their wheelchairs and showing everyone their new boots. Debbie said that she *never would have thought* to donate them, but I did; and she was now proclaiming to everyone present. I could not help but cover my face. I was completely bowled over. Neither Debbie nor I could believe the impact that a simple pair of boots could have on a person. I'm glad that they were appreciated (Matthew 6:1-4) and I thank God that I was able to give *to one of the least of these.*

A PEACEFUL STAY

As mentioned earlier, the Chinese people take the time to go back to their hometowns to spend time with their families. Therefore, everyone in Beijing —or should I say every Chinese person- had left Beijing, unless of course, their hometown was Beijing, in which case they'd stay home. For the remainder of the city, shops would close, as all the owners would pack up and go home. It was proving to be a boring time for those who would be left behind in this city which turned from bustling to boring overnight. Meanwhile, Bunny had invited me to her place. Now, for those of you reaching for your Bible and prayer cloths, let me finish my paragraph. She too was going back to her hometown to see her family, and seeing as the city of Langfang 廊坊 was not going to be as drained as Beijing, there would still be places open and I could stay at her place for a while. To me, to get away from the bustle and noise of the capital was seeming more attractive. I could spend some time alone in a place where no one knew me. In fact, I could spend some time in the city where there were no other people who looked like me. I was excited.

As usual, Bunny booked the train ticket for me. I had planned to leave on the Saturday before the holidays stated, as I saw that even the little kiosks on campus were selling out their stuff and packing away things to shut down the stores.

John, who is the leader of the English Corner had asked me to fill in for him on that same Saturday. I decided to lead the English Corner for him, and then leave for the train as soon as I can, in order to meet the train at a reasonable time. English Corner that Saturday was not difficult to lead, but I found myself humbled that my God would allow me to see a glimpse of my dream. I was standing, surrounded by Chinese, teaching them the Bible, under the guise of an English learning platform. The lesson for that day was "Unity in Diversity", and I figured that there could be no greater example of unity in diversity than having a black person teach Chinese people. I used that as an illustration of the unity that brings Christians together by the Love of Christ.

UNITY ASIDE

There are many people who have been trying to answer the question as to whether we as the body of Christ can have unity in diversity. I had one day posted on Facebook that the Apostle Paul had encouraged the Church to be "of one mind". He had so emphasised this point that he said that it would make his joy full. He makes mention of it in Romans 15:5-6; Philippians 2:1-2 and 1 Corinthians 1:10. The reason I had uploaded that post was that there was an organisation of which I was a part, and it was going through a troublesome time, in which some particularly zealous people, in their search for true doctrinal teaching, left their love behind. Some joined them, and the body began to tear down the centre, dividing the members between the "know-its" and the "know-it-nots". There were even relationships which were shattered because of this divide. Men who jumped on each other in brotherly affection now passed each other with a mere nod of the head. Couples who couldn't get enough of each other were now separated and broken up. All around me, I could see the destruction that this disunity was causing, and I was feeling grieved, knowing that splitting was not the Godly way. Moreover, as I had friends on both sides of the divide, I was completely dumbfounded and didn't know how this would be fixed, especially as either side had developed a gross dislike for the other. Eventually, the radical group left, and the numbers in the fellowship cut in half. It was no longer "we are family", but us versus them.

While at Urbana Student Missions Conference 2015, I got my hands on a book by Dr Christena Cleveland entitled **Disunity In Christ**. While reading this, the author had really illustrated the psychological reasons behind why people think Christianity should be approached like "Us four, no more. Shut the DOOR!" When people see others "them" and themselves as "us", then any difference that is encountered is seen as a threat. Instead of engaging and focussing on the similarities that bind us together, differences are emphasised and even invented, in order to keep others away. If different "others" are kept from us, we will be able to keep our sub-identity, instead of focussing on the larger, more encompassing identity of oneness in Christ. What this means is that we should keep Jesus' prayer in mind. In John 17, when Jesus was praying, He particularly asked for the Father to keep us in unity, with the same togetherness that He and the Father have (verse 20). While in China, in a church congregation that had people from 70+ different nations, I got a greater appreciation for those who are different from me in Christ. It has been a tremendous help for me in China as I interact with Christians who, though they view God the same as I, their interaction with Him is different.

It is impossible to read the scriptures without coming to the conclusion that humility is one of the main ingredients of Christianity. You cannot get along without humility. We cannot study the Bible without humility; we cannot serve each other (or God, for that matter) without humility. In Romans 14, the person who only eats herbs can only get along with the one who eats everything if they are humble. If they see themselves as higher, or closer to God than the person who "contaminates himself", and they condemn them, then unity will never occur. So, humility must come first, then unity will follow. Speaking of unity, I met a man one day on my way to get my internet sorted out (this is going on a month now that it still hasn't been sorted). I was walking and reading a book which I had recently bought on Chinese Idioms and set phrases, when a man eyed me and the book. When he eyed the book, I angled it so he could see it better and read the title. After reading the title, he asked me about my interest in it, and where I am from. When I told him, he inquired as to whether it was a Christian country. This man was tall (yes, a tall Chinese man), and seemed to have a number of years on him. When he asked about the Christian nation of Barbados, I couldn't help but be sceptical about the direction this conversation was going; especially seeing as though he was wearing colours green and gold, reminiscent of someone working for the authorities.

He then expressed his deduction that I was a Christian too. As to how we got from Chinese idioms to Christianity in three minutes or less of conversation meant to me that either he was anxious to fill his prisons with believers, or he was eager to meet another believer in Christ. When I said I was a Christian, he stretched forth his hand and loudly congratulated me. From there, we talked until the cold got too much of us, then we ventured inside for warmth. We spoke about everything, and I could tell that as old as he was, he still humbled himself to listen to what this boy had to say about the Bible. His main concern (and this is why this story is mentioned in this aside) was that too many assemblies are not permitted to let Chinese in to worship with them. The government regulates that only Chinese with an international passport can enter certain assemblies, and he was adamant that the church here was rolling over and obeying man rather than God. As opposed to encouraging unity in the Body, division between sets of people was created and this, he believed, is not the will of God for the Church. This, of course, is much easier said than done.

Meanwhile, back at English Corner, as I had prayed for a smooth session, I found that the lesson was excellently executed, and the time was adhered to with on-the-dot precision. I didn't know why, but it seemed as though the Lord was making sure that I was early for the train station. When we got to the end, we said a prayer, and headed to lunch. There, Raissa, one of my friends from Ivory Coast sat next to me as the others found their seats around the table. I was just sitting there, and pretty much keeping to myself. The Chinese were chatting away in their native language, and I was content with just listening, and picking out the words and grammatical structures that I know from the conversations I was overhearing. Raissa on the other hand, though she too was studying Chinese, did not see it that way, and it was not long before she got too overwhelmed by the others' speech. I was quiet. I was just itching to leave and get on my train to Langfang 廊坊. Just as I was in thought, my friend burst out for everyone to speak English (she said that in Chinese, I'll have you know). They all chuckled, and one of them turned to her and asked her what it was that she would like us to discuss in English. *Please don't say marriage, please don't say marriage.* She then said that she would like to know more about the Chinese culture as it relates to marriage and marital relations. It seems as though that is the only thing on the minds of Christian young people, and though I refuse to leave any further thoughts on that here, I sighed deeply and forced myself to remain seated.

As the conversation pressed on, I kept looking at my watch to see if I still had enough time for the train. Sometimes, in my thoughts and daydreaming, I would pop back to reality to see if the topic had changed. *As if that were going to happen.* One lady that was there mentioned that a popular question that is tossed around is 'who would you save, should your mother and wife both fall into water?' Now, Stefan Lorde could sit there and let them speak among themselves and arrive at whatever conclusion they see fit. I could have even taken that time to leave and head off to the train station. To me, the answer was simple: the man is the representative of Christ in the marriage. Christ gave up Himself to save the Church; therefore, were I in that position, the answer would be obvious: save my wife. Of course, somebody disagreed, and said that he felt a duty to his mother. I said that you will be faced with situations in which you will be forced to make a decision between what you feel and what you know is right. Now, I cannot aptly explain my position or his in this paragraph, so if you readers disagree on what my position states, you too are entitled to an opinion. But there have never been any cases that I have heard or seen where that particular situation happened, nor do I think that it is likely to happen. Let us move on.

I left the restaurant, and headed to the train station. When I got to Beijing South station, I checked in and proceeded to look for my gate, so that I could be early for my platform. I was about an hour early, and I thought that I could take the time to catch up on my reading; but no matter how much I searched, I could not find my platform. It was only when I asked the third guard that she told me that I am at the wrong train station! I was at Beijing South Station, and not Beijing Station. I had to run to the subway station, take the subway from Beijing South Station to Beijing Station and check in all over again, to then find my platform. Now I know why it is that I got to the station over an hour before schedule. I made it to the correct station 20 minutes before my train was to depart, and made it to the train just in time for it to hit the tracks. In China, there are three types of trains which are available. Two of them, I have experienced already when I went FAR AWAY AND BACK AGAIN. As I was late in booking, all the tickets for the high speed train had been booked, and I was stuck with the baseline train.

Inside this train was hot and crowded. There was a repugnant odour that filled the carriage, and I felt my nostrils being ravaged by the unwelcomed fumes. *Must be that raw garlic that people just chew on.* Everybody seemed to be carrying more bags than the train could hold, and it was very uncomfortable. I managed to manoeuvre my two small, albeit cumbersome bags into the small space around my seat, pull out my book and a snack. This is also the slower train. Unlike the High Speed one that would have me in Langfang in 20 minutes, this slowpoke will chug along the tracks and would take 3 times as long to get to the same location.

An hour later, I arrived in Langfang. Disembarking the carriage, I was walking along the poorly paved embankment, and was immediately struck with the differences between this humble city and my belovèd Beijing. Straightway, a random guy struck up conversation with me. I believed that this was the start of a very talkative vacation, as I continued the conversation. When we were parting ways, he told me that I should find myself a Chinese girlfriend. I laughed it off and bade him adieu as we left the station. Bunny met me a few minutes later, and we caught up for a while before the bus came. As the Langfang government wants to limit the number of cars on the road, public transportation is free. However, as the bus was yet to arrive, the bitter winds attacked us with a vengeance. When we arrived at the apartment, Bunny walked me through how things worked before taking myself and two of her other friends to lunch at a nearby restaurant. The restaurant's specialty was beef noodles, and I could see why. It was very tasty, and I was very disappointed when I got to the end, because I wanted more. I determined that I would eat there again. One thing that I could not help but notice is the portions of meat in dishes like beef noodle soup. The pieces in the bowl were few and far between, as if to only add flavour to the dish.

CON TE PATIRÒ

The next day, Bunny left, and I alone was in the apartment. The level of peace that I found in that solitude was incredible. I found myself meditating on God's Word, taking long walks and praying, and even doing morning and evening stretches. The apartment was a good way's off from the main road, so there was much quiet as well. I was very pleased with this getaway. That morning, I boiled some eggs and drank some water. I've got to hit the supermarket if I'm to survive. When lunch time approached, I found myself at the same restaurant at which I ate the night before. I ordered the same thing, and sat down. While I was sitting, there was an old man who worked in the kitchen, who wanted to use the bathroom. Seeing as the bathroom was already occupied, and I just happened to be at the table closest to him, he dropped himself in the seat opposite mine and looked at me with a smile. He smiled with a particular curiosity that seemed to wonder if I spoke Chinese. I satisfied his curiosity by greeting him in Chinese.

Conversation ensued, and he got more and more enthused. Like most people, he inquired as to the length of time I was studying in Beijing. "Old Beijinger" 老北京人(lǎoběijīngrén) is the term used to describe persons who have spent a long time in Beijing (maybe a generation or two), and who are very much accustomed to the culture and language of Beijing. I told the gentleman that my friends call me this when he asked me how many *years* I was in Beijing. When I said more than 4 months, he slapped the table in disbelief and exclaimed "no wonder they call you Old Beijinger!" He even grabbed a nearby waitress and pointed at me, shouting "foreigner!" **As if the wonderful colour of my visage wasn't proof enough.** I then indicated to him that the bathroom was now available, and he smiled, leaving me. When I was finished my delicious meal, I took my bowl and made eye contact with one of the waitresses and smiled. In my best Chinese, I asked "is this your specialty dish?" She said yes. I responded by saying "no wonder it left me so satisfied". Her warm smile could be felt, as she took my bowl and left for the kitchen. I couldn't be sure, but I thought there was something in the way she looked at me. I brushed it off as all in my head, and headed out for my afternoon walk.

That evening when I returned home, two things occupied my mind: the food at that restaurant, and a particular television series that I've been watching over the past few weeks. Of course, however, when I thought about the food, that particular waitress would come to mind, and I would wonder if there was really anything going on besides plain customer service. Let it be made clear that I had no intentions of entertaining any 'flings' or 'flams' while on this vacation. Therefore, with that in mind, and the fact that I had convinced myself that it was all in my head, I found myself at that very same restaurant the very next day, ordering the very same thing. This time, another waitress had taken my order. *See?* I told myself, *this is all in your head.* I sat down and I ate this wonderful beef noodle meal. It was nice and hot – perfect for warming up any weary travellers like myself. I sat there eating. Around the time that I was finished eating, there happened to be very few patrons in the establishment. My favourite waitress took it upon herself to begin sweeping the floor, before more patrons could enter. When she got around to my table, I moved my feet that she may get better reach with her broom. I then opened my mouth, just like they do in the movies, and said "you know, in my country there is a saying that no one will marry you if someone sweeps a broom over your foot." She stopped and looked at me. Her head gave a slight tilt as she rose from looking under the nearby seat.

"China has no such saying," she said, intrigued now by the topic of conversation.

"I know," I said, smiling back at her. "China has no saying so strange. This is my country's saying." Leaving the name of my country out of the equation was the perfect lure, and she clung to it: bait, line and sinker. Fortunately or unfortunately, I was a child that was gifted with the ability to guide a conversation to a mutually desirable topic. As what I suspected was all in my head, I had nothing to fear, right? Wrong! What happened next convinced me otherwise, and swung me the opposite direction. Seemingly unconscious of her actions, she reached back and grabbed the end of her hair and twirled it in her fingers, before catching herself and grabbing hold of the broom. As her hand was on its way down, she asked me the name of my country. Of course, when I told her the name, she expressed that she had never heard of Barbados. I knew that it would be unlikely that she would have the foggiest clue as to where or what it was that I told her, but she turned her now bright red face away, and resumed sweeping. If I were not convinced before, I was then. Though it were that nothing concrete can be pointed out as being "a spark", and though I could be wrong and this could all very well be in my head, throughout the conversation, I pinpointed at least 5 instances where I could have asked her when she got off from work or when she was taking a break. The more I thought about it, the more opportunities I saw that could lead elsewhere. I left the restaurant.

For the next two days, I avoided the restaurant. The first day after that, I went to another restaurant that specialises in pizza. I thought to myself *it's been a while since I've had pizza*. I went inside and the food I ordered came up to three times what I would spend in the previous restaurant. The next day, I went to a fast-food place, thinking that it would be at least more economical, even if not as filling. That was still close to twice as much as I would pay for beef noodles. Again, I convinced myself that I am just imagining all these things, and that being in that apartment by myself for so long has played on my brain. On the third day, I went back to the beef noodle restaurant. By now, it was well into the Spring Festival holiday, and the restaurant had altered its opening hours. It was a Friday, and I was planning to return to Beijing the following day. I was beginning to miss my friends in Beijing, and I couldn't spend money so loosely on food every day for very much longer. When I arrived at the door, I tried my best to decipher the sign posted on it. *Were they closed?* I could see people inside, but they all seemed to be the ones who work there. I returned my gaze to the sign. Knowing only about 40% of the characters, I pieced together what I was reading, and concluded that they were still open. I could have simply pulled the door like normal people. Upon pulling the door, I gazed inside and found that only the workers were in. I stepped in. No one objected to my entering, so, I figured that they were still opened. When I got in, one of the guys sitting called someone's name and alerted them to my presence. As if on Lifetime Premier, or some other *romcom*, who should get up and turn around to find me there but the waitress in question. She practically skipped over to me, and I ordered the usual. There was no longer a blush in her face, but her smile was ever beaming. I would go on to describe her more and how that interaction went. I could even go on to the many times she snuck glances at me as I ate and chatted on the telephone with my friend Daniel, but I can already feel some of my readers sending me messages about this "mystery girl", asking questions or even questioning my motives.

Whatever else happened or could have happened in there left me fully convinced, and I left still on the phone with Daniel. When I got to the end of the road, I turned around and proceeded to head to the mall. Little did I remember that the restaurant I just left was closing around the same time; and upon heading back that way, I saw two persons coming my direction. She was one, and her colleague was with her. As these two young ladies got closer, she waved at me with bubbling excitement. This seemed to be an expression absent the confines of professionalism and work ethic. In a second, I realised that if I left for Beijing without telling her, she may spend a long time looking out for me to come into the restaurant. As they walked by, I told her that I was leaving for Beijing the following day. Looking back at me, she stumbled over her friend as she stepped. "Beijing?" Her smile so quickly went, and her countenance fell so far down, that I could feel her disappointment as it pierced her. All the colour seemed to leave her face as she stood there with her mouth slightly ajar in disbelief. I too felt sorry to see her like that, and the few seconds that passed felt really slow. I, then did the unthinkable. I broke eye contact, turned around and continued my walk.

A NEW DAY HAS COME

"...and be ye not conformed to this world: but be ye transformed by the renewing of your mind, that ye may prove what is that good, and acceptable and perfect will of God."

– Romans 12:2

Since the last chapter of my life, or at least that last one that I have written, I've returned to Beijing. When I came back to Beijing, I was ready to take the New Year by the horns and ride the goodness out of it. I was well rested, and I had finished the homework that we were given to do during the vacation. The homework was as such that the first forty pages or so were very simple: multiple choice and such. However, when those were over, the more difficult ones came. They were not as the multiple choice that took all of one to ten seconds per question. No, these were the ones which required thinking and analysis. Grammatical syntactic, yea even morphological analysis was needed in this second section. Then, each page's content was taken from that which we did in class, according to the chapter of the books we studied. As if that weren't arduous enough, the bottom of the page had fifteen new words which we had to write sentences. Particular grammatical structures had to be used, which would therefore warrant more complicated sentences. It took me quite a long time to complete, but when I did, I was quite satisfied.

I mentioned all of the above mainly because I was under the impression that though the work was intense, the time given was more than enough to complete it. The first twenty pages could be done in one day, the second twenty another, and the last two dozen pages could be done two per day, and you'd still have all the time in the world to do your gallivanting. I was never so wrong. I am sitting now sixteen days after school resumed, and there are still some students who haven't completed their homework. *Who am I kidding? Homework is for nerds.* When I had returned to campus a week before school was to resume, I asked my friends about the homework. I got the same answer from all of them: "I will do it tomorrow". I thought to myself that it is impossible to do and complete all that homework in such a short space of time. Given the amount of thinking and writing that one had to do for the last few pages of the homework book, it would take too long. But, some still had it in them to procrastinate, and now their homework was still not done. While I cannot believe that some are squandering their opportunity and potential, some of you readers cannot believe that I took up two paragraphs of your time complaining about slackers. Ah well, I promise the next paragraph would have something different.

[***]

So, here we are in the next paragraph, and you dear readers are expecting something different. I came home from Langfang and opened my door to find a new roommate. Some of you may remember my first roommate from when I got here, the one from whom I sought to flee. When I arrived at this new room, my new roommate was a guy called Chabni Muhammed Zoheir (or Zack, for ease and simplicity). He was cool, helpful and all-round a good guy with whom to share a room and to call buddy. We often spoke and shared music and movies. His girlfriend would come over and bring food for us, and we'd all sit and eat together. She didn't speak much English, so I took the opportunity to practise my Chinese with her whenever she came over, while I'd speak English with Zack. His brother, whose name slips me at this moment, would also come over, and it would just be a grand time whenever we were all here having a good time with lots of laughs and food. Though his real name slips me, he said that he calls himself Jack in English speaking countries. . Someone having more than one name, and being called something else in a different country or language is really cool to me, and I'm glad that I can join in on the multilingual and multicultural fun being had by the rest of the world. Unfortunately, Zack had graduated and finished studying at BLCU, and was just waiting out his days before he left. From the time he said that he was soon to leave, all the good times flashed before my eyes, and quickly puffed out of sight as I snapped back to reality. I couldn't believe that all this goodness was to be so short lived. To me, he was the standard at which a roommate should be in terms of maturity and compatibility. I prayed. I prayed hard. I prayed to the Lord God not to give me another roommate, because I know from experience how miserable it could be when you're living with the wrong person. Needless to say, the Lord God deemed it fit to have me live with another roommate. *breathe* I did not want another roommate. The dorm manager said that they were moving people from other dorm buildings and putting them in Building #1 a.k.a Guantanamo, so it wasn't a question of "if" but "which one" I was going to be getting. The other students in the dorm called it Guantanamo because the beds and facilities there had gone a while without being repaired or replaced. That, plus the cockroaches, and having to live with someone that you may not really like, inspired the students to give the dorm building that nickname. I still prayed to the God of the impossible to get my way, but he would not have it. When Zack left, not even 48 hours had passed before keys were rammed into my door and, swinging open, this large, broad muscle man entered my room with not one, but four pieces of luggage, and a backpack. *My poor heart.* Not only did he take up a lot of space with his luggage, but by just standing, his frame seemed to take up the entire doorway. It was only when he moved to come further in that I saw the friend behind him who was helping him with his luggage. My countenance sank, and my smile quickly shrunk. I was not happy.

Upon seeing me, he looked back at his friend and uttered the words "oh good, he's black. I'll be okay." I wondered what experience he would have had in the past to make him utter such a statement, but that thought was quickly expunged by the fear of the discomfort which would accompany him as he lugged his things into the room behind him. Back story aside, now I was back in Beijing and after much prayer and petition, I noticed that he was still in the room. It was ten in the morning, and he was still in bed. He spent the remainder of the day sleeping, and got up at night only to go to the club, get drunk, and come home to repeat the cycle until school resumed. I would say more, but this is not a forum for complaining; God hates complaining.

THE LORDE RETURNS TO THE CASTLE

Changing the topic to something less distressing, I was sitting quietly in my now not-so quiet room when my phone vibrated with a message. When I looked, I beheld a message from Lisa. Lisa is the person in charge of the Kid Castle in my district. For clarity's sake, I had left Kid Castle in 2016 when I had counted the cost, and discovered that it was taking more out of me than I was willing to sacrifice. I was "in training" and I was obviously not being paid for it. When I did my first class with them, though it was at this nearby Castle, it felt to me like a complete failure. I told them that not only was my entire Saturday being used up in travelling to and from training (three hours total), but after training for about three hours, and then to return home, I would be exhausted. Moreover, I would be spending too much money in transportation. Anyhow, that was in 2016. This year I got a message from Lisa asking me if I would be willing to be a substitute teacher for the month of February. As the two branches are hours apart, my first thought was that Lisa was uninformed about my resignation. When I informed her about my departure, she told me that she was well aware, but she still believes that I have the potential to do an exceptional job, and she believes in me. It didn't take me very long to make a decision after such encouragement. When I was at the other base in Chaoyang District, I couldn't help but notice the slight fear in the eyes of the colleagues there. There was no encouragement from the leader there, and the others just seemed to "do their job". The atmosphere seemed to dim slightly whenever the lady in charge was in the room, and I thought that it was just me. However, upon reading the message from Lisa, I was more willing to give it a try. I didn't take long to think about it. I responded to her within the week and told her to count me in. As God's Providence would have it, the College was not resuming evening classes until the next month. So, I had all the opportunity to teach in the evenings, while being a student in the morning. I thanked God for the time and opportunity, and I decided to give it a go!

My first class was on a Sunday. Though thoughts ran through my mind about working on a Sunday and all that, I concluded to myself that God gave me this opportunity to enhance myself in gaining some valuable experience. I thought that it couldn't be coincidental that I'm being presented with this opportunity at the same time that all my evening classes are erased. So, I got up, brushed off my shoulder and headed to church that Sunday morning. After church, there was Bible study and lunch as usual, and I went to work in the afternoon soon afterwards. I prayed. I prayed that God would give me the creativity to teach these kiddies with all enthusiasm. I remembered in the Old Testament when the Sanctuary was being built. I remember that God said that He will give certain people certain skills (Exodus 35:30-35). Therefore, I figured that God is more than able to inspire me in the same manner.

I went to the institution, and got the books which I would use to teach the content of the class. Luckily, there were many teaching aids there at my disposal. I guess that you, my belovèd readers would like to know about my first class, so here goes:

I got to the classroom and started with the one student that was there named

Zosima. He was a very attentive student, and he learned the work well. If memory serves me correctly, we did some dialogues and consonant blending. Ann soon joined us, and we continued. Their level of English was pretty high for their age (7 or so), though I believe that Ann needed more encouragement and practice. When I was finished with that particular class, I left the classroom feeling on top of the world. I thought to myself *I can do this. I can actually do this.* I went to the staff room afterwards (because I am on staff now, ha-ha) and I sat down to do my write up. Each student has a book in which the teacher writes their notes regarding said student, their behaviour and conduct. I believe the parents would read these notes, like how we have report cards in Barbados. I had nothing but good to write to about those two students and thought to myself that I could really get used to this job. It was having a good impression on me thus far, and from the students' work, I could see that they actually were learning. Needless to say, I walked into my next class with a smile so big that the top half of my head would fall off, had I no ears.

When I got into the next classroom and was met with the rowdy, misbehaving hyperactive boys of the next class, I thought to myself that it was going to be a long evening, and it was only just beginning. This second batch of students were so very difficult to control and to teach, and it seemed obvious that they came from homes which reflected a kind of laissez-faire style of parenting. If I had longer hair, it would have been all pulled out because of the level of stress they would have caused me, if I let them. The attitude I did not want was one of mediocrity. I didn't want that I would believe that once I am getting my money at the end of this month, you could act in whatever manner you choose, and I really could not care less whether you spend an entire year here and leave still being unable to spell your name. Such is the attitude of some, and such is the attitude I will avoid, as long as the Good Lord grants me the Grace to do such. When I was finished with that class, I headed to the staff room, where I was met with a sympathetic teacher, who reassured me that I was doing a good job. She was very encouraging, and I felt much better afterwards, though the children were too disruptive, to the point where I hadn't managed to complete the allotted tasks for the evening. I rested assured that I had done my best, and went on my way.

As I spent more time there at this Kid Castle branch known as Mirror Edu where *your achievement is our Pride*, I couldn't help but notice that one of the teachers here was reading a particular book. This book, which shall remain unnamed, is as such that I was warned about it. It was many years ago that I was privy to reading a short article written by a young gentleman who had found the Lord, after living in sin. He made mention of the book, and how he had read it. When he was saved by Christ, he then said that the book is complete nonsense. Though this could be seen as a frivolous thought, I held fast to the opinion that even though a large number of Christian Theologians disagree with a large number of *other* Christian Theologians; for a person who read something as a sinner, and then come to Christ and count said book as nonsense has to have some merit to it, given the total transformation power of Christ's shed blood. I decided then, based on this, and as Christ as my witness, that I would purchase for this teacher in question a book which I deem suitable for someone seeking God to read. The reason that the aforementioned book remains unnamed is for the simple reason that I haven't read it, and it would be remiss of me to name something as nonsense, having not read it myself.

TOTAL DEPRAVITY ASIDE

Some Christians, upon hearing those two ominous words up top, begin to get all antsy. Here, I will be bold and write to you a little about what it is, and why I chose to bring it up here. The reason I wanted to bring it up is because of the previous paragraph when I mentioned the total transformation power. I mentioned it because "the one who is forgiven much loves much" Luke 7:47. For the cleansing power of the blood of Jesus to be appreciated, the sinner would have to realise that they are completely helpless without Christ when it comes to approaching the Father. There is an old song which says "souls in danger, look above. Jesus completely saves" For this to be true, and for all the Scripture regarding salvation to be true, the sinner would have to be completely in need of Salvation. From my understanding, people upon hearing 'total depravity' think that this means that mankind is completely wicked and every human being is the most wicked person in the entire world. They misunderstand it to mean that this doctrine teaches that all people are immensely wicked, and every thought, word and action of every human being is ultimately evil, with no shred of good in them at all. This is not accurate.

Some people go to another side of the spectrum, believing that man is good, just a little broken by sin, and that Salvation is just that little boost that man needs to reach 100% righteousness so we can see God's face. This also is inaccurate. That being said, I would like to address what I believe the Bible says about total depravity. This would only be a very basic, short and precise exposition about it, because to go deeply into what total depravity means —or any doctrine, for that matter- would take up more that I am willing to address here. Therefore, if I miss anything, it is because it wouldn't be considered "basic".

Firstly, man was made perfect. In Genesis, we see that man, as he was created, was a perfect being, without fault, and without sin. Man was made with two abilities: the ability to sin, and the ability to not sin. Unfortunately, when man thought it was a good idea to reach for more than what he had (namely, God status) he sinned. He sinned in that he disobeyed God. His purity was then tarnished, and he was no longer 100% righteous. Furthermore, nothing less than 100% righteousness is required to see God's face, and so, man was banished from God's presence, no longer able to see His face. Sin, having entered man, affects all the facets of man. This means that your intelligence is affected by sin; your world view is affected by sin. The fact that we get sick, is as a result of sin being in the world. This might not mean that every person is born believing in Amun Ra or Zeus; neither is it to mean that the reason for sickness is as a result of someone's individual sinful actions. It means that man by nature is sinful in all aspects of his being. The reason we would have sinful thoughts, even if they are few and far between, is because our mind is corrupted by sin. You may be saying that you don't have that many evil thoughts, or that you don't think yourself to be wicked like Bin Laden; but when you read through the commandments, you would see that even the first one you have not kept perfectly. This is because we were born sinners. Sinning does not make us a sinner; being born a sinner makes us sin. If that is the case, and we are born sinners, that would mean that there is absolutely nothing that we can do to please God who requires 100% righteousness to be in His presence. If you look at the commandments, any of them, you would see that the exact opposite is the norm in any society. Take this commandment for example: you shall not steal. Not only have we stolen things from pencils to human organs, but we have evolved more complex and sinister ways to swipe things from under people's noses. It comes natural to us because…we are born sinners; we're good at it. Since we are born as sinners, and every aspect of our being is affected to one degree or another by sin, it would mean that nothing we could ever do would be able to suffice, because no matter how "good" our motives or intentions might be, it would come from a less than righteous heart, and it just would not do. Our good is just not good enough. We are totally depraved. (Jeremiah 17:9; Matthew 19:25 Proverbs 20:9) What then? What hope is there? Salvation through Jesus Christ.

对牛弹琴- PLAYING THE LUTE FOR A COW

There was once a man in ancient times who could play the lute very well. Everywhere he played, people would laud him, and he was known all throughout the land for his talent. One day he saw a cow grazing in a field, and figured that it would greatly appreciate his playing too. After all, who didn't? So, he sat himself down and began playing for this beast. However, no matter how well he played, nor which tune he rendered, the cow just stood there staring at him and chewing its cud. The man then went away feeling very sad. This proverb is the illustration needed for the following account.

There was a young man in my class. For his sake, I wouldn't mention his name. We will call him Max. Max and I sat pretty close together in class, and I would help him on occasion as he doesn't learn as quickly as the rest of the class. We began to be friends, and when we went on the school trip, the teacher saw it fit to bunk us together. We would talk, and enjoy each other's company. On the trip, he admitted to me that were it not for being my roommate on the trip, he would have found himself in trouble like the misbehaved ones. He said I "had a positive influence on him". I was glad that I could have such an influence on him, and I thanked the Lord for our friendship. However, I noticed something about him. I noticed that while trying to explain something to him, he would cut you off by saying "this is too hard" or "man, this thing is confusing" or the like. *Big man, I am trying to explain something to you, just shut up and listen; then you'd understand.* I also noticed that he was the king of conspiracy. For example, when on the trip he came up with the notion that we were moved from a good hotel to a not-so-good hotel because of the behaviour of some on the train. As to how we could change the hotels and arrange the lodging of 400+ students in less than twenty-four hours after months of planning, and still have enough money to buy the expensive train back to Beijing is beyond me. However, there was no convincing him otherwise. I just let it slide as simply part of his personality, and give a little chuckle whenever he brought it up. Aside from that, Max and

I would get alone well in class, share food and exchange music. All was going well.

One day, Max was looking a little down. I was not too bothered because, being a drunkard, hangovers are common, and so I just let him be. He and I often see who could get to class the earliest. I use 'earliest' because there was another guy from C12 who would get to class early too. So, that day when Max was there, I went next door to C12 to see my other friend. As we were talking, Max arrived at the door. We were in the middle of saying something funny, and so when he arrived at the door, the laughter died down and we both looked at him. Given the nature of our usual conversations, a one-liner or some joke would be expected, so I was waiting for him to say something funny or ask what we were laughing at. He just stood there. He looked angry. I was confused. He walked away. *Ooooookay!* I continued talking with the other guy until class started. When I got back to our classroom, Max looked furious. I asked what the matter was, and got no reply. I was really confused, but I sat down and we had class. While class was going on, I received a message from the other guy asking what the matter was, and if it was a good idea to apologise. But I still did not know what was the matter or the offense, so I didn't know what he would be apologising for. I suggested that it would be better to apologise, just in case. At break, I left the room while the other guy came in and apologised to Max. This did not help the situation, as he still did not budge, neither would he say what was wrong with him. After class, he snatched up his bag and stormed out. The next day was worse. He came into class believing that whatever I was discussing with the other guy was obviously about him, and now our entire school knows about it. He said that he went outside to smoke, and everyone outside was "looking at him funny". He then accused me of creating a group chat on social media to make fun of him, because he went to sleep at 4 am that day. I was beginning to get really frustrated, as I tried to tell him that I have no idea what he was talking about. It moreover seemed that the more I tried to convince him that this was all in his head, the more he became convinced that I was somehow trying to turn the school against him.

I decided that playing the lute for a cow was not for me, as it is really pointless trying to argue with someone who has made up their mind about something. My father always told me as a child: "a man convinced against his will is of the same opinion still" and this is something regrettably that I had to face many a time. When people are closed-minded, then it is hard to teach them anything. Max would see me in the hallway: "man that thing you did spread like wildfire." I am still confused. On one occasion my temper slipped and I yelled at him for his delusions. In class, he would burst into fits of laughter. As soon as the teacher turned their back, he would laugh at something. Nobody else was laughing, and when the teacher would ask what the matter was, nobody had anything to say because the one who was laughing was not responding to the questions asked. While this is going on, Stefan Lorde decides that this is not worth his happiness, and so spends more time in bed when the mornings come. I took to making myself some oats and cinnamon for breakfast and spend a few more minutes chatting with persons who don't share a time zone with me. I thought to myself that it's better to be at least happy away from him and get to class at my usual 45 minutes before schedule, than to get there and have to face Max. One day, after the first class period, I walked around the hallway, greeting friends and chatting, when I glanced at my phone. To my surprise, I saw a missed call from an unknown number. I ring them back, and when the other person picked up, I was even in greater shock. It was student affairs.

So, your boy Stefan got called to the office. In the beautiful island of Barbados where I'm from, should you be called into the office, and it be not for a reward, you would have a beating to look forward to when you get there, and when you return home. A little while before that call, some of us in the college had applied for an extra scholarship that the college had. The case was that the funds allocated for student sponsorship still hadn't all been given out, though all the students were covered. So, a notice went out for all the good students in class to apply for said extra scholarship, to use up the remainder of the money. Of course, every Tom, Dick and Stefan applied for this extra money, and I felt a glimmer of hope that it was the Student Affairs office which was calling me to tell me secretly that I had been granted the money. Nah, I was wrong about life yet again. The office told me to come to them as quickly as possible; so, I quickly made my way to the office. When I got there, I was asked to sit. The teacher there in the office looked over her table at me and asked me a question that made me heave a great sigh, "Now, Stefan. What's your relationship like with Max?"

I will give the reader time to breathe as I took a few seconds to gather my thoughts before writing that last line. I even sighed just now before writing this one. I began to explain to this very understanding teacher all the things which transpired between us from before the trip till then. She hummed with intrigue, and listened more. She told me that he had reported me for creating a group chat on social media, and making fun of him. In truth, I told her that I have created no such group chat, and not only could she check my phone, but the phones of any of my classmates. I assured her that if such a chat existed, I wasn't its author, nor was I in it. I had even told Max that if I hear anything about a group chat, I will let him know immediately. I let the teacher know that Max was not eating, he was not sleeping, and his diet comprised mostly of plain Vodka and cigarettes. After listening to me, the teacher responded thus: "I have listened to him, and I have listened to you and I am now of the view that this is his problem." I sighed a sigh of relief as she sent me back to class, just in time for the second one to start.

I returned to class and sat down, thinking that it was only a matter of time before Max's mind snapped and he got expelled and deported back to Sudan. Maybe that was wishful thinking; maybe that was too much punishment for something so relatively small. Anyhow, things started to get more interesting. The funny thing about paranoia, is that people will soon start to notice. If you walk around thinking that everyone is looking at you funny, soon enough, they will start to look at you funny. Some friends from other classes started talking about 'this weird guy from my class', and asked me what the problem with his brain was. After class, Max would snatch up his bag and storm out, giving the rest of us the opportunity to talk about him, each of us bringing another story about him to add to the discussion. One guy who lives in my building told me that he was even scared to stay in his room, because Max was on his floor, walking up and down screaming "Lucifer's here!" I laughed out loud, and here's why. 罗(luó)思(sī)凡(fán) is my Chinese name. From the pronunciation, you can clearly see how "Luó Sīfán" could turn to "Lucifer" in the mind of someone who only feeds themselves nicotine and alcohol. As I am somehow the one to blame, my name would be the one used. It just sounded like the name of that fallen being. Of course, by the time the news came to me again, it was changed to "Satan's coming to kill me". Amazing how a message can change over time, and over number of messengers. If people weren't looking at Max funny before, they were definitely looking at him funny now. As the days rolled on, Max was concerning me less and less, as he got more and more crazy. When he wasn't crazily bursting out with laughter in class, he was furious and quiet with veins pulsating out the side of his temples. People who sat next to him moved to the other side of the classroom. He would send drunk texts to the class group chat, and to others individually. He sent me one asking if I was "satisfied with my accomplishment" and wondering what I "had to gain from doing all this to him". One week, he didn't show up to class at all, and we were all quite relieved that he wasn't there, making us uncomfortable.

Max finally showed up one day and told me that he stopped drinking. He told me that the reason for his behaviour was his lack of sleep, along with smoking and drinking heavily. He said that combination made him start "seeing things, man". I said okay, but still kept my distance, as my trust was fully betrayed by this man. I could not talk to him after that, I could not even look at him after that. I was sorely disappointed in this 32-year old's behaviour, as he is setting a very bad example for his kids. Yes! When he declared that he "was off the bottle", another classmate, Pam was quick to agree with him, and say "yes, he really stopped drinking. I know, I'm there to be his probation officer." Stefan Lorde believed neither of them, but continued to keep my distance, to the point where one day, he asked me if we're okay. I was like WHAT DO YOU THINK, DRUNKARD!? All in my head, of course. I always hear the stories of people who do bad things to you, and then act as though it never happened. I've seen the Facebook posts of people ranting about "being hurt" and blah blah blah, but I never thought that it could happen to me. I was not really hurt by it, but I would admit that I had to pray for him, and take a few breaths before going to sleep, and before entering the classroom on mornings. I don't think that I answered his question directly. I sure didn't give him the cussin' that other people thought he deserved. I rejoiced. *What?* Yes, I rejoiced. Many of you who are reading this now would be familiar with the teaching of Jesus in Matthew 5 when He preached the **Sermon on the Mount**. He said "Blessed are ye when men shall revile you and persecute you, and speak all manner of evil against you falsely for my sake. Rejoice and be exceedingly glad, for great is your reward." There was nothing I could do, but exercise self-control in not retaliating, and so I have the Holy Spirit to thank for His fruit. Needless to say, Max was at it again soon enough, and it wasn't long before he was drinking and smoking and sending drunken messages in the class's group chat -and to me, of course. Some others also indicated that he messaged them privately as well. I was glad that I hadn't wasted any time with trusting him again, and wondered what Pam thought about her friend now. I then concluded that trying to talk to him, or anything of the sort would be like playing the lute for the cow.

万般皆下品，唯有读书高。

All other professions are of low degree;
only reading is of high degree.

– Confucius

One day, at Bible study, we were all gathered at the table reading the Word of God, and eating the food of China. However, when it got my turn to read the passages, there were obviously characters which I did not recognise, and therefore was unable to call them. This was the last straw for me when it came to the decision to purchase a Bible with the Pinyin pronunciation in it. The only other factor which would prevent me from purchasing one with pinyin was that it was about 4 times more expensive than the regular bilingual one (as it is printed and then imported). I sent a message to my Bible study leader and asked if she thought it was a good idea to buy it. Not only did she agree with the idea to purchase it, but she forwarded me 60% of the money needed to buy it. Needless to say, I went immediately and purchased it the very same afternoon. I thank the Lord that I was able to receive such a blessing for the sake of me understanding of his Word. I smile to myself as I think back on the blessings that God has bestowed upon me.

Another such thing for which I give thanks is Mirror English (Kid Castle). I remember when I prayed and asked God for a new phone. Knowing Him, I believed that the things which we deem as unimportant, God actually pays attention to. I figured that as He is concerned about every facet of my life, that a cell phone which has been mine for years, embarrassingly slow and frustratingly outdated, needed to be replaced. I trusted that He would either provide me one for free, or he would provide the wherewithal to obtain one. The latter was His will, as He providentially brought Kid Castle back into my life. The "wherewithal" they gave me allowed me to purchase a new phone. I thank God. I pray that He continues to enable me to trust Him for bigger and more 'important' things in my life.

TEACHING RESUMES

For the new semester to start (yes, we had class before the semester actually began), we had to sit another placement test. This placement test was set with the content of HSK 4. HSK stands for Hànyǔ Shuǐpíng Kǎoshì 汉语水平考试, and it is the standard test for Chinese language proficiency. Having an HSK is your ticket to most things study related in China. Many universities require this certification, and it's the word on the lips of all students in Beijing. From HSK 1- very basic proficiency, to HSK 6- Doctoral candidate proficiency, you are sometimes looked up to or looked down upon, based on the HSK level which you have attained. For me, it is not necessary now for me to worry about HSK, as I have already been accepted into the University of my choice, and only need to pass the exam set by the China Scholarship Council (which is easier than other exams).

However, the college had seen it fit to use the content of the HSK4 exam to gauge where we as students are in terms of proficiency, and separate us to suit. I have got so very accustomed to the students and teachers of C11, and though I would have preferred to have some of our classmates moved to other continents, it would not be my lot, as I would see later, after the exam. We had already sat this particular examination, but my result was as such that I felt very bad upon seeing it. My teacher even was greatly surprised, and we went up to the office to review the exam paper to see where I went wrong. Even though the result for the end of term last semester was satisfactory, this was slightly more important. I was a little discouraged (okay, a lot discouraged) and I was not too confident in sitting it again. I had drawn a conclusion that I was not good at sitting exams, because I would confidently sit in the exam, and write it. When the results would come out, I found that my result would not match the confidence with which I wrote the exam. For example, out of a possible 300, I got 194. I found that the persons in class with the least admirable attitude to study, and the most hideous characters would be getting more than that- even more than 210. My disappointment was inexpressible.

This time, I walked into the exam room feeling casual. I did not think too highly of my potential grade, and did not even study that feverishly. However, when I saw the results, I laughed at the fact that I got the highest grade among the males in the class, and second highest overall. 238.5 was my grade this time, and it was the perfect grade for staying in the class which I was in from before. I liked that. I was very grateful to God for that. One of the reasons I wanted to write about this, was that one of the students in the class got 179.94. Stefan, why is that important? The pass mark is 180. I was most hysterical that he would get such a mark. He was one of the more careless lads in the class, so it does not really surprise me that this would be the result. I was only hysterical at the infinitesimal difference between his grade...and the passing grade.

As the new semester rolled on, I was fighting the temptation to worry about not being able to pass the course, or even finish the degree. The new words which we have to learn every day, from their tones and stroke order, to their meaning and context. Moreover, it would be the stumbling block in any language learners' path, should they think to allow their first language to influence their production of the target language. Students studying a foreign language should be weary of what we in the Linguistics world call "L1 interference" where one would use the sentence structure, vowel pronunciation or grammar of their mother tongue to produce the target language. Fortunately, it is postulated that simply knowing of this phenomenon could be enough to avoid it, as the language learner, fearing error, would seek to put aside their mother tongue for the sake of the target language; but that's just a hypothesis.

As the teaching resumed, the results from the test we did were used to separate us again into classes. Also, those whose majors were business, accounting or finance would also be separated into classes according to their proficiency, and according to their major. During the previous semester, some studied hard, others partied hard. So, now, in this semester, every student is given the same book for business and mathematics, irrespective of Chinese proficiency. For this reason, many who didn't study hard before, have had their rude awakening now, as the mathematics book is in Chinese, and the business book has vocabulary and grammar on par with that done in classes of mid to high proficiency. As Errol Barrow would say, they're now "catching their royal[10]" because the words

10 A phrase I first came across in a speech by Errol Barrow (Father of Barbados), meaning to be left running helpless.

in the business reading book (which is all in Chinese too, by the way) are far more in number, and far higher in complexity than those of normal reading, as theirs are the jargon of the business world. Before, friends of mine would ask me for the translation of certain words of which they were uncertain. Now, because their major is different to mine, I am unable to give them an answer. For this, I am grateful. Because they are forced to look up and learn for themselves the words which they do not know. As my major is Chinese Language, I would learn the words according to Language and Linguistics; and as I have already studied linguistics as a degree, I at least know the terminology in English. All I need to do is apply it, and learn it in Chinese. For this also I am grateful. One of my classmates (actually one of my favourite classmates; or rather my 'partner in crime') was moved up to C12, because, as she had studied Chinese last year as intensely as we're studying now, she has a proficiency and vocabulary way above mine. Therefore, as far as the HSK results were concerned, she got a whopping 278, while I was gunning for second place with a 238. Not only that, but she has to do math and business as well, whereas I don't. So, regrettably she is no longer by my side, as I sit alone at the top of my class. I thank the Lord that He has allowed me to be of such a high proficiency, and I pray that He continues to bless my studies as I continue to give my utmost for his highest.

Not only has teaching resumed for my teachers; teaching has also resumed for me. Though the person for whom I was substituting has returned, and though the month of February was over, I was still "volunteering" at Mirror English, teaching English to little children. Granted, I was only teaching two days a week, a total of three and a half hours: two on Mondays and one and a half on Tuesday. The Monday class is the one that is a little easier to teach, because they are older, and they have a little bit of English under their belt already. As I have asked the Good Lord for wisdom and creativity to teach these kids to the best of my ability, He would put ideas in my head that I would not have otherwise thought of. I would use flashcards and invent games and competitions for the children to exercise that which they've learned to gain the most points. Kid Castle has designed a reward system in such a way that points earned in class could be rewarded with point cards. Accumulate enough point cards, and they could be redeemed for toys, puzzles, stationery, among other fun things. The students, therefore will be more active in class, should they be rewarded with stars or points. I remember studying a school of thought called Positive Reinforcement, made famous in the world of Psychology by Jean Piaget and B.F. Skinner. As a little with content is great gain, so too, a child with encouragement is great progress.

As I conclude this chapter of my story in China, I endeavour to keep my light shining. All around me, people are smoking, drinking, wasting money and swearing. I rely only on the grace of our Lord to keep me from falling into the same habits. I was once told "the best man...is a man at best". I use this saying, albeit secular, to remind myself that because I am born a sinner, no sin is impossible. The seed for every sin is in my heart, and should I for one minute lose sight of the One who sent me, I would quickly slip into the huge abyss of sin, and my witness will be lost. I remember Peter when he took his eyes off Jesus, and allowed the sound of the raging seas and howling winds to frighten him. He allowed the things of the world to distract him from the One who has conquered the world. These accounts in the Bible were written there to be our examples. We are to keep our eyes fixed on our Saviour. We are to continue pressing toward the mark for the prize of the high calling in Christ Jesus. We are to resist being conformed to this world, and continue being transformed by the renewing of our minds that we may prove "what is that good and acceptable and perfect Will of God". One last story before I go:

One evening, my new roommate was about to leave. He asked me a question that took me quite aback. "Are you married," he asked. I was laying on my bed, and what I did not want was a topic as broad and as touchy as that. Though it is a topic that I seek to avoid, I was intrigued as to why he asked such a strange question. "No," I obviously replied. By now, the reader should have their head tilted slightly in curiosity. He saw Kunal's picture which I always keep atop my table. Under his picture are the words "your child", and I had already told him that I had adopted Kunal. He wondered how it was that I could have adopted a son without being married. I explained that "sponsored" is a better word, and that I didn't need to have a wife to sponsor him. Quenching more of his curiosity, I went on to explain that GFA takes the poor children off the streets and educates them in the name of Jesus. I further explained that my sponsorship of Kunal allows him to finally go to school, receive education and food. My roommate looked puzzled. "I don't get it," he said. From my point of view, I could not perceive why he could not understand. I thought that I explained it simply. "I was educated for free," I finally told him. "Why should I not provide for another that they be educated for free also?" I could see from the vacant expression on his face that he still was not getting it. I did not know how much simpler I could make it. Scratching his head, he asked "so, do you receive any benefits from doing this?" I could not want this conversation to end any quicker, as midnight was quickly approaching. I told him no. I was going to add that my only reward was that Kunal was getting to be a child free from poverty, hunger; and free to pursue an education, but I figured that if kindness confused him, selfless investment would make brain juices ooze from his ears, so I kept quiet. After a few more seconds, it finally clicked. He said, "So, you're doing this for free with no benefits?" I said um-hmm.

"DAMN," HE SAID. "YOU REALLY ARE A CHRISTIAN!"

A world of Culture

"If all that we say in a single day with never a word left out, were written down each night in clear black & white, it would prove strange reading, no doubt. And if, just suppose, 'ere our eyes we would close, we'd read the whole record through, then wouldn't we sigh, and wouldn't we try a great deal less talking to do? And I more than half think that many a kink would be smoother in life's tangled thread, if half that we say in a single day were left forever...unsaid."

– Anonymous

THIS POEM FINDS itself being brought back to my memory with great force as I sit here at my computer for the first time since Spring 2017 was in full swing. I have not touched my computer in weeks. I have been discouraged, disheartened and just too darn busy to be available enough to start, and you know what they say about the journey of a thousand miles. I know that this document would be more than a few thousand words in length, and so the discouragement to even start is seemingly a lot greater. Notwithstanding, some things have been happening to me as of late which I find too significant to leave the memory of such to chance. I was encouraged further by a brother in the Lord, Brother John, to write down the experiences that God has allowing me to have recently. I will start with the one that I told John, the one which triggered such a response from him. But first, the reason I put that poem up as the first thing you see under the title.

I had just finished eating supper with the Japanese congregation (yes, the Japanese congregation) and I had told someone a certain story in my past. The reason I had to is because she asked. She asked me about my country and where it is, and I used the map on my phone to show her. Before I knew what was happening, I was telling stories from my childhood, and unfortunately had her full attention. The more I told, the more she asked; and the more she asked, the more I told. You know those times when people give their opinion on something they didn't experience? Does it seem as though their solution to your problem is ever so simple? Well, yea. I came home thinking to myself, *maybe I should have just left with the others, or only show her the map and shut my mouth there and then.* However, I didn't, and I left feeling as though I dug myself deeper and deeper into a slimy hole —one which I have no means of escaping. It is only when I got to the shower later on that night that the poem above hit me. Maybe I should start responding to people using that poem instead of actually talking myself into a hole. Anyhow, enough of my meandering —on to the stories.

WITHOUT THINKING

I had found myself in a nice, little routine when the weeks came. I had class during the week, along with two classes per week which I teach on evenings. I was going to church on Sundays, and participating in small group with other believers, and English Corner with John. However, something else has become a part of my routine. Something strange. Something that even most Christians do not even think about. Something powerful. Coming home from teaching one evening, I stopped by the corner shop to grab myself a pancake. Now these aren't your regular Aunt Jemima pancakes with the flour and the syrup. These pancakes are: made with a heated batter; topped with egg, sausage, and a crunchy centre; and wrapped neatly in a nice, tasty filling snack. I was riding my bike to the corner, smacking my chops all the way. I bought myself the pancake, and resumed peddling my bike home when I spot a homeless couple laying on the ground. I pulled over my bike. I looked. I went over, and reached for 10 kuai[11] from my wallet and placed it in the hands of the man, as was my custom whenever I pass anyone homeless (the woman was covered and presumably asleep). The thought hit me as soon as I touched his hand, *this man cannot eat money; he's probably hungry.* I took the hot tasty, scrumptious pancake, and with watering chops, I

---

11 Kuai or Renminbi (RMB) is the currency of the People's Republic of China

handed it to the man. "I give you something to eat," I say to him. He grabbed it with both hands and thanked me profusely. When I looked up, a security guard was staring at me. To see someone of my…persuasion speaking to someone who everyone ignores –maybe he himself as well, and not only talking to them in their own language, but also caring for them in giving them food was probably strange for him to look at.

Though I left there and went to buy myself something else to eat, I decided to make this a new habit of mine. What I would also do, in the event that, without food I come across someone homeless, I would put 10 Kuai inside a Gospel track and hand it to them, being sure to tell them that the money is inside, and all I ask for them to do in return is to read. One particular guy's eyes lit up so brightly when I handed him the pancake. Someone else was scrimmaging through their purse to gather their 1 Kuai bills together to hand to him. His eyes shifted to the food I was giving him, and he reached out his hands to gratefully grasp the warm package. The woman next to me with the 3 Kuai was also very surprised. I also gave him a little money and rode off.

The next day, I repeated the process, this time, I bought two pancakes, because I still hadn't had any for that week. I left Kid Castle one Tuesday evening, and went, as was my custom to the corner of the street to grab myself a pancake (well, two). When I started describing what I wanted on the pancake (everything) the lady doing it remarked on how "good" my Chinese was. After asking where I studied Chinese, she inquired as to whether the second pancake was to give a classmate. I smiled at her and said that it was to give to a stranger. She froze. "A stranger?" she asked, almost as if to confirm that my Chinese was as good as she had previously thought. When I confirmed that the second pancake was indeed for a stranger, I explained that the poor guy doesn't have the means to get anything to eat, and so I have no choice but to get something for him. Even though I was speaking as one obviously would, seeing as I am talking through the little stall window to her, I noticed that as she stood there, she seemed only to be moving her hand making the pancake, while her face remained pensive. Her colleague looked over and saw her facial expression. "What did he say?" she inquired. The woman could barely talk now, but what she could muster she said to her colleague, and she too took a while to understand. She also peeked over her hotplate to glance at me. Handing me the pancake after what felt like half an hour (it was 3 minutes), the woman thanked me for looking out for the people on the street. I thanked her for the two pancakes and rode off.

While riding, I prayed and asked the Lord to provide me with a homeless person to give the pancake to. Sure enough, there he was. Now, sometimes, in order to maximise the amount of money given to them, you may not find two homeless persons on the same side of the street. So, I had to pray that anyone was there at all. When I got there, sure enough he was there. I rode around and handed him the pancake. When he looked up and recognised the face of the person handing him this food, he frantically searched in his pile and gave me something, as if in exchange for God's kindness. I went into my bag and handed him a track with some money in it at well, and thanked him for his token of appreciation. This time, it seemed that God's kindness spread, because there were at least 4 other food stuffs there on the mat around him. However, I felt good to think that mine was hot food, and that he may have eaten it immediately. I went home rejoicing, having met Jesus on the road.

FEELING USED

Have you ever felt that you were being used? I felt used one afternoon when I went out for lunch with a Chinese lady. She had admitted to me that she was asked to lead a discussion on the work of the Cross of Jesus. I was stunned. "… and you only have an hour to present and discuss?" I asked with great disbelief. I was thinking that there was no way in the world that you could take the topic of the Cross and compound it into a one-hour presentation. It just seemed too impossible for me. Furthermore, I would think of myself as too lowly to bear a burden as great as that of the Cross. However, when I expressed this, she jokingly said that it was too late to tell them no, so I decided to help her with her task. The following hours were spent with myself and the lady going through scriptures, praying together and preparing for the bible study which she had to lead the following day. While we were having lunch, however, she had admitted to me that she was being oppressed by a demonic spirit, which she could hear cursing her and discouraging her daily. I, Stefan Lorde, from a position of first trying to understand and not cast my own judgements, explained to her from Scripture the nature of the Lord Jesus, and how the jealous God of the Bible would not allow anything to come between Him and His own. "So, that demon could terrorise you all he likes. Once your faith is in the saving power of Christ, there's no demon that can overpower you, or take control of you. You are God's, and nothing can pluck you from His hand. God will also give you the Grace to endure this trial, if it is that He doesn't remove it immediately." As I went on, I was really humbled to see that her eyes were wide open, and she was on the edge of her seat. She was soaking in every word I was saying, and I made sure to be very careful to explain as clearly as possible what it was that the Bible says.

Suddenly, she burst into tears and laughter. "I am so happy," she exclaimed. Turns out that this information was good news that she was longing to hear. She began to tell me about the long time this thing had been terrorising her, and she actually noticed a difference in its presence, and her attitude towards it. It is unfortunate that the words I type out here as I sit in my room reflecting on the transpiring events, lack a great deal when it comes to expressing what really happened in that Pizza Hut in Wudaokou. Reader, just know that she felt liberated from whatever it was. She was so transformed by this liberation that she was skipping and dancing and swinging her hands as we walked back to my campus. I thought to myself that it would have to be a liberation indeed that this 43-year old woman would take to dancing in the busy streets of Beijing.

When it was time to have the Sunday Bible study session, she led and constantly gave thanks to God for using me to give her examples and hand her the knowledge that God has to free given to me. All the while, and even on the Saturday in which we met, I had no inkling of a feeling that any of this was my doing. I felt as though this was just an ordinary conversation. I was seeing this woman being liberated before my very eyes, and all I did was talk to her.

Meanwhile, just a few days prior, I was talking to young gentleman, and bringing the archaeological and historical proofs of the Bible, and its accounts and all he did was sat there and agreed that it made sense. He didn't crawl to the foot of the Cross, tearing his clothes in repentance and faith. This woman, on the other hand, felt the power of God wrap around her and tear the grave clothes of sin from her and she practically floated back home. This brought home to me the point that it is not me that does the transformation. This brought home to me that it is not me who does anything, but it is God who works within a person to bring about regeneration and salvation. I felt the same way before, during and after the conversation. There was no hint in me of a feeling as though any credit was to be taken. Therefore, I concluded that this was, and is all God's handiwork.

SUNDAY SCHOOL EXPERIENCE

"The trials that those men do meet withal,
that are obedient to the Heavenly call.
Are manifold, and suited to the flesh; and
come, and come and come again afresh."

– The Pilgrim's Progress

As I go to church weekly, I remember something that someone told me about cadet camps. When I was a cadet, I used to stay behind all the time, and more so when I became a Cadet Officer (because it was my job to). Staying behind, however, was no problem for me because I really loved being in the atmosphere of the cadet camp and being around the people that made it worth being there. One evening after a camp, I was almost knocked over by someone on their way out. When I inquired about their hurry, they responded by saying "when you remain in camp, you're given work", and with that, he dashed out from the camping ground. Sure enough, as soon as he left, my name was called, and I was given some work that almost made me regret staying in camp. In like manner, I was in attendance in the Chinese service one Sunday morning. After the service, I usually attend the Bible study with the members of the congregation. One day, I was approached by the wife of the Pastor, and asked if I would be willing to help with the Sunday School, because she sees from my interaction with her children, that I am "good with children" (she actually did the air-quotes). I thought for a few seconds before responding…

ETERNITY ASIDE.

As a Christian, I understand that there is coming a day when Jesus, because He has risen from the dead, will come back for those who are in Him, and take them up to Heaven with Him. Following this, there is described in the Bible a judgement where God gives to each man according to his work. The parable in Matthew 25 comes to mind of the man who gave his workers some talents and told them to go to work. There is a servant who, because he was afraid of how his master was, took it upon himself to bury his talent, and gave up on the opportunity to please his master. He paid the price when it came time to receive his reward. With this in mind, whenever I am presented with an opportunity to serve the Lord, the image comes to mind of me standing before the Lord. All the heavenly host is behind Him, standing, looking at me; all the saints are standing behind me looking at me too. I am standing there, and God opens His mouth to speak, "I presented you with the opportunity to serve me in this particular regard, why didn't you?" I stand before God, with the entire host of heaven and earth standing around me. What do I say? I didn't feel like doing it? No!

Therefore, when I was approached with the Sunday school, I told her that I would try my best to help them. She said that I could start out by reading to the children. I agreed.

It was a horrendously boring experience for the children. I thought that they would like the book I was reading to them, as it was the same one that they were reading for the last few weeks (as I was told). I could look at their faces and see that they couldn't wait for me to finish. I in turn couldn't wait for me to finish either. I wanted to just run and get out of there. The feeling of failure was encroaching on me, and I wanted to run away. One little boy stood when I was finished and said "read two chapters". The other children seemed to resent him for saying that, because they slouched all the more and sighed all the heavier. While reading, I was thinking to myself, *what have I gotten myself into? I think I better quit while I'm behind. I thought these children were accustomed to reading. Where is the nearest window through which I should thrust myself?*

This discouragement was weighing on me to the point where I was considering telling the people in charge of the Sunday School that I was going to "take a break" (quit) from the Sunday School, because I clearly am not fit to be in any position to be part of this team. Moreover, there was a meeting after that reading session with the Sunday school team, and it was fully in Chinese. Of course, Stefan is picking up and understanding almost 45% of the conversation being held. For something as important as the souls of the children of the fellowship, 45% of a meeting is not enough –so, I'm feeling downtrodden again. They encouraged me, and told me that they believe that I would be able to do what I have to do. "I believe in you," the pastor's wife said.

> "The hill, though high, I covet to ascend,
> the difficulty will not me offend; for I
> perceive the way to life lies here: come,
> pluck up, heart. Let's neither faint nor
> fear. Better, though difficult, the right
> way to go, than wrong, though easy,
> where the end is woe."
>
> – The Pilgrim's Progress (Bunyan)

TEACHING EFL

AS MENTIONED IN one of my earlier letters (or chapters), teaching English here in China is one of the main reasons why foreigners come; and it is one of the main anchors that keeps them here too. Some of them are in it for the money. Some? They are in it because they are actually having fun, and see purpose in what they are doing. As I sit here in my room, which is, for the time being, peaceful and quiet, I reminisce on the time when I first started teaching. I thank the Good Lord for the Grace which He has given me over the weeks and months of teaching these bright young minds of my class. I often pray that he would provide me with the skills and creativity which would be needed to aptly teach these students, as the teaching method here is far different to that which I am accustomed. I thank God immensely for all the opportunity which he has given me to practice my language proficiency, and to meet new and exciting people. At first, teaching the little ones was a headache. Whoever wasn't running around aimlessly was crying, was hopping and screaming they wanted to go Niào niào *(kid-speak for "Might I please have permission to utilise the lavatories?")*. It was a nightmare. Slowly, I was able to get them under control, and learn what made them tick –namely games. So, with a clear focus on getting them to remember the words and letters at hand, I would play musical chairs and have them chant the different letters, for instance: D- dinner. Dinner, Dinner, hot hot hot. E- egg. Egg, Egg, eat a lot. F- fish. Fish, fish, don't get caught. Then, they would hop twice for the word, and then stamp their little feet for the chant. So, over a couple of weeks, I went from a boring teacher to a fun pal to learn English with. My prayers were answered. Furthermore, as I only taught two evenings a week, I still have ample time to study for my midterms which I passed in blazing glory. There seemed to be a balance of teaching and study, which I still am thankful for to this day.

よろしくおねがいします

Of all the words I have written here in this chapter, and even in the ones previous, nothing took as long to pronounce as the ones above here in this title. It is Japanese *GASP!* Yes, ladies and gentlemen, I just wrote Japanese in this document after being a die-hard fan of "The Continent". Before your eyebrows remain ruffled, allow me to explain. *Aaaannd exhale!*

One clear, bright Sunday morning (there aren't that many in Beijing) I went to church as was my custom, and praised the God of my soul with my Chinese brothers and sisters. I was greatly surprised to see a few of my international English-speaking friends there also. I always invite my foreign friends to come with me to the Chinese service, but the majority of them just come up with an excuse as to why they didn't make it; the most annoying of which is that it is too early. If it were that we had classes as 11 a.m., I would understand 9 a.m. being considered early. However, seeing as regular classes are 8 a.m., and sometimes 8:30, I don't see why it is that they cannot make the sacrifice to come. Another excuse was that they "wouldn't understand what is going on". My mistake which I make constantly throughout the years is thinking that other people care as much as I do. I first went to the Chinese service within a month of coming to China. Of course, I couldn't understand more than 25% of anything that was going on, but I still went…because I wanted to go. Now, I am a member, and even volunteer with the congregation in helping to setup, reading for the Sunday school, among other things. The other bird killed with this same stone is that I get to practise my

Chinese listening, reading and speaking, as I go there and learn more and more; not only do I learn the jargon associated with the Bible and Christianity, but while the songs play and the sermon is preached, I listen out for the grammatical structures which I am taught in class. This way, I get to fellowship with other believers, and get better at Chinese, so I can better fellowship with believers, so I can get better at Chinese. However, not everyone would think this way. Seems no one else thinks this way. I concluded by thinking that no one is coming because no one wants to come. So, I stopped inviting anyone at all. So, you could imagine my great surprise when I saw not one –but four of my friends at the Chinese service one Sunday morning, bright and early and sitting on the other side of the room from me.

After the service, I greeted them and hurriedly left with the Chinese to go to the Bible study. At the Bible study, it is all in Chinese, as expected, but I fear not. I have my Bible which is in English and Chinese, with the character pronunciation (or pinyin) above the characters. This way, when I come across a character which I haven't covered in class (which happens a lot, if I'm honest) my eyes don't have to look far for the pinyin, and I simply read along without a hiccup. I thank God so very much for all the knowledge of the Word which He has given me. I thank Him for all the times my father and I would sit together and read the Bible together, researching and understanding; praying and encouraging. I thank Him even for the times I read the Bible alone. I thank God so very much for the knowledge of His word. I cannot thank Him enough. I thank Him because when I am with the Chinese Christians, I am already familiar with certain passages because of God's goodness, and so all I have to do is look for the passage, and read it to them in Chinese, using the pinyin to guarantee fluency, and to ensure that I am understood. This way, God greatly uses me to explain His words to His people. While I feel at home in the Scriptures, the ones around me are amazed, and constantly give thanks to God for bringing me here to help them in our quest to understand Him more and more daily. Even as I sit here on a Thursday, and think about the fellowship, I look at my calendar and long for another Sunday to come again where I can be with the Lord's people and speak the Lord's words in Chinese with my brothers and sisters in the Lord. The more I try to express here, the more I hesitate to write, because I don't want for my words to be interpreted as anything other than thanksgiving to God, nor do I want them to be taken as self-aggrandizement in the slightest degree. God is the source of all my knowledge, all my wisdom and all my boldness. When I started out, I didn't want to get involved in anything. I wanted to just sit in the back and absorb the Word and practise my Chinese listening. God apparently had other plans. I am reminded of Ezekiel 36: 25-27[12]. I see it slowly playing out as I try

---

12 "A new heart also will I give you, and a new spirit will I put within you: and I was take away

less and less to resist it.

When Bible study was finished that one Sunday, the others were planning on going to the prayer meeting which had started half hour before we finished. This meant that we could still go and enjoy another half an hour of prayer with the other believers. I decided to go and pray with the others, as it has been a long while since I have attended a prayer meeting. When we got there, we separated into the groups that were already there and praying. I sat down, and the pastor smiled at me and asked me how much of the sermon I understood this toss[13]. Whenever we meet, he asks me to give him a percentage of the sermon which I understood, so he could track my progress. These past few sermons, I was glad to report that I understood a whopping 80%! He then pointed to the screen upon which were written the prayer requests of the members of the church, and asked me if I could read that which was written. I took a look, and began reading. After reading 9 out of 10 words correctly, he then proudly said "Good. Now that you've read, you can clearly understand what is written. So, you will pray in Chinese first". I somehow had in mind that he would have asked me that, and so I was not surprised in the slightest, but prayed in the best Chinese that I could. As I pray in private in Chinese to God as an act of thanksgiving for giving me the utterance in the first place, it was not a new thing, and I was not afraid.

The prayer meeting finished and I was sent a message by my roommate at the time requesting the room for himself, and whichever young lady he would have over at the given point in time. I was actually getting tired of his shenanigans, and I was trusting in God for the Romans 12:18[14] to be made manifest in me, to keep me from getting too agitated. Luckily for me, someone had said that they were going to head out for a walk along the riverside, and I told him that plans changed, and I would allow him to have the room again this time. When I left the prayer meeting, others were waiting outside, and the men of the congregation were going to meet outside with the pastor for a time of fellowship. I, however, had decided already to lend support to a sister Wu who was going to give her testimony for the first time…in Japanese.

The Japanese service was starting in about an hour and a half, and I had enough time to catch up on some reading of St. John's Gospel. Even when the Japanese service was about to start, I was still head down in my Bible totally consumed in the words as the. Somehow, sitting there, the text was easier to read, and I could almost picture the scenes as they unfolded. I had to take a break, however, because I was wearing a black shirt, and it was getting hotter in the

the stony heart out of your flesh, and give you a heart of flesh. And I will put my spirit within you, and cause you to walk in my statutes, and ye shall keep my judgements, and do them." (KJV)
13 Time
14 "If it be possible, as much as lieth with you, live peaceably with all men."

room. Luckily, I had just collected a package from the post; the shirts which I had ordered online *for such a time as this.* I opened the package and took out one of the shirts. From the time I felt the material, I knew it was a ￥10 well spent. I excused myself from a conversation I was having by the way, and made my way to the men's room where I changed my shirt. I felt an amazing relief and came back smiling and showing off my new clothes. Even Chinese were amazed at the cost of the shirt, as well as the quality. I decided, once I was satisfied with the shirt, to purchase three more, in varying colours.

Four p.m. came, and it was time to start the Japanese service. For reasons which escape my memory right now, the service is done in Japanese and Chinese. While I was getting myself comfortable in my chair at the back, a talking Sister Wu came close to my seat and pointed at me, as she was clearly speaking to someone else. "Maybe I could ask Stefan to help…" she said. I could not believe I was being roped into something already, and this was only the second time I was at this service. I looked up to Heaven, and then braced myself for whatever it was that I would *gracefully* acquiesce to doing for the sake of the Body's edification. Constantly in the New Testament, we are encouraged to do everything for the edification of the Church, and with this in mind, I looked up at Sister Wu to see what it would be that she would ask me to do.

She looked down to me, and smiling, she asked me if I could serve as an interpreter for a visitor who was in the hallway, who was to be joining us for service that day. The reason I was chosen ad hoc was that the congregation is very small, and the person who would usually interpret for the monolinguals among us was already busy with the projector. I was therefore asked, and humbly responded by saying that I am in no way capable of this task, as I barely understand for myself, far less be able to understand for myself *and* someone else. Despite my attempts to disincline, they pleaded and said that they believe that I can do a good job. I could never boast of such a thing at this time. I was barely able to grabble onto an understanding for myself, and my language skills are not as high as I would like. However, as there was no one else to do this task, I figured that it would be better for me to do this for them, than for no one to do it at all. I sat behind the two monolinguals, in the seat between them, and whispered the English to whatever was said in Chinese. Whatever was said was in Japanese first, then translated into Chinese, then English. It was Acts 2 all over again.

When the singing part of the service was over, and the better translator arrived to take over what I was doing, I sat back and experienced a mental tiredness. Switching my brain to think in another language was something that had become less difficult to do; so sometimes I would be speaking in English, and the Chinese words would come to my mouth as I spoke as it felt easier to express myself in Chinese. However, to have to think in both languages at the same time, listening in one and practically responding in another for the sake of somebody else's understanding was a mentally tiring exercise. Not only was I changing Chinese words into English words, but I had to transfer the Chinese sentences into natural English expressions for the gentleman. Sometimes, admittedly, I had to tell him "sorry, I totally missed that one" and move on to the next comprehensible sentence. He was just too grateful, and also encouraged me saying "That's alright. You're doing great. Keep going." It came time to pick up the offering, and everyone reached for their money bags; yet I noticed that no one reached for the offering basket. I dashed towards the front of the room and snatched up the basket and began collecting the offering. This brought an eruption of laughter to the congregation, as someone leaned to the person who was supposed to collect it, and reminded her that she was supposed to be the one collecting the offering. Before she could cover her mouth in shock, I was already in the second row passing around the offering basket. We all laughed.

At the end of this service, as it was for the Chinese service, we had a time of food, fun and fellowship in a nearby restaurant. The conversations, as you could imagine, were in Chinese, English, Japanese, and I believe even Korean. Because the congregation is fewer than 20 people on average, the conversations are much closer and intimate. I sat amongst them, and tried to deflect the praise compounded on me for humility's sake. They were telling and retelling of how I translated for the visitors, how I took the initiative in collecting the offering, among other things which to me are not worthy of honour; but they were ever grateful to God for bringing me there in their midst, and I too was grateful. Is there a future for me in the Japanese service as well? Of course, I can help them, as many of them have Chinese as their second language already. The meaning conveyed in the title "Yoroshiku Onegaishimasu" speaks to people having met, trying their utmost for the betterment of the relationship from now on. Before, the only thing I could say in Japanese with any manner of fluency was "I finished drinking the juice", and that was what I would say to the Pastor whenever we shook hands. Now, a very good friend of mine was gracious enough to bestow "Yoroshiku Onegaishimasu" on me. I am now that much closer to my Japanese brothers and sisters.

The second time that I went to lunch with the Japanese congregation, or maybe it was the third, I sat next to a young gentleman from Korea. South Korea. While we were chatting and eating and having a wonderful time in the Lord, he leaned over to me and began to speak. "Ya know," he said. "I would always remember the time you sat next to me in the Chinese congregation."

By now, Stefan Lorde is listening intently to what he is saying, waiting for the conclusion with baited breath. He went on to describe one particular Sunday when the offering was being collected, and I needed to go to the restroom. After tapping his shoulder to get his attention, I put my offering into his hand and told him that it was my offering, and that I was going to the bathroom. I nodded as I called to mind the morning it happened. He then went on say that the offering felt heavy in his hands. He said it felt to him like a tremendous burden was placed on him, and a huge responsibility laid upon his shoulders. Your boy Stefan was completely taken aback by all of this, and sat there with my eyes wide opened. Here I was thinking that my ￥12 was a simple offering, and just needed to be placed into the offering basket, just like his offering; but it was proving to be something much bigger than I had conceived. The Korean guy went on to describe how relieved he felt when he finally put it in the basket. "I almost dusted off my hands," he said. "I sat there sweating in my chair, feeling God watching me as I held the money in my hands."

After picking my mouth off the floor, I looked around, as he translated the story into Chinese for the people at the table. I was in awe that he would think so highly of something as simple as putting my offering in the basket. To my great surprise, the others at the table were equally amazed by what he had described, and were smiling at me. I could not, and cannot understand why, as I saw nothing in what I had done. I just wanted to use the bathroom.

STEFAN SQUARED

While writing thus far, I took a look at the page and word count to see how much longer I have before I have to cut this document short and try at Chapter 11 –whatever that would be. Before I started this particular chapter, I was thinking that there was not much that I would have to write, and then I had the experience with the Japanese, and that took a while to describe. However, I remember the people who kept on telling me that they want to read all about what I'm doing in China. They want me to record all the happenings and let them know what is going on. There is even one friend that wants me to read them while he listens. Even though there are times when the discouragement comes along hard and fast, the friends I have make the story more unforgettable. While we are on the topic of unforgettable friends, there is a friend who I will introduce in the following pages.

When I was in Barbados, just before I left the island, I bumped into him on the streets of Bridgetown, and upon shaking his hand, I told him that he must come to China with me, and I will go up and wait for him. What makes this friend special, as you can guess from the title of this paragraph, is that his name is Stefan…. like me. My name is Stefan Lorde, his is Stefan Forde. When we signed up for Chinese studies, the name given to me was 罗思凡, and his was 付思凡. He is also a believer in Christ, and that seems to be all we have in common. Hold onto your socks, readers, he is quite shy.

I actually spent a few seconds thinking about the vast difference between us, as I consider his quiet and reserved nature. His voice doesn't go above a certain octave or pitch, and he does not speak as much as I do, though just as passionately when he does. I knew that he wanted to get to China, and so pushed and encouraged him to get here, and all the more when I got here myself. When things started to fall into place for him to get here, I rejoiced daily with him. For example, one day, he would send me a message telling me that he is not sure that he would make it; the next week, he would say that he got a message from someone telling him that he made it. Another day, he would message saying that he doesn't have any money; the next thing I'd hear is that he was given money through some random circumstance and is back in the game. In fact, just yesterday, he sent me a message –well, a picture of a message from him school- saying that they were glad to inform him that he had been accepted. I thank God for this, because he will be in the same district as me, Haidian District. His school will be a short bike ride away from mine, and I get a bubbling nervousness in my chest whenever I think about the fact that in just a few short months, Stefan will be joining me in China. I feel relieved that God has answered our prayers. I am glad that he didn't give up.

In China, from the time I heard/ thought that he would be coming, I started to think and plan what I will do when he gets here. Of course, he's going to need a place to call home, in terms of church fellowship; and of course, I mean no other place than where I go, to BICF. He's going to need to know how to order food on his cell phone, how to take the public transportation, where has the most delicious Chinese food. He's going to need help in his administration at the school to which he's going. He's coming up here to do animation, and I know that, because of how the study situation is here in China, he's going to have to attend a language school for a year before he starts his degree. I pray that he comes to my school, even though it makes sense that he comes here because of the close proximity. I would be so very happy if he were to come to my school. That would be so great. I get excited just thinking about it, and it is still four more months until I see him. I try not to get too anxious, but I still have a mental check list of the things that I would do for him when he gets here. From picking him up from the airport, to treating him to lunch…to helping him with his Chinese to translating for him at church, should he come to the Chinese congregation. I just thank God for the opportunity for him to come here, and for bringing him here safely whenever he *does* arrive.

A WORLD OF CULTURE

My school, Beijing Language and Culture University, was soon to be holding the 14th Annual World Cultural Festival. Why this is a big deal is that my school is one of the most famous in all of China, and the most renowned for teaching

Chinese language. People come from all over the world to study here, and even the Chinese study here too –it's that good…apparently. Therefore, a plethora of about 100+ countries will be participating in it this year, and your boy decided to give it a try. When I was approached about it, the first question that crossed my mind was "how on earth did you guys find me?" This question was quickly followed by countless others, none of which I dared ask out loud.

I prayed. I knew that as the only Barbadian on campus, that it would be difficult. But I know that I would be given volunteers who would help me to get things set up and prepared for the day's festivities. Moreover, I know that the Barbadians who came up to China with me would be more than willing to help me, not to mention the ones already here at the universities within the district. I felt more and more capable of pulling this off, and yet, thought more and more that I should just pull out in the early. Then, days turned into weeks, and I still hadn't quit. I thought that God will help me to get this thing done, namely setting up a booth to display Barbados to the world. Even if I don't get things done as wonderfully as I would have liked, I would have the experience and the preparation time to get things up to par for next year. So far, my volunteers have been nothing but nice to me. They have been nothing but helpful to me. They are putting a lot of themselves into this, and it is really making me feel a lot more enthusiastic about it. I thank God for them, and pray for the success of the day.

ALL OF HIM, SOME OF ME

When Jesus was on the road to Calvary, and even on the cross, He was being beaten and whipped from the moment he left Pontius Pilate earlier in the day. He was dripping with blood and forced to carry His cross. Just 12 hours before that, He was with his disciples and told them that the cup of wine which He was sharing with them was the symbol of His blood. He commanded them to drink all of it, representing the fact that all of His blood would be spilt for the remission of sins (Matthew 26:27-28[15]). This was further illustrated in His death on the cross, when every drop of blood came out. How is this possible? We know this because when Jesus was pierced, water came out as well, medically indicating that my Jesus was totally spent. Every drop was spilt and my debt before God was paid in full, on account of this great sacrifice.

It was this thought that comes to mind now when I was going to a picnic in the park with others from the Caribbean. On my way in, I noticed a bus where blood donations could be freely given. I walked up to the guy on the outside and asked if I had to fill in a form before I give blood. He was more fascinated about

---

15 And He took the cup, and gave thanks, and gave it to them, saying, Drink ye all of it; for this is my blood of the new testament, which is shed for many for the remission of sins.

how "good" my Chinese was, than he was answering my question. Even as I was writing and filling out the form, he was "interluding" every question on the form with an exclamation about my Chinese proficiency. I had to laugh at it all, though as I sit here writing, I cannot believe that "interluding" is not a word. When I had completed the form, the gentleman escorted me into the bus and I sat down. There was so much equipment in this one bus, it was amazing. I had to help the poor guy at the computer scrolling through the list of countries there, looking for mine. While I was doing this, I was trying to ignore the two guys behind me who were talking about me rather loudly, though we were sitting shoulder-to-shoulder with each other. When I called my country, they even repeated it out loud behind me. I let that roll off me, and continued the procedure. The needle was large, but I have a secret. I take the thumbnail of the opposite hand to the needle, and just bore it as far as possible into the index finger of the same hand. This causes more pain than the needle itself, and so my brain doesn't count the needle as pain. While there, the nurse was chatting with me, and was equally amazed that I could understand what she was saying. As the needle went in and the blood came out, she asked me if I wanted to donate 400ml. I just said yes to everything. I couldn't help but snicker when the guy opposite me was gnashing his teeth at the sight of the needle which had yet to enter his body. I was given a stress ball and a box of ice tea to help. The stress ball would help with the pumping of blood, and the juice was to help keep me from feeling dizzy afterwards, I suppose. When I was finally done, I was given a free umbrella, and I went to join the others for the picnic. When I got to Kid Castle that evening, the other teacher announced to the children that their teacher is a hero because he gave blood to save somebody. I smiled as they examined my arm, but I only know that some time long ago, someone gave a lot more of their blood…to save me.

"But God hath chosen the foolish things of the world to confound the wise; and God hath chosen the weak things of the world to confound the things which are mighty; and the base things of the world, and things which are despised, hath God chosen, yea, and things which are not, to bring to nought things that are; that no flesh should glory in His presence."

- Paul of Tarsus, I Corinthians 1:27-28

Never Give Up

When you feel like giving up, remember
why you started.

-Anonymous

I START THIS chapter by reminiscing on the happenings of yesterday for me, namely the 北语世界文化节 (BLCU World Cultural Festival). I was a little anxious during the days coming up to the event, because I feared that I would not have that much to offer with regards to showcasing the culture of Barbados. However, God gave me two of the most hardworking young Chinese volunteers from the school. I have ever seen to help me set up and run the booth for the festival. In the blazing heat, they neither complained nor bickered (rarely sat down) and they worked feverishly to make sure everything ran smoothly. When one of them sat down, one of my country mates marvelled, saying "whoa, she's human. She gets tired". I also marvelled.

A few weeks prior to the event, I was feeling rather discouraged, and tried my best to remind myself of why I started, and why I committed to this venture. I started because, when they asked me to, I thought to myself that the Lord would not allow me to do this if He had the slightest doubt that I would succeed. I believed He was more than able to help me, and so I asked him to. There are plenty of instances in the Scriptures where the odds were stacked high against the people of God, and God showed up and showed off. This, if I may say so reverently, is another one of those cases. As the only one from my country, I had to manage a booth, and lead all the proceedings and make all the decisions and delegations to make sure that everything went smoothly. There was lots of money to be spent in purchasing items for the booth, and late nights being up and painting the billboard, cooking Barbadian delicacies and organising tasks.

On the actual day of the event, I got up feeling most unwell and unclean. I knew that I hadn't got enough sleep, as I was up a little later than I wanted to be. After being kicked out of a neighbouring university for staying past curfew (yea, we were cooking past 10 pm) I came home to seeing my good friend and sister in the Lord in immense pain and tears as she complained of being tremendously unwell. I had notified the others in the Christian circle, and we prayed for her, while one of us went to the hospital to accompany her. That kept me up a while. Later on, my roommate came in, in the wee hours of the morning (presumably drunk) and kept a bit of noise for an hour or two before falling asleep. From 5am, the volunteers were outside helping to put up the tent, and I was to join them at ten minutes to 7. Needless to say, I got up a little later than I was supposed to, and therefore got out there a little later than I was supposed to. I felt really miserable, and I was hoping that I wouldn't carry that miserable feeling all throughout the day. I was cheered up a little when the representative from Argentina offered me a coffee, but back to misery when I realised that the country flag was back at the University of Science and Technology (from Where I was removed the night before). Had I the chance to finish what I was doing, I would have the chance to get it, but I had no time to grab it. I thought that it would be brought by the Barbadian students who would be coming from that campus, but as they had many a thing to prepare, I didn't think they would make it on time for the parade, and therefore I pedalled from my school to theirs to get the flag, to pedal back just in time for the parade. When I got to the entrance of my school, I was stopped by the police. They told me that I could not bring my bicycle inside, due to the day's festivities. After much beseeching, he then told me to park it by the teaching building, and walk the rest of the way. While walking my bike, I looked up and thought to myself. I felt the temptation to ride back to the pasture where the booth was. I then thought that if I disobey the command of the guard, though he would never know, God will still see, and I would have sinned. However, if I walked the bike, there was the chance that I would not make it in time for the parade which was soon to start. I chose to park the bike. I quoted Romans 13:1[16] to myself and walked briskly to the booth to collect the one Barbadian student who had come, to walk back to the parade starting point. Feeling unprepared, unkempt and unwilling, I went and stood in my place.

More than a hundred countries were represented in the parade, all decked out in their national colours and playing their national music. I was cheered up a bit to see that the guy from Costa Rica was showing off their national dress... literally, with frills and all. He used balloons to accentuate the feminine parts which he lacked, and he stood upon a wheeled pedestal. When the music started

---

16 "Let every person be subject to the governing authorities. For there is no authority except from God, and those that exist have been instituted by God." (ESV)

to beat, I forgot all my worries, and jumped and chipped all the way to the pasture with the flag, posing for pictures, and hi-fiving people as we passed by. When we got to the end of the parade, two representatives from each country were to go up on the ceremonial stage to show their flag. Barbados was among the Latin American countries, and I was glad that I was not completely lost when they Hispanics were chatting among themselves. When we got on the stage, and the music was still playing, there was a moment where we were just standing there. It was then that I shouted "BAILAMOS!" the Spanish word for "let's dance!" We laughed and started jiving on the stage, much to our own amusement, and, I'm sure, that of the people watching.

When the others came, and the booth got up and running, it was packed. The school had about twenty thousand people flowing in and out of the compound. There were little "passports" on sale which one would purchase and get stamped as you went to a country's booth. Each stamp had the English name of the country, the Chinese name of the country, and how to say "hello" in the native language of the country. One would then walk around and visit different booths, and would get the passport stamped. This, to me was a fantastic idea, and had me busily stamping passports for hours. We also had rhinestones which the girls and ladies lined up by the dozens to have stuck to their faces. A few men also joined the line. I had seen some little stickers of the Barbados flag when the Science and Technology University had their culture festival, and decided to buy 400 for mine. I would stick them on the hands and faces of people who passed the booth, and was pleased to see that all four hundred of them were given out within the first hour of the festival. I am thinking that for next year, I would have to purchase a thousand or so, because people were disappointed when all had gone. There were also the delicacies which were made by the others who had come, and they too were graciously accepted by the visitors of the booth. I had decided not to give them away, and even then, people paid a small fee to taste them, and even to purchase the little flags which I had bought for the event as well.

At the end of the day, I was tired and hungry as expected, and still felt as though I was being supported all the day through; I hadn't even eaten anything but was hard at work all day long with my volunteers and the country mates who *did* end up coming and participating. I felt that, regardless of the day's draining activity, I was still being held up. I have no choice but to conclude that it was not in my own strength that this was done. I am sure that I would have been completely spent by midday; but I didn't tire, and I didn't stop for the sake of the heat. I am certain that it was the Lord who supported me throughout the day.

WISDOM ASIDE

I would love to be able to say that I have wisdom. I would love to say that the wisdom of God permeates my life to the point where I speak not an idle word, and my actions are all well thought through; but that is not the case. In fact, the opposite seems to be true most of the time. When I was little, I would see those gurus on the television and admire them for being so old and wise. I would watch those cartoons of people climbing very high mountains, in search of the wise one who sits at the top. Upon seeking the advice of this wise one, it would make so much sense, and they would descend the mountain feeling most enlightened. From then, I didn't seek to find such a person...I sought to become such a person. Of course, I sought out where I would be able to ascertain such wisdom, and the Bible was right there to show me God's route to wisdom. Looking in the Bible, I saw many a passage which admonish men to pursue wisdom. The Teacher in Proverbs speaks of wisdom as a "woman crying in the streets", a beseeching mother calling to her child saying "come, come"; and a best friend that should be always at your side. Reading this vivid description and understanding the benefits of being wise, I endeavoured to find out from where I can get this wisdom.

It was then that I came across the verse in James which speaks to anyone, saying: "If any of you lack wisdom, let him ask of God, that giveth to all men liberally, and upbraideth not; and it shall be given him" (James 1:4). I thought to myself that this must be it! Here lies the key to wisdom. You're saying that all I have to do is ask God for wisdom, and no matter how often I ask, he will more than willingly give me an abundant amount of wisdom, and never hold back as long as I ask? Wow, this is great news, I thought to myself. I then spent many a prayer asking God for wisdom, fasting for wisdom and reading the Word of God for wisdom. I came across passages like "Where no counsel is, the people fall: but in the multitude of counsellors there is safety" (Proverbs 11:14) and "Wisdom is the principal thing; therefore get wisdom: and with all thy getting get understanding" (Proverbs 4:7) and was seeming more and more like the Bible, and God by extension were encouraging me to pursue wisdom above all other things that I would pursue in this life. And then...the cycle started...

I went to God one day and asked Him for wisdom. The Bible had said that if I asked for it, He would be more than willing to give it to me, so why not, right? God began to pour wisdom on me, and I started understanding things. Biblical things, spiritual things and even interpersonal things. I was beginning to grow up faster than I was growing older. I began seeing meaning pop out from Scripture; and more so, I was being more and more enabled to explain that which I had been shown. It was seeming like a lot of fun at first, and I was pretty much enjoying this precious gift that the Good Lord had given me.

Then, there came a surprise. While riding and floating on this new-found wisdom, I started to feel some pits and speed bumps along the way. I remember when I was leading a small group on the book of Exodus while I was at University in Barbados. I that I was teaching them as the Bible taught, and very little opinion was given. I had about 5 people in my small group, and I was feeling quite satisfied just being there, reading the Bible and being with the children of God. That which had me a little perturbed was when I had decided to visit the small group of the other leader, to see what I could learn from it. When I sat down on the outside, I had to scratch my head when I started hearing things which had no Biblical origin at all. I heard him talking about "gates" to the spiritual realm being at crossroads, and T-junctions in traffic and such like. The sources from which he was taking his material were things printed from off the internet, and no Scripture was mentioned. I looked around to see if I was in the correct place for the Christian gathering, or if I had taken a wrong turn. What had me more perturbed was the throng of people that sat anxiously at the edge of their seats, seeming to salivate for more of this guy's teaching. That was why I was sitting on the outside, because there was no room for me to get in. I am not going to say that all the people within his earshot lacked wisdom, but what I will say is that when you are wise, and see people doing or subscribing to things that are not, you tend to feel uncomfortable. The point in all of this was to illustrate what the man in the book of Ecclesiastes was talking about, when he said that the wiser a man is the more miserable he becomes.

THE LAST FEW WEEKS

Over the last few weeks of school, I have been having practice exams for the China Scholarship Council. Two Saturdays ago, I sat the exam that we have all been waiting for. Maybe I should have said that this was the exam "for which we have all been waiting" just to satisfy my inner Grammar Nazi. Anyhow, we were all very excited to take the exam. There were a few of us sitting on the corridor, studying and trying to cram the last bits of information into their desperate minds before they entered the room. I couldn't help smiling. I felt prepared for this exam, and I saw no need to be cramming. While in the exam room, I felt that there were some questions for which I was not prepared, as in there were some words which I didn't recognize but overall, I believed I did fairly well. A while after the exam, I got a text message from my class teacher saying that I had fulfilled the requirement for the exams, and can now go on to start my degree. In case some of you are a little confused, or hadn't read that section I will remind you of the requirements: the first year of school for me was spent at the College for Preparatory Education. Here, we learn the basics of the Chinese language: how to read, write, speak and understand; and are prepared for the degree for which we've applied. So, seeing as the degree for which we applied will be taught in Chinese, we are taught…how to be taught in Chinese. After the language year, we move on to our respective universities to start our degrees, depending on whether we fulfil the requirements of the China Scholarship Council. Luckily for me, my major is Chinese language, and so, not only am I more than being equipped for my major, but I don't have to move all my belongings to another campus. I simply stay here and merely walk to a different part of the school come this September.

After the exams, there was a graduation ceremony for all the students in the Prep College. The ceremony was bitter-sweet because it reminded me of the reality that out of the two hundred plus students here, most of which have become treasured acquaintances and even friends, will leave BLCU, Beijing, or even China, and head off to pursue the rest of their lives. The young men I'd hang with, and the young ladies I'd smile with will all be gone, and I will be left here with a clean slate to fill with the friends of my future. I sat for a while and only realised I was lost in thought when one of those same young ladies sat beside me and asked me what the matter was. When I told her that I was saddened at the fact that I won't be seeing her again, after visiting her class every day at break time, she assured me that I should visit her in Shanghai whenever I am in the area. I faked a smile and kept thinking that it wouldn't be the same as how it was during the semester. After she got up, I decided that it would be better if I allow myself to enjoy the few minutes left with my peers, taking selfies and making jokes in Chinese. Looking back, I really had a great time overall in my year in China, and particularly in BLCU.

THE END OF A GREAT YEAR

God has been blessing me over the past year in ways that I have never imagined. I examine myself to see if I am in the faith, and I notice that I am frail and weak. Based on the blessings that God has bestowed on me, I should be happy all the time, and always laughing and smiling (genuinely) and thanking God with and for everything. There should be nothing that gets me down, and there should never be a sad or disappointing moment in my life. However, as I have heard, and as I have experienced, even though I am saved, even though I have been redeemed from the power and penalty of sin, sin no longer reigns… but it remains. I find that "sin, taking occasion by the commandment, deceived me, and by it slew me." "For I know that in me (that is, in my flesh,) dwelleth no good thing: for to will is present with me; but how to perform that which is good, I find not." One day, someone asked me what my dream was in life. I told her that I have already been living out my dream. My dream as from childhood is to study and master languages. Even though I have far to go between where I am and the mastery of Chinese, I am doing what I want, where I want, and everything I could ever need is taken care of. Yet, though I have been blessed with everything I want and more than I could ever dream of having, when I try to live a life of thanksgiving to God; and to trust, obey and imitate Jesus, "the good that I would I do not: but the evil which I would not, that I do." The words of the Apostle Paul bring comfort to my eyes as I read Romans 7 and remember that he also had struggles. Because God mightily worked through Paul in His work, we are tempted to put Paul on a pedestal and think that he was somehow more of a Christian than we are today. What I have learned in the past year, and have had reinforced in me is that "if I do that which I would not, it is no more I that do it, but sin that dwelleth in me." I am glad to know that though there are some things which I do that I'd rather not do like doubt God's providence and care, or dwell on thoughts that make me worry and grow weary, that it is sin in me that needs to be put down, and not my spirit.

Also in the last year, God has allowed me to lead one of the sessions for small group. God has allowed me to help many a person, friend, enemy and even homeless guys. The image comes to mind as I think about this paragraph. The image of a mountain climber taking a break and wiping his brow. I look over my shoulder at the hike I've just come. I see a vast expanse of terrain which God has brought me through and then I turn and fix my gaze at the path that lies before me, most of which is still shrouded in cloud, hidden from sight. I do not know where I am going. I think I see a path, but I can't be too sure. All I can do is "be confident of this very thing, that he which hath begun a good work in you will perform it until the day of Jesus Christ."

Let us hear the conclusion of the whole matter: Fear God, and keep his commandments: for this is the whole duty of man.

– Ecclesiastes 12:13

The End of Preparation

THE DAY IS Saturday, August 12, 2017. In a few days, I will reach the end of my first year here in Beijing. Luckily, it didn't take me as long to come up with a title for this chapter, and this should be the last chapter I should write until my new year starts next month. If memory serves me correctly, I should have given a conclusion in my last chapter about the more recent happenings of my existence, and some more will I put here. Sometimes, by the way, I think that I that writing is my only way to keep my English Grammar in check, as I am not on Facebook that often to be correcting the grammar of others. Other things I have done to occupy my summer time, and therefore, my writing has suffered a bit. I have been occupying myself with the company of friends, church family and travel, so forgive me if my sentences seem a little incoherent for this chapter (or any of the others, but I only have an excuse for this one).

INT'L STUDENT SUMMER FUN

> "The Lord works in mysterious ways
> His wonders to perform; He plants His
> footsteps on the sea, and rides upon the
> storm."
>
> – William Cowper

For those of you who pay very close attention to the characters within my China story would be quite familiar with Jane. For those others of you who have lives, and therefore would not be able to recall, you would do well to read or reread CHAPTER 6 - A CHANGE OF SCENERY for further details and familiarisation with the aforementioned person. Back to the story. So, one day I was at the house of Jane and her family, talking to her in the kitchen during the afternoon, when she looked up from the stove and expressed that she would like to organise some fun activities for the international students who are in Beijing that haven't got anything planned to do with other students. Later that week, at the English service at BICF, Jane and her husband Luke were on the platform advertising the Summer Fun initiative to bring international students together for the purposes of fun and fellowship. They proceeded to outline some activities that they had discussed, and heartily invited everyone to participate in them.

Before I could get the chance to be skeptical, there were days at the park, Frisbee games, trips outside of Beijing, and even baking classes. People poured in from all over Beijing to take part in sports days, women's brunches; and international dinners on a weekly basis, with dishes from all over the world coming together in one large banquet for all. Christians and sinners alike were laughing and having a good, clean time; and to be honest, there were some days that I was out for hours due to the activities held.

Something else was happening too. Something that could not be seen on the surface. Something the laughter hid; something the smiles covered: God was working. God was proving Himself to be true within the activities as He worked on the hearts of the unbelievers. He seemed to be working behind the scenes and drawing people to Himself through the love that was being exhibited among the believers. The Lord Jesus once said "by this shall all men know that you are my disciples, if ye have love one for another."[17] One day, one of the members of the group came up and said that there was a friend who was not really that interested in Church, but after the first and second activities had for Summer Fun, they wanted to see what church was like and asked to come along. When they got there, the sermon for the week was on Hospitality, and it just showed me how God uses the littlest and simplest things in our lives to bring us to believe in Him. One of my favourite passages of Scripture tells us just that when Paul speaks to the church at Corinth.[18] God has shown me that He can use anything for His purposes so that no flesh can boast in His presence. This, actually helps me to humble myself and not to put people on too high a pedestal (especially myself) when it comes to the gifts which they possess.

---

17 John 13:35

18 1 Corinthians 1:27-28: "God hath chosen the foolish things of the world to confound the wise; and God hath chosen the weak things of the world to confound the things which are mighty; and the base things of the world, and things which are despised, hath God chosen, yea, and things which are not, to being to nought things that are…"

EGGS, TOAST AND OJ

One Saturday morning, I was honoured to have joined the men of the church for a breakfast meeting. So, the OJ in the title stands for orange juice and not that Simpson character. As someone who is still in mid-twenties, sitting among these big boys always has had with it a feeling of being a fly among frogs. The men seated there were elders in the church; deacons and such, all with decades of experience serving in the church. We ordered, introduced ourselves and thought about what was to be discussed that morning. One of the gentlemen there started out by saying that he would like to propose looking at the book of Jonah. He went on to ask what everyone at the table knew about Jonah, and each of us gave our experiences with the book, and our understanding of the characters involved.

One particular thing happened which stood out in my mind: the question was asked concerning Jonah's reason for not wanting to go to where God had called him. From the time the question mark hit the floor, it was brought back to my memory the genealogies from the first book of the Bible, about the descendants of Noah, and how Ham's descendants were cursed. I had come to the conclusion that having known this part of history, Jonah as a prophet knew more than anybody that the cursed descendants of Ham went on to build the city of Nineveh in Genesis 10, and these people- these Assyrians were thorns in Israel's side for centuries. Jonah, knowing how wicked these people are already, added to the fact that God declared that their sin had reached high heaven was more than convinced that these people were anything but deserving of God's mercy. Not that there is any such thing as being "deserving" of mercy, but Jonah had weighed the situation and decided that he was having none of it. After my long and detailed explanation, I sat back in satisfaction. Maybe it was in pride, but I was glad that I could bring biblical history and scripture, and so confidently lay out the points upon which my answer and contribution leaned. Two of the men leaned back and folded their arms. They had looks of inquisition on their faces, and I braced myself for whatever question they would hurl at me. Luckily, their question was the same: are you sure that the Ninevites are descended from Ham? While I was defending myself, the guy who brought up the topic in the first place was flicking through his Bible, looking for any evidence that would support what I was saying. When he found it, he read it aloud for all to hear, and I could see the two men with inquisitive faces slowly nod their heads. It was only at this point that I was beginning to feel a little nervous.

But, Stef. Why would you be getting nervous? I can't say that I know; I am not too certain.

AFTER THE HICCUP

The last time this particular chapter was looked at or edited by me (or anyone else for that matter) was the 21st of August, 2017. That would make it one complete year and a day since I wrote the above paragraphs. It would take a book to describe what happened in the months that followed that Saturday morning at men's breakfast. What had happened to my writings? Well, my memory stick had been corrupted, and I had lost all the documents which I had written. It was only a miracle of technological dabbling that I was able to get them back. I had even started to do a paragraph here, but I don't know what happened to the train of thought. Did I do the paragraph somewhere else? Did I forget to finish this chapter? God only knows. What I do know is that this chapter has to be finished because there seems somewhere to be other chapters that come after this one, and a missing chunk out of this one.

I would strain my brain to recall what would have happened last summer, but luckily there is somewhat of an account of that in the previous chapters. What happens for sure is that a lot of people leave.

I often refer to Beijing as a 21st century Jerusalem. For those of you who are not too familiar, Jerusalem in the 1st century was a haven for all manner of international Jews, speaking a vast array of languages. Beijing is such a place (minus the abundance of Jews, of course) in that it is home to people from every corner of the globe, somewhere in the range of 100,000. These are just the estimates of Beijing. Heaven knows what the numbers are like for the rest of China. That being said, and most of them being students, it wouldn't be too much to imagine that the summers here are bitter sweet for everyone: the ones who are leaving are sad, not to mention the ones who are being left by their friends; while the ones who are coming are happy. Hence, that summer, as I had finished my introductory course of Chinese language, the vast majority of my classmates would go on to study at different universities across China, and never see me again. Even now, an entire year later, the void that some of them left in my life remains unfilled, despite the shallow excuse of an encouragement that "you'll find new friends". They never seemed to fit into the space that was left. Furthermore, of the new ones that have come, some have left too, making it many voids unfilled. Now, looking back at that, and another summer that has gone, the point is reinforced that the transience of Beijing is bitter-sweet. Tears a-many were shed in the summer Sundays at church, when treasured members announced that they were no longer going to be attending; and while church numbers filled back up in the coming autumn, those who were gone still were missed dearly, and yet, there was a hope of seeing them again. Christians know what I mean.

"Your first hello begins your last goodbye"

– Anonymous

Seeing Double

> *"So, Barnabas went to Tarsus to look for Saul, and when he had found him, he brought him to Antioch. For a whole year they met with the church and taught a great many people. And in Antioch the disciples were first called Christians."*

> *–Acts 11:26 ESV*

FOR MY NAME'S SAKE

FROM THE TIME I came to China back in August 2016, I was completely enthralled by the glory of the country, and the wonderful things which can be found here. I was taking pictures like crazy and sending them to people and friends that I have back in Barbados. Just like how I was encouraging people to learn Chinese when I was at my first University, I started encouraging people to come up to China to get fresh starts, or to simply further themselves. One such person is a guy that I met at church a few years ago. In Barbados, when I was at the church, I was told of this guy who has the same name as myself. To make matters funnier, his last name only differs from mine by one letter. I was told that he was also one who was passionate about the things of God and His Word; and that I have to meet this guy: Stefan Forde. Naturally, I was drawn to the idea of meeting a guy with the same name as me and so I agreed to meet him. Just before I was leaving Barbados, I ran into him on the street and held him by the shoulders. I told him that I was going up to China, and that I will be looking forward to seeing him there as well, come 2017.

While in China, I got wind of the time that he was coming up, and found it no surprise that it would be on the same date that I came to China the year before. I went to the airport and waited for him. The "trust God" operation had to come into activation, in that his flight was badly delayed, and I had a class in just a few minutes' time. I was checking my watch, and trying not to become anxious. I was already waiting for him for four hours, and his flight had not yet landed. When he finally *did* come through arrivals, I got us a taxi, and we made our way back to BLCU, before I rushed off to Kid Castle. I got there just a few minutes late, and had to push the class past the regular finishing time, much to the displeasure of the kids. Shaking that off, I went back to the school where I continued to help Stefan settle in. My greatest concern was getting him to move to my dorm and us living together. The following days were nice, and well enjoyed by us both. We went out to many places in the area, and I had the pleasure of introducing him to many of my friends. Unfortunately, however, the roommate that I had at the time didn't pass the examination set by the Chinese Scholarship Council, and so had to redo the year. This put me in a position where I had to move my belongings to where Stefan was staying for the time being, as opposed to having him move in with me. Patience on my part had to be taught, in that I saw it as unfair that I had to be the one moving out and it was my roommate who was the one who failed. To me, failures are the ones who move out, and winners keep their place. I took a breath, got up early one morning, and started packing my things to move up two floors to be with Stefan.

When I was finished moving, I took a few breaths and reminded myself that this was a fresh, bright new room that was prepared for me and him. Stefan himself told me that he was grateful that I moved, because he didn't want to have to sleep on the bed in my room, knowing what my roommate used to do under the covers. I bowed my will and felt better. As if God was teaching me a lesson, the day after the move, I read a notice on the dormitory's 1st floor stating that the floors 1-5 will have to do without cold water for the next few days, and the floors from 6-14 will be getting new mattresses. I was on the 5th floor before, and moved to the 7th floor with Stefan. Stefan saw the notice and believed it to be a sign from God.

Romans 15: 2 tells us that we should all please our neighbour for their good, and not for our own benefit. Though the context described by Paul is somewhat different to the one I am describing here, the idea is that when you see someone in need of help, you ought to help them. 1 John 3 puts it further into perspective by telling us that if we have the world's goods, and close off our hearts to our brother, how is it possible for the love of God to be in us? Sometimes, you may have to go out of your way to find opportunities to help out people. Other times, you could just literally be standing there, and a change hurls itself at you. When I was yet younger, and was in the Cadet Corps, people had the habit of by-passing other people and coming to me to ask questions about things. It could just be me being paranoid or it could have been that my uniform was flashy, but sometimes, a person may come up to me and say something like "you look like you know what's going on, can you help me with this?" and being here in Beijing is no different. Even now, outside the uniform, I am here in China, and people are looking my way, and as soon as our eyes meet, they would approach me for help. Fortunately, the Lord has placed in me a "spirit of helpfulness". I give credit to Him because helping people has caused me some serious pain in the past, and naturally, I would gravitate away from it.

HELPING ASIDE

While sitting with Stefan in the office for international students here on my campus, a guy comes into the office tattered and torn. He looks like he just stepped off the plane and is covered in sweat. He was lugging his very heavy suitcases, and he had his blazer trying not to sweep the dust from the floor, as it was desperately flung over the dragging suitcase. I took one look at him and said "just stepped off the plane, did we?" He responded between breaths and wiped the sweat from his brow. I took a look at the forms he had, and was able to tell him where it was that he had to go. I got up and took him to the place where he was to be, and even bought him water and a small snack.

Another afternoon, Stefan and I were heading off to meet up with some friends, and amid the plethora of foreigners traversing the Wudaokou 五道口 area, I couldn't help but notice one particular young lady trudging around with two very large suitcases behind her. She went north, then south, then north again. When I saw her the third time, I leaned into her line of sight and asked her if she was lost. We spoke for a while and then, I directed her to the correct bus stop from which to take the bus to her school, and the nearest location from which to hail a taxi. When she left, Stefan and I stood and marvelled at the interpenetrating hand of God, working in and through the little decisions we make daily for the perfection of His will. It amazed us both, and we started discussing it at length. It seemed as though we were merely standing and waiting for another friend to meet up with us, but it just so happened that we were in that particular spot, at the time that Amber (that's her name) passed that way. Had we been at the bus stop at our regular time, we would never have seen her, and she probably would have taken a lot longer to get to her school.

The ideal situation for helping people is for them to accept your help, appreciate your help, and then show gratitude for your help. After all, who doesn't want to be helped? Who doesn't want to have a burden lifted from their shoulders? During the time that I've been here, I've helped many a person, and, most of the time, they are pretty grateful for the help I render- however little. Unfortunately, there are some times when people are not as they appear on the surface. There are some times when someone would look like someone in need of help, and when the help is offered, it blows up in your face. It may seem like a complete flip of the script, that someone helped could respond in such a manner, but I was quite surprised to find out the hard way that people can be like that. I guess the problem isn't that I was not cognizant to the existence of those kinds of people, but that I, in my blissful ignorance never thought that it could happen to me. Here's a taste:

There was one day when I saw someone in need of help. It was evident that this person needed a friend to lean on for a while until a particular situation in their life settled down to a norm. I decided that if it were me, I would appreciate a friend coming to be there for me if I were going through a difficult time. So, I went to be there for this stranger. This stranger then became a friend; and this friend became rather close. I was like a frog in the pot of slowly boiling water. The water became warmer and warmer, and I had no idea what I was in for; and before too long, this friend- this close person to me looked at me and told me that I was never there for her. She began to lash out at me verbally and physically, and shouted hateful words at me. She lied and manipulated me, and then loudly declared that she hated me, and never wants to be associated with me again. I am making a bold move in putting these things in my story; and with every word, I feel the temptation to delete this entire paragraph. In telling of this to you guys,

I run the risk of you questioning what I did to have triggered all this, or what I said to her to make her blow up like that. In writing this down and opening up this part of my life in China to you, I run the risk of being seen as the cause for this young woman's explosive reactions, and it would have to be something that I did. Of course, you are all entitled to your own opinions; and neither the full story, nor her side of the story are included in this paragraph because my point is to illustrate that helping people will not always guarantee gratitude. Again, the reason I would say that it is all God that gave me the spirit of helpfulness, is that, even after that hurtful ordeal, I was still more than willing to help people register for rooms, point them to where they needed to go on campus, and use my best Chinese to show people around. It is for Christ's sake that I do these things. The memory verse from when I taught the Chinese Sunday School comes to mind when I think that in whatever you do, it must come from the heart (however hurt or damaged), as if you are doing it for the Lord, and not for man.[19] This way, when you look at the situation that brought you much hurt, and confusion; when you know within your heart that you did everything without evil intention, and you know that ultimately, you do what you do because of what you believe, then you do like Peter tells us: not to be surprised when trials come, but welcome them as friends.[20]

PARAGRAPH OF MANY COLOURS

As the new semester starts, I find that the trouble in registering that I encountered in my first year at BLCU, somewhat tripled for Stefan as he tried to register for the same place. It was seemingly trouble upon trouble as he was sent to and fro, from one part of the university to the other. Just as he was getting accustomed to one set of circumstances, things would change, and he would be sent to another part of the school, and told to settle down there. He finally was put in into a class fit for his program, and had even met great friends along the way. I am sure that he is more grateful for being here, than he is frustrated with all the running around.

---

19 Colossians 3:23
20 1 Peter 4:12-19

Meanwhile, I simply had to appear at the office, show them my transcript from last year, and receive my timetable for my year's courses. When I started my courses, I was put with some more international students from mostly Asian countries, with varying levels of Chinese proficiency. One thing which was surprising to me was that a teacher walked in, and the first thing she did was to call out the names of about seven students and told them that this class is too hard for them. She then handed them a new time table, and sent them away. The remaining 21 of us began studying the courses for that week: Cambodians, Koreans, Russians, Bangladeshis and more gathered under one roof, to be united by the language of the one teaching. People caught speaking another language were fined ¥ 1 and had to pay it to the class monitor. When I say class monitor, I believe that the post goes a little further than what we see in primary schools with one/two persons keeping the class quiet when the teacher leaves the classroom. I believe that the teacher had explained the roles and responsibilities of the class monitor(s), but either I totally forgot by this point, or she will go into further detail at a later date. For right now, I don't think that I would be willing to take on that responsibility- whatever it is. However, as much as we haven't even decided who ours will be, a student who missed a class came up to me and reported the absence to me. I stood in confusion and was wondering if it was that he was asking me what he would have to do. To my bewilderment, he addressed me by the name of class monitor in Chinese, and I had to correct him. From where I sit, it seems as though even from that short encounter with my classmates (only one week has gone by this time) they -or at least that one- have already put in their minds who they think will be the favoured one.

Sometimes, the thought comes to my mind of this cycle: classmates don't speak when a question is asked. Out of respect for the teacher, or just to break the silence, I would say the answer. The answer is either right or wrong. The one's who don't speak further refuse to speak, either out of intimidation or pure disinterest, and it continues to circle down from there. Then, the ones who answer are perhaps looked at with scorn or jealousy. Or maybe not. Maybe they don't really care at all, and I'm just here sitting down worrying over nothing. Maybe I should just forget about them, and answer all the questions when they come. After all, we are here to learn Chinese; and if you don't want to participate in the class freely offered to you (we're on Scholarship) then it would be nobody's fault but your own, should you not receive a favourable grade.

But then again, I could also be right in my assumption that being too much of a know-it-all would have a negative impact on the others in the class. It wouldn't be the first time that being over-enthusiastic made people like me slightly less. I pray for the balance to still answer questions enthusiastically, and yet not make the other students feel as though they're any less than human because of my enthusiasm too.

Before leaving Barbados, I had the pleasure of meeting a Chinese lady named Lisa. When I told her that I was leaving Barbados to go study at BLCU, she found it a remarkable coincidence, and told me that she was the person in charge of the Department for International Students at that very school. She told me how my classes would be structured, and that she believes that I would have a successful time at this school. I was speaking with the teacher in charge of my class, and she told me that she knows of a Chinese teacher that is still in my country. This teacher, who is Lisa, as you would have imagined by now, had told my teacher about me before I even entered the classroom, and she told me that she is tasked with taking very good care of me.

WHY ME?

The above question is one that I am sure a great innumerable multitude of people have asked themselves, and even asked God. Some people, I'm sure, don't even believe in a personal God of our lives that cares about every facet of our being, but still sometimes would raise their fists to the heavens and scream the above question. For me, this is a question that I try my very best and hardest not to ask, if it is that I trust God for His perfect will to be done. Last week, for example, I was approached on social media and asked if I were a small group leader. I had mixed feelings about the question. I didn't know if to feel proud that someone would think me small group leader material, or aggravated that I would be thrust into responsibility. Within forty-eight hours, I was asked the same question by another person. This time, I was worried. Why are people asking me this? Being a small group leader –or any manner of leader for that matter- takes a certain amount of responsibility, and should anyone lack the responsibility needed to lead in a particular capacity, they are automatically disqualified from leading, on account of their lack of responsibility. I have not asked why these people assume that I have said responsibility to lead a small group. When the second gentleman asked me if I am a small group leader, I told him no. He responded by saying "you should, you should". I was most confused. Why should I lead a small group, when there are already plenty small group leaders? I told him that I am already a member of the small group at my school, and that group already has a leader. As if he was rehearsing for this moment, he responded by saying that I should then start another one, and then lead that. My confusion reached new heights as I searched for the logic. What was the premise upon which his point was based? There was never a time where I would have been a leader of anything that would show him that I was capable of being a satisfactory or even capable leader. Did he think I would make a good group leader because I seem to know a little about the Bible? These are merely my thoughts as I reflect on the whole issue.

For anyone who is confused, I realise now that I haven't told my dear readers what small groups are. Upon entering church, they immediately start encouraging new-comers to join a small group in their area. Small groups are –as their name suggests- small groups of people who meet up once a week for Bible study, discussion and prayer. The leader, therefore, must be responsible for the members of the small group: their spiritual needs, level of maturity, and even if they be saved (Christians) or not. These are all things which the small group leader must both know and handle. The small group leader must avail his time, energy and efforts for the benefit of the members of his group.

Meanwhile, the second week of school has started, and it is time to choose the class monitor. The teacher instructs us to take out a small piece of paper and write the names of the male and female class monitor who they'd like to have. While in the West, the position of class monitor is something that is left behind with one's childhood, here in China, it seems that even at the University level, the position is one that takes high honour. I take out my paper, and in an effort to shift the inevitable tide coming my way, I write the name of the French guy who sits in the back. When we had all written down, I and a girl from Kirghizstan went up front to count the votes. I read out the names and she wrote them on the board, with the number of votes beside them. I stood there as I opened the papers and saw each of them with my name on them. Out of four guys whose names were on the board, one was the French guy that I voted for, and the other guy had switched classes. So, it was only my name really, and another guy's name. I got eleven votes, and the other guys got one each. I somehow knew it was coming, along with knowing that I had a greater chance to be voted in. There is a Chinese idiom: 蚍蜉撼树 (pífúhànshù). This idiom describes an ant trying its best to push down a tree; and that was me when I was voting for the French guy, trying to shift the focus onto someone else.

Concluding this paragraph, I and the person who I tried to help in earlier paragraphs, have come to a decision which I think, for right now, is the wisest and safest, albeit not the most comfortable path for us both. Stefan and I are growing and learning more and more each day. Up to a few nights ago, we took a walk around the neighbourhood, and sang hymns aloud in the streets as our voices harmonised to His glory. We went to the small group in our school, and we enjoyed reading the Bible and sharing with our friends. There was even a guy, David, who asked about the inspiration of Scripture, with reference to all the other extra-biblical sources out there. The credit goes to the Holy Spirit for my answer, because I took him through the Bible from the beginning, and showed the fine story line that is traced by the hand of God from the Genesis account, down to the revelation prophesy. What is sometimes missed is that the entire book, is the script of God's eternal plan to bring man back to Himself. From the fall of man, I showed how every book or set of books was just another layer taken off to the identity of this man, this agent of God who will be responsible for bringing back the world to God. Pray with me that the Holy Spirit uses my imperfect articulation for the perfecting of the faith of the young gentleman.

EVERY – ISM THAT YOU OUGHT

Today is the day after my birthday, and I must say that it was just as well-enjoyed as any other day. The day before, the pastor of the Chinese congregation had asked me if there was a time that I would be free this week to meet with him for a lunch. I had taken out a time, which happened to be my birthday, and figured that it was just the right time for that kind of fellowship. As Providence would have it, he didn't know that it was my birthday, though I must admit that it had crossed my mind that the entire church would be meeting me there at the restaurant for a surprise birthday party; but alas, it was not the case. I went there, and the two of us sat and talked for a while about my life in China, my plans for my future in the Church, how life in church is back in Barbados, among other topics. When it came to my role in the church here in China, he told me that he has noticed my level of Chinese proficiency has risen to a very… (I'm trying not to reuse the same word "proficient") level. He noted that my Chinese has improved greatly in the last year, and encouraged me to join one of the small groups of the Chinese congregation, so as to hone the skills of speaking outside the classroom. I could feel the pressure rising as he mentioned another brother in the faith who has joined the small groups, and he is even an American. "When he first joined, his Chinese was not as good as yours is," he said; and it was as though he was saying that if it is that someone joined who wasn't as proficient as I am, how much more should I join. He ended by encouraging (challenging) me; telling me that I ought not to waste the talent for sharing in Chinese that the Lord has given me.

Also for my birthday, I had oral Chinese class in the morning. I find it a perfect place to practise my Chinese idioms that I have learned over time. While there, I find that the teacher provides ample opportunity for speaking; and she is very good at making sure that we get our tones and pronunciations accurate. On the whole, I find that the teachers here are much better than I had previously anticipated, and there are some of them who, when they're teaching, no one ever cares about the time. Sometimes, the hours go by, and no one is sleepy, no one is feeling uncomfortable, and no one complains and moans. I am noting these things because these teachers are completely different from a lot to whom I am accustomed. There are some teachers who show their true feelings about teaching, and it reflects on their students and their attitudes as well. In my undergraduate thesis, I noted that the language teacher is "not teaching Spanish or French, but students" (Lorde). I don't know how it works with citing one's own document. I am not even sure if my document is cite-worthy, but I will cite it nonetheless, and maybe when it comes to publishing, I would know whether it could remain or not.

Anyhow, the day continued, and I went to small group here on my campus in the evening. Small group was good at first, but I kept battling myself to not let emotions get the better of me, as I was trying to block out the thoughts of past hurts; and not to let what I think about people stop me from concentrating on the reason for small group –namely, for fellowship, and for the edification of the brethren. The Bible tells us that we ought to commit ourselves to the frequent gathering of ourselves together, and to not neglect it as some are in the habit of doing, but rather to help build up and encourage one another in the faith.[21]

A few weeks ago, I had told the teachers at Kid Castle that as most of my classes this upcoming year will be in the morning, it will free up my time in the afternoons for teaching the little children. I was also praying for more classes, that I would not only gain the much-needed experience for the betterment of the classroom, but also the additional cash that would "grease my pockets", as I'm sure all foreign students want. As providence would have it, I got the extra classes to teach, and I was looking forward to seeing how they would pan out. The class I had before, which was actually the class which I liked teaching the best, was taken from me, and I was left with the more difficult class to teach. This class wasn't only difficult in terms of the age of the students (4-6 years old), but in terms of the number of students to be taught. When I first started with that particular class, there were three or four students. Then, when I thought that this class was just about right as it is, and beginning to love my "job", then my favourite class was taken from me, and four more students were added to the tiny tots that were already difficult to handle. These new students, regrettably were not as enjoyable to teach as the four previous ones, and seemed to delight in making the classroom into a zoo. Added to that, the other two classes which have been added to my shoulders have been of people of similar age, and even one guy who is autistic.

I find myself in a bind. When I started teaching the class with the autistic child, the other teacher had to remove the clock from the classroom because it was all that he was looking at; ever asking what time class was finished (we hadn't even started). Whenever we got one of them to sit down, another one would get up and leave the class. When that one would finally sit still, another one would get up and start running around. One parent had even tried to control her own child for the class, who then proceeded to literally run circles around her mother. I stood there stunned as to how she would take her child, who she herself cannot control, and place her in my care expecting me to control her. This is not a

21 Hebrews 10:25

new situation for me in terms of trying to get a figurative grip on the children of others. Amid the confusion, I looked over at the administrator and when her eyes caught mine, I said: "this is going to be difficult, isn't it?" The expression on her face changed very little as she nodded and said, yes it will be. I had a ball that came in very handy with getting the kids' attention. Seeing as they all wanted it, I made it clear that no one was getting to touch the ball until they sat still and participated well in the class. This was a good method to get them to sit well, as I remember Pavlov and his Operant Conditioning; every time I would bounce the ball and hold it up, the children would sit and pay attention. This behaviour was rewarded with points and an opportunity to catch the ball and bounce it while saying the letters on the board.

I thank God for the ideas and the training that I have received, as I find myself able to grip their attention all the more, and still get the content taught in a timely fashion. Moreover, the classes are not the original two hours, but one and a half, as the children involved are of smaller ages than my previous class; and smaller attention spans. This being the case, I would have to incorporate more games into my classes, as well as other activities to keep their little minds from wandering off into their own little worlds as mine once did. And the little kid with autism? Here and after known as Bill, he caught on to the words, and I felt like one of those whisperers on television when I got him to match the sound of a word like pencil, to the object on the flashcard.

PATIENCE ASIDE

There is something that I need a lot more of in my life. It's not cake, though that would be nice (I didn't even have cake on my birthday). It's patience[22]. Patience is one of those things that the Apostle Paul advises us as Christians to clothe ourselves in, and it's one of those things, regrettably that you cannot buy at the store and just put on, but it something that has to be honed over the years. It is something that is also very difficult to attain, as it only comes with trials. The Bible tells us that trials work patience[23], in addition to building character[24]. I happened to be in a situation with a pastor, in which I witnessed that he was displaying so much patience and understanding with the persons involved that it was amazing for me to watch. He seemed not to flinch or to be affected, but listening, understanding and patient. I marvelled

22 Colossians 3:12
23 Romans 5:3
24 1 Peter 1:6b-7

because, were I in his shoes, I would have lost my cool a long time before he did. The thought hit me then, that if the Bible says that tribulation works out patience, and he is this patient, then it would mean that he would have had to had gone through a great deal of tribulation.

When I think that patience is something that must be attained and personified by the Believer, I find it easier to look back upon events and people in my life that have been a rather large pain, and be grateful that dealing with them was a gift to be welcomed and cherished. When I come across that colleague who believes me to be about 6 years old, and speaks to me as such, I feel annoyed, taken for granted and emasculated for about an hour or so, and then I take some breaths and let it roll off. I know that these things will happen, because Jesus said that if anyone seeks to live righteously, they will suffer persecution. It's amazing that sometimes, these persecutions don't always have to do with your faith, but as they happen, your faith will be reflected in how you face them, and your attitude towards the person involved.

IF…THEN

While Stefan and I were on vacation, we often met with another Barbadian. Over lunch, we would talk about the ways in which Chinese culture differs from Barbadian culture. One afternoon, the topic about creation came up in conversation. Dwayne, as he will be known in this document, purported that there has to be an intelligent design behind the universe. He, coming from an architectural background, thought it obvious that, based on the manner in which things work, there has to be a creator. Stefan and I saw the opportunity and swallowed it up, bait, line and sinker. We began reasoning with Dwayne about God, and about how if there is a creator, then his signature has to be on his work. It was only a matter of time before Jesus was in the conversation, and we used the same logic Dwayne was bringing, to make the case for God, and salvation. When we left the restaurant around midnight, we encouraged him to think seriously about the things discussed that night. When Stefan and I got home, we prayed *hard* for Dwayne to think about Jesus. We prayed for Jesus to remember Dwayne, and to draw him to salvation. About two Sundays later, my phone buzzed and I looked upon it, and behold, it was him. He was on his way to church, and wanted to know if he was at the right place. I smiled brightly, and ran outside to meet him to take him inside. I am overwhelmed with joy to have had him come to church *more than once*. We even had him for lunch, and we continue to pray that God draws him to Himself.

More good news, Stefan finally got his documents sorted out, after much running around. His situation was quite different to mine; and therefore, we had to go through a completely different procedure for him. These inconveniences cost us a lot of time, to the extent that he was quickly approaching his visa expiration date. We thank God for His timing, because, had he been two days later than he was, Stefan would have been in deep trouble with the authorities. Along the way, however, we met several friends, many of which we still hang out with to this day. Stefan breathed a sigh of relief deep enough to blow the roof off any building. I was relieved too; but I kept on telling him, that if it is that God was the One who brought him to this wonderful land of China, He wouldn't short-change him. Sure trials would come, but none so as to derail the purposes of God.

TWO GUYS; ONE GOAL

I sat for a while thinking of a good way to conclude this chapter, a good way to land this plane. Looking around the dorm room, it was just another average evening after class. Stefan was editing some animations on his computer, and I was finishing up some homework. Already, the school has taken my class to see some Beijing Opera, and will soon take Stefan's class to see the Great Wall. I asked him how he would describe his experience in Beijing thus far. He said that despite the difficulties and challenges that Beijing presented, he is enjoying himself and making every effort to master the Chinese language for his academic and personal development. Church wise, he has been attending the Mandarin and English services with me, and has begun to serve in the Christian Fellowship here. There is not a day that passes that I am not grateful for God bringing Stefan here to Beijing, and to my school, by extension. I have shown him around as much as I could, and we should be travelling to another part of China to celebrate the coming New Year (Chinese one, of course) if all goes according to plan. Helping him with homework, praying together and just enjoying each other's company has been the highlight of my school year.

"...and let us not be weary in well doing: for in due season we shall reap, if we faint not. As we have therefore opportunity, let us do good unto all men, especially unto them who are of the household of faith."

- Galatians 6:9-10

CHAPTER 14

The Start of a Major

"三人行，必有我师"

If three are travelling together, I'm bound
to learn something from one of them.

– Confucius

THIS IS NOW November 2017, and it's the third month that Stefan is here with me. I've learned a lot about him, and a lot from him. What I find most interesting of all is the grand differences in how we two see the world. We watch television a lot, and very often he intently watches and points out the aspects of the film with regards to colour, lighting, angles, etc. Sometimes, it is very hard for me to see what he is talking about. However, when I am listening to the words being spoken on TV (Chinese TV), and spying the Chinese subtitles, I learn new words, and even discover how certain words are made. Often times, he asks me how I remember all the characters. This leads into a discussion where I, like him, begin to point out the various intricacies about the subject, namely language, and how this language of Chinese (Mandarin) is so vastly different from that of English, or any other language for that matter. Whenever he speaks, there is no doubt as to the level of passion with which he speaks about film, and the various techniques used in film. When I speak, there is the same passion, but different focus. When you even check his browsing history (not that I'm telling you to) you would find speeches and tutorials and symposia among all other kinds of film related material, whereas in my browsing history, Ted-Talks about language acquisition, language in children and language evolution permeate my computer. To have two people, though named the same, be so vastly different in point of view and thought, fascinates me. Up to yesterday, I was taking the time before class to explain to the two other students who usually come early to class certain things and idiosyncrasies about language, and some of the differences between our language English, (though I am the only native speaker of English in the classroom) and that of our target language, namely Mandarin Chinese. Even though I am now learning Chinese, and I have so much more knowledge to attain, I find that I speak in a manner as to arrest the attention of those listening, to the point that when others started trickling in to the classroom, even the teacher herself, they too are entranced by the doodling I had drawn on the chalkboard, and the vivid description of what I have said.

Stefan F. on the other hand, would say that he is introverted. He doesn't speak as often, or as loudly as I do, and some days he could absorb himself into what he's doing to the point where people would even forget that he is in the room. When asked about public speaking, I inquired if he would be willing to speak in front of a thousand people. He shivered at the thought. Knowing that many people would prefer death to public speaking, his reaction did not surprise me. However, when asked about his willingness to speak to a thousand people about film, all the anxiety in the world suddenly vanished, and his eyes lit up like Chinese New Year. He seemed almost to float above his bed as I could tell that he was imagining himself in that very circumstance.

WAKE UP AND SMELL THE FLOWERS

The school has yet again given us the opportunity to travel on a school trip. A few weeks ago, they had taken us to see the famous Beijing Opera. This time, we were privileged to go see the Beijing Botanical Gardens. As it was the autumn season, the leaves were all turning from yellow to orange and red, and it was indeed a lovely sight to behold. Like every attraction in Beijing so far, it was huge, filled with people and bustling with activity. However, at the Botanical Gardens, the people there besides my schoolmates were all retirees. Sure, there were a few babies too; and a primary school had taken some of their students there, but the majority of persons there were elderly folk. Our teacher had told us to go off into groups so as not to get lost. My group of choice was that very teacher, and another teacher from our department. Before I could break off and join them, however, I had gone with a few classmates, and toured the place a bit. An Indonesian classmate, J and I had crossed a bridge, and heard music. We followed the sound and came across a large group of elderly men and women singing and playing instruments. I took out my phone like a good millennial and began recording what I was seeing. They stood around a tree where a man stood on a pedestal conducting the entire affair, and the people stood around with their music sheets singing at the top of their lungs, songs of praise to their country. I managed to have a glance at the music sheet of one of the ladies, and from what I was able to understand from the characters I knew, the song embraced the vast differences of the people and cultures among the different provinces and cities of China, and how they are many, yet one in the sight of the people. Every man is a brother and every dialect a speech. The lyrics were, to me, the complete embodiment of patriotism, and I appreciated the experience.

When the first song was over, the person with the microphone called the page that they were going to sing from next, amid the chatter of the people after the first song. One of the ladies started turning to the wrong page (maybe because amid the chatter, she didn't hear clearly) and I reached out and stopped her. I told her that the person said turn to page 42, and she was astonished! Turning to the lady next to her, she said "not only is this guy's speech fluent, his ears are better than mine, for even I didn't hear which page to turn to". We all laughed and I attempted to sing the next song with them.

After I had parted from the company of the lovely patriotic ladies, I caught up with my group of choice: the two teachers. The three of us walked and talked, took pictures and basked in the ambiance of the area. They asked me a lot of Barbados, and taught me a lot about China. On our way, we came across about six elderly ladies walking in the opposite direction. Mrs Tang (one of the teachers) told me to talk to the old ladies. It is only when I responded asking "talk about what?" that one of the ladies turned and exclaimed that my Chinese was good. Mrs Tang then told the ladies that they could ask me anything, because there's no problem with my Chinese. We talked for a bit, and it seems like these ladies were only old in age, but not in attitude. They all had up-to-date smartphones, selfie sticks and all, and they were walking with a jazz in their step. After we took a few selfies with them, we parted ways and my teachers and I continued our stroll around the Gardens.

I don't know why it is that I always preferred to be with people older than I, rather than with people my own age. From as early as I could remember, I would always prefer to be talking with adults, than with persons in my class. For instance, I remember when I was in primary school, I would be in the carpark talking with parents while they wait for their children to come to them. There was even one instance when I was talking with a classmate's dad, and I asked him if he wants me to go and tell his son that he's waiting. He told me not to, so we can talk a while more. He wasn't the only one. Many a parent and guardian would stand and talk to me as we wait for the children to finish playing on the field; and even now as an adult, I find myself still talking to older people, and finding conversation with them much more fulfilling than that with younger folk.

ABOVE AND BELOW

As it is quickly approaching December, one thing is guaranteed: the cold. Unfortunately for most people, the cold that comes is the virus, just as much as the drop in temperature. My beloved teacher, regrettably, was one of those trapped under the net of influenza, and she missed two days of class. For the two days, we had two substitute teachers, one of which was quite cool; the other… let's just say that we preferred the first one. When our beloved teacher came back in to class on the third day, we were understandably relieved, as she is quite the talented one in her profession.

More on the cold, I myself had woken up one morning with a sore throat, and knew immediately what my next move was supposed to be: the pharmacy for some Chinese medicine. Now, the thing about foreigners and all things Chinese is that most of us take a step back whenever the idea comes to partake in something of the Chinese nature, especially medicine and certain foods like rabbit brains. There seems to be a stigma attached to the things that Chinese people have been taking and doing and saying, and Stefan Lorde does not see it. From my viewpoint, Chinese, as humans, have been getting sick for the last 5000 years. If it is that they have a medicine that is said to treat the common cold (notice, I didn't use the word "cure") why is it that you would not want to try it? A lot of the foreigners I have had encounters with have boldly expressed their disgust at the food they see here, and the manner in which Chinese people live out their lives. I see no problem with the food, clothes, medicine or music that I have found here, and maybe this readiness to open up to the culture of this great people is the reason I would be getting 97.3% in my midterms this semester. We thank God!

Anyway, I went to the pharmacy, and purchased myself a box of Chinese medicine. I took it home and began drinking it. As it is natural and herbal in nature, it took a while to work, but it sure did. It was almost as though the medicine is rationed in such a way that you're given just the amount that would treat the cold, so that there would be none of it left over when the cold is gone. That's exactly what happened. The day that the sore throat (and soon to be nasal congestion) was over was the day that the medicine had run out.

Why are people all around me getting so sick all of a sudden? Well, the answer lies in the atmosphere. As the weather in Beijing changes from cold to colder, added to the fact that the weatherman on the news does not give advice on what to wear, people either don't wear enough clothes, and are affected by the cold, or people don too many clothes, and are affected by the cold. The trick, apparently, is to put on clothes in accordance with the weather change. For instance, when it is autumn, one is advised not to throw on the entire wardrobe. Similarly, in spring, one is advised not to fling away all the clothes and start wearing bikinis in the street (other than that getting you arrested). This is to allow your body to get more and more accustomed to the weather as it changes. So, with the cold settling in, colds come knocking upon the doors of our bodies. Luckily for us, and whoever comes into Beijing for the first time, the church takes two or three Sundays to donate winter clothes, and give them to one another in the church.

FRIDAY JOYS

One day in class, there was a guy who had told me that since we finish classes at around ten thirty on Friday mornings that it would be a good idea for us to go out as a class. To me, it seemed like a good idea, so I took it into consideration. Unfortunately, it took me a few days to come to a firm stance on it, and I decided that I would like to go ice-skating. I thus presented this idea to the class, and the few of us interested persons went to the Guomao Mall to skate in their rink. It was a rather rewarding experience, as I haven't been on the ice in quite some time. I went with a Turk, a Bulgarian and an Indonesian, and it was the beginning of a lovely habit we'd form. Thus, our friendships grew stronger, from ice skating, to bowling, to tennis, we spent the next few weeks chatting and laughing with each other. Usually, after the week's activities, we would gather in a restaurant and eat various foods.

One particular Friday in December, I was privileged to go to the Christian Church in Beijing to perform in a skit for their Christmas celebrations. I played the part of a father who, after realising that there is no peace in the spending of money or the togetherness of family, finds peace in Jesus. In the play, the daughter comes home for the holidays, and is ashamed to admit that she lost her job, and was out of work for a whole month without telling her family. Her father (me) is flown into a fit of rage and the family starts yelling and quarrelling with each other. Just then, the uncle passes by with presents, and a message about peace, as he correctly guessed that we were fighting as a family before he arrived. That was the story of the play.

After the performance, and the lights dimmed, some of the people in the audience left, while others stayed to discuss their notions of peace in groups. I was standing at the back with Stefan waiting on another friend of ours to split the taxi fare. While we were waiting, there came a man to me and stood there, looking at me. He started signing to me, and I thought that maybe he didn't think I would understand him. I told him that he's free to speak Chinese to me, and he went on to explain that he too was out of work just like my daughter in the play; to the extent that it was the same amount of time too. I stood there in utter amazement that God would use something as simple as a bunch of kids on a stage to bring people into the knowledge of His ever-loving care for creation. The fact that he was so moved and convicted that he sought me out to testify to me about how God has convicted him through our play really drove me to tears.

The days seem to be going along so fast now. It seems as though there would be a month's break between my paragraphs, and that I am not making much sense. Sometimes, it gets so discouraging to write things down, and to document what things are happening, that I would be tempted to give up and simply make do with the little that I have already. Then, I remember my readers. I remember the people that are actually willing to read or listen to my writings, and that keeps me going.

Speaking of writing, here's something that I thank my God for. In my week, there is a Rudimentary Writing class, which, as its name suggests, prepares us for writing essays in Chinese. During the first few weeks of class, the teacher would explain to us the basics of Chinese essay writing, and how the various punctuation marks work, etc.; and then he would task us with writing essays of our own. To me, I enjoyed the experience of putting my thoughts into words and putting them on paper. It was almost intoxicating to take the structure and grammar and words which I've learned and put them onto the sheet given. I found myself going over the word limit, but luckily not by very much so as to draw out the task, and therefore waste precious time. The following week, the teacher would take the time to talk to us about our essays: our good sentences, our mistakes and areas needing improvement, and help us with it. What I particularly like about every other week is that the sentences which the teacher deems as "good sentences", he would insert into his PowerPoint presentation to show the class. I dare say that it was my aim every week to have at least one of my sentences posted upon that slide.

Whenever there was a writing task for us to do, I would make sure to master as many complex grammatical structures as I could, along with 成语 Cheng Yu (Chinese 4-word proverbs) and use them in my essays. Often times, I would breathe a sigh of satisfaction when I was finished with my essay, and hand them in with a smile. After submission of my work, I would eagerly await the correction of the essays by the teacher to see where I would have fallen, where I was strong, and whether the writing methods I employed were accurate or not. With this knowledge, I would seek to make my next essay more impressive, and see if I could make the slide again the following week.

WINDING DOWN

Another semester has come and gone with me at the Beijing Language and Culture University. It cannot be overstated how much I've learned in the last semester, both academically and spiritually. When we had taken our final examinations for the semester, I was a little nervous about the oral exam, because the teacher had told the class that maybe one in twenty had the chance of getting above 90% in the exam. Seeing as there were approximately 20 of us in the class in the first place, I, knowing how easy it is to make errors in language and have them ruin your entire presentation, became rather downcast, as my odds for an above 90 final grade were statistically lower than I had expected. When I went into the exam room for the other finals, I wasn't nervous. It was only the oral exam that had me a little anxious. When I got back the results, I was rather elated to see that every result was above 90%--especially the oral examination. I was so glad that I had "beaten the odds", and had come out on top.

When it was coming down to the end of the semester, a brother of mine, Coleman came to me and told me about a mission trip to Guangzhou, which involved the teaching of English to some kids at a summer camp. I was interested in going, added to the fact that I didn't have any other plans for the upcoming vacation. I signed up, and there were some sessions to prepare us for the trip, and I was growing more and more excited about it. More of what happened will be described in the upcoming chapters.

"As I journey through the land, singing as I go, pointing souls to Calvary, to the crimson flow, many arrows pierce my soul, from without, within. But my Lord leads me on. Through Him, I must win."

– Rufus H. Cornelius

To Kunming with Love

THE HARDEST STEP to writing about my experiences in China is always the first line; and this is no different. In fact, I would dare say that this particular chapter was one of the hardest ones to start. Every day that passed since I came back from Yunnan was riddled with the mixed feelings of what happened when I went, and laced with the hesitancy of beginning to document it. On the one hand, I was anxious to start writing in order not to forget about it; on the other hand, I was sure that such an experience would be most unforgettable, even if some minor aspects were lost to history.

This chapter of my life describes my first missionary trip. First in this document, however, comes the purpose, and background to this glorious adventure. I was sitting in Church one Sunday morning, when a friend of mine, Coleman, came up and sat by me. He proceeded to describe to me a trip to Guangzhou which involved the teaching of English to children in a Christian-run camp. I expressed my interest, because I had no other plans for the upcoming winter holiday; and, knowing how Beijing is quite the ghost town during Spring Festival, it would be most advantageous to take an adventure elsewhere until the place reopens. The more Coleman talked about it, the more I was interested in it, and the more I began to mentally prepare myself for it. As the trip got closer, the team of us that was going started to meet up and get to know each other more before the trip. Familiarising myself with the other teammates was in order to work better together once we had landed on camp.

About a week before the trip, I got a message from Coleman saying that the camp got cancelled. According to the organisers, only about 10% of the expected number of children actually signed up for the camp, and therefore the camp could not continue. I was disappointed. I had gone to the meetings, I had gotten to know the other teammates for the camp; and now I was to learn that it was all for nothing. Now, it seems, as soon as my motive for going shifted from wanting to get out the house to actually looking forward to participating, the camp got cancelled, and I wouldn't get to meet all the little children.

While I was yet thinking about the disappointment I was feeling, behold, the pastor came up to me and Coleman the following week after the service and took us up the stage to the head of the Korean team (they have Korean service in the same place, after the English service). When he took us up, he spoke to the team leader, telling him about our current mission-trip-less situation, and then proceeded to explain something that I didn't expect. He said to the now three of us that he and the leadership of the English congregation had been praying for the English to join the Korean team for a number of years. The Koreans apparently go to the southern villages of China to build up the churches there and teach the Sunday school kids, and this is the first time that the English congregation had the chance to finally join them. He, though he expressed regret that our trip was cancelled, concomitantly suggested that we are the answer to their prayers.

I stood there confused. My head was almost swirling, because I had heard of the Korean trip that was coming up. It was actually around the same time as the one in Guangzhou. I was still getting used to the fact that there will be no trip, then to be faced with another one just as quickly as the first one vanished. I reluctantly agreed to go.

Not knowing the gravity of the mission ahead of me, I went to the meetings that the Koreans had. I went, obviously, for information. I wanted to know what I was getting myself involved into, and I wanted to know everything. The week before the trip, the team met every day for prayer. Coleman and I went when we could. It was intense. Everything was conducted in Korean, with a volunteer translating into Chinese for us. The linguist in me tingled with excitement as two groups of people, whose language are mutually unintelligible, got together, and used a lingua franca[25] to communicate. All manners of linguistic theories and historical data flooded my mind. Questions also. Questions such as "what am I doing here? I don't speak Korean." "Their Chinese is probably as faulty as mine. How are we to communicate?" I tried not to worry, and focus on the Lord, especially during the Korean style prayer meetings. "Korean style" is a form a prayer where the one at the front prays on a particular topic, and then everyone in the room prays out loud on the same topic. Really loud. This then repeats, and many topics are covered in prayer.

The day for the trip was getting closer, and I felt more lost than ever. I didn't know what to expect. I wasn't given a timetable; I wasn't given a checklist. Nothing. I was completely out to sea, and the people around me didn't speak English, save one (two, come to think about it). Even most of those who spoke Chinese were more limited in their vocabulary than I was, and so, even when I spoke in response, it may not all be understood. *What am I doing here?*

---

25 A language that is adopted as a common language between speakers whose native languages are different.

THE TRAIN RIDE

To get to Kunming, we had to take the train. What I learned afterwards was that the reason we took the slow train wasn't because we didn't have the money for a flight; but was for us to have the time to get to know one another before the mission. There were activities planned for the trip there, and we admittedly got closer- or rather, more familiar by the time the train ride was over. I had written in my diary about the first day. Here goes:

[Tuesday, January 30th 2018] Thank God!

I wasn't feeling very excited to go to Kunming, seeing as my Guangzhou trip had been cancelled. I decided to wait until we reached Kunming to then see how I would feel. I still feel a tinge of solitude when with the Koreans, especially when they are speaking with one another. Yet, going off on my own still seems like giving up. Though I think, or thought that it would be too overwhelming to attempt Korean, from the time I opened my mouth to speak, it felt quite fun, and they all said it was good. I am indeed grateful to God for the gifts which He's given me. We've been broken into two teams- three groups per team. There're more people going this year than ever before. With these large numbers, may God reap a much greater harvest than we ever imagined.

During the day on the train, we would have our devotions, and lunches. I had previously imagined that there would be little food on this trip, but I ended up eating more often with them, than I would were I at home. While on the train, Coleman even had the opportunity (or should I say took the opportunity) to share our faith with a young Chinese gentleman seated with him on the train. With us, as well, were two of the other teammates from the original Guangzhou trip. They were from Nepal.

As we got further and further from Beijing, I started to notice some differences in landscape. Not only in landscape, but I realised that there were many more houses, and much fewer apartment buildings as well. It seems that the people living in these parts were so few that they could afford to have their own houses. I couldn't remember the last time I had seen a house just standing on its own. In Beijing, all the people live in high-rise apartments, so, the change in scenery was quite noticeable. Because Beijing isn't as mountainous as Kunming is in the south, the roads here face north, south, east and west; whereas in the south, where there're lots of mountains, the roads are bendy and wavy. The way people give directions also reflect this, so when people go to Beijing (even from other parts of China), and ask directions, they are struck that people would say things like "turn east here" or "go north here". Another thing I saw in the south was snow. It turns out that Beijing was the only part of China that didn't have any snow that year. Disappointing, I know. Something strange also happened on the train. I was sitting on my bed when I noticed that a woman was looking at me. Being different from the average Chinese, I could understand that curiosity would cause one to look at me. What I couldn't understand was why she was crying while looking at me. Before I could get too worried about that, however, we passed the mountains that were the scenery in James Cameron's Avatar. It was really awesome to see. It was as if I were watching the movie again from the train window.

SECOND JOURNAL ENTRY:

[Wednesday, January 31st 2018] Almost there!

If my sense of direction is any good, we are still heading south. It should take us another 18-20 hours to get there. I find myself sleeping more and more often; and eating snacks. We've had some more meetings regarding the camp preparations. It's quite unimaginable the length of time and the amount of materials needed to create these railroads. We have been on the same train, on the same track for the last 24 hours.

We spent another 21 hours on that train until we got to the city of Kunming, Yunnan. However, the time for relaxing and settling down was not yet. We still had another 7 hours of travelling by van, up the mountains. We exited the train station and met up with the Korean pastor there who was helping with the organisation of the whole thing. He took us to a street where would have 2 choices for food: we had Chinese rice noodles on one side of the street, and McDonald's on the other side. Of course, the younger ones galloped to the McDonald's side of the road, while I enjoyed my bowl of rice noodles. I'm made to understand that the place in which we were was the rice noodle capital of China. These were supposed to be the best, and they certainly tasted so; so much so, that the leaders of my group bought me another bowl of noodles because of how I reacted to the taste.

We left the city, and got on the vans. Divided into two teams; three groups per team, we set out through the countryside. The road was narrow, and sometimes, we were the only ones on the road. It was so bendy and narrow, that one of the vans almost toppled over the cliff when evening was setting in. Sometimes, we passed through some alleys in the town that were so narrow, I could reach through my window and touch the buildings on the road beside us. Before I could ask what time it was, the sky was dark. Also, as we were moving further and further from what we city kids would call "civilisation", our mobile signal vanished. I watched (though not in horror) as my "bars" got lower and lower, until there was nothing there to be had. Darkness. A dead phone battery. No signal. What did I sign myself up for?

Though it was dark, I could still make out the fields and hills which belonged to this vast land. There were many different kinds of crops that fed the people and perhaps people in other parts of China. The vans carried on over, under, around and through the ever-bending roads and hills. Rain water sprinkled the windshield as we began to get more and more tired. The already-faint moonlight was further clouded by the altostratus that blanketed the night sky… Cold set in. We were trying to keep warm in our jackets, and huddling close to each other in the van. Every so often, we would ask the driver how far we were from the campsite just to reassure ourselves that we were soon there.

AT THE CAMPSITE

When we thought we couldn't take it any longer, a familiar sight emerged from the darkness. It was a church. We reacted with awe as we laid eyes upon the edifice. But the hard work had now begun. We still had to set up our sleeping arrangements, and put some finishing touches on the classes we had prepared for the weekend. Unfortunately, all the kids were not to have vacation until the next day, so we had to make adjustments of our lessons. The ones who were not helping with that, were busy moving around bunk beds and luggage. One or two children had already arrived, and we said hello. At the time, I wasn't sure how I felt about approaching them, and so I didn't. I waved. I thought about talking to them, but thought it better to wait until the morrow.

We were told where the bathroom was. Well, I should say that we were told where the toilets were, because there was no shower. Come to think of it, it wasn't really a toilet per se, but that's all that I will say on the matter. There was really a sense that this was more than just a trip for us. The sense of a calling greater than oneself touches the heart when we thought of why we gave up the comforts of this world for these kids. I mean, we know the grace of our Lord Jesus Christ, that, though he was rich, yet for your sakes he became poor, that [we] through His poverty might be rich (2 Corinthians 8:9). We gathered, and discussed how we were feeling about the trip so far, along with our expectations for the mission. These kids, we were told, knew about Jesus, and it was our job to teach them what He had commanded (Matthew 28:20). Those kids would start pouring in the next morning. I knew that I would be writing this, and I didn't want to leave out any details so, at night, I recorded the main things that happened during the day in case the memory of them fade over time.

THE EVENING AND THE MORNING WERE THE FIRST DAY

The following morning, we woke up early and cold. Another difference between the north and south of China, is that the central heating is only on for the Northern provinces, where it is colder. Therefore, though it wasn't as cold as it would be in Beijing, the temperature was still low enough to freeze the water caught in the outside buckets. I ended up sleeping under a blanket, comforter, sleeping bag, and my jacket was thrown over me as well, and I still woke up feeling too cold to carry on. My extremities were all numb and so was my will to move, but I was reminded of the reason we came there in the first place. After brushing our teeth and having breakfast, we went out to meet the children. To be honest, I didn't remember them by name, but by face and behaviour. It was easy to get to sit with a lot of them at once, because all humans were gathered around a fire or around embers. We were all covered in jackets as if they were t-shirts, and we sat around the fire talking. Though their language is one of the 50+ dialects spoken by the many ethnic groups in China, they are taught Mandarin in school, and I was therefore able to communicate with them. They asked me to sing for them in English, and while I was thinking of an appropriate song, one of the girls encouraged me saying that even if I sing the wrong words, they wouldn't understand, they just wanted to hear me sing. I asked what made them think that I could sing, to which they replied they just know I look like one who can…whatever that means. I sang for them, however, and they liked it, though it was the alphabet song.

From the very beginning, I was amazed at the level of happiness and contentment that was seen across the faces of these little children as they stood and sat around the fire. I couldn't help but think that we who live in the city not only have a lot to be thankful for, but a lot to think about. Though these kids here aren't necessarily poor by definition, there are certainly people in this world who live in abject poverty, and China is no exception. Sometimes, I would sit on a log and stare into the fire thinking about these children, and the other children I know. I thought about Kunal- my sponsored son in India, and wonder how he was getting along these days. I long to see him.

Every now and again, one of the adults would bring a handful of logs and placed some of them upon the fire, and then shovel some of the embers into the bowl that we sat around. On this day, while the others who came with me were busily working with the decoration of the church, I felt a little bit on the outside. Every person had something to do, and people were helping. I went inside to see what I could do to help. I was blowing up some balloons for them, when something happened. I saw a baby. All my concentration went out the window as I saw this little bundle waddling around behind the balloons which littered the church floor. I dropped what I was doing and went to her. At first, it was a little awkward for her because I was a stranger with a strange look. I was different but the same. I didn't speak like she did, but I had a familiarity about me that was expressed in how I interacted with her. It took me a while, but she finally warmed up to me, as the music in the background played. I took the opportunity and grabbed two balloons and started waving them in rhythm with the music. She did the same. This little baby could barely walk, but was dancing and twirling and waving balloons with me on the stage of the church. I dare say that she was actually leading me in the dance moves, the way she carried on. I was the one being taught by her. I was the one following the steps of this child, and reminded with every beat, that we are to become like little children (Matthew 18: 2-4). I was reminded that I am to not think of myself higher than I ought, and to bring myself down willingly in order to please God. Hours after, when I was back out by the fire, the little girl whispered into the ears of one of the children that she wanted me to go back and dance with her again. This is now four months since then that I am writing this paragraph…*what I would give for another dance*. This to me was more important than decorating the church.

When that was all done, we gathered all the children on the inside and introduced ourselves. We also had taught them from the Bible about the life of Jesus, and some of the things of Jesus they already understood. When the evening came and we gathered, there was a message from the young leader who went with us. When I was listening to him, I was relieved to hear that his words were from the Bible and not from other sources. I would be rather distraught if it were that he brought unbiblical doctrines to these kids so far away. Even with the formal sessions, it was clear that the children understood the things being taught, and were responding with eagerness.

Another thing that stood out to me while among the people was their level of hospitality shown by the locals. They served us with gladness every time we had meals. Before we got there, they went out and caught little songbirds to fry for us. One of the ladies even let me stir the meat in the 4-foot-wide frying pan. Watching them as a whole, as a community working together was something that brought home the idea of family. It gave me a taste of what the Church is supposed to be like, with everyone doing their part, and harmonising roles and responsibilities. With Jesus, you can have little, and be just as content as if you have much. I saw in their eyes, the same sparkle of joy that I see in the eyes of those who have Jesus where I am from in Beijing. The kids play the same way, the adults talk and laugh the same way, and the teens carry on in the same manner with Jesus, though in different parts of the world.

The thing which will be etched in my heart the deepest is what happens after the message. The message was delivered, and then the importance of prayer would be emphasised. After this, the teachers would be first instructed to get up and pray for the kids. This was followed by the kids being instructed to do the same for their teachers. The children would clasp on us so tightly and squeeze our hands as they prayed to Jesus for us. As we stooped to get closer to them, we could hear and understand what they were saying. We could feel the pitter-patter of their tears hitting our hands as they cried unto Jesus for us. However, as is the case for most groups of people, sometimes behaviour is infectious and learned, and I saw that one or two seemed to be crying for crying's sake, or maybe they just didn't understand what was going on. Some, on the other hand were visibly moved by their praying and prayed from a sincere heart. This obviously drove the teachers to tears too. We never would have expected this manner of response from the children. They were then asked who had unsaved relatives back in their households, the majority of them raised their hands and we prayed for them too. One by one, they said who wasn't a believer in their household. Then, the kids, little as they are, knocked upon the doors of Heaven for the salvation of their relatives. This moved my heart to witness.

After some more praying, we dismissed the children and sent them to bed. The Korean teachers and I sat in a circle and the pastor led us in a discussion about what we did, learned and liked about the day we experienced. While we sat and talked, my friend would sit next to me and translate in either Chinese or English, depending on which language was easier to use to express the particular idea at the moment. During this time, I was most surprised to learn that one of the high school kids who went with us wasn't a believer. Later, he would express that he was inspired to follow Jesus, after seeing how much love was poured onto these kids. I was very moved by what he said, and wondered secretly how many more were in similar positions. When we were finished that discussion and went to our beds, I tried to keep warm in the freezing temperatures. I had a blanket thrown over my wooden bed which I laid upon, another couple blankets on me, with my sleeping bag spread over them. My winter coat was also spread over the sleeping bag, and I even had a hair dryer blowing hot air on my feet before covering them over to keep in the hot air. It was still cold. I took my phone and made a voice recording of what transpired during my day, so I would easily forget. Though my ribcage trembled with the cold, the reason for me being there kept me from complaining (though I hence learned the Korean word for "cold"). After recording myself, I rolled over and tried to sleep.

THE EVENING AND THE MORNING WERE THE SECOND DAY

I awoke the next morning feeling cold, and the water that was on the outside had all frozen. The temperature had dropped a bit, and even the many layers of clothing we had donned weren't enough to keep out the blasting cold air that, though fairly quiet, still chilled us to the core. During the morning, the teachers and kids all danced together with music that sung about Jesus' love for children. Lessons and breakfast were had just as the previous day, and we sat again around the fire for warmth and comfort.

On this day, we took out some I-clay, enough for each child to have a kit with a huge set of I-clay, carving tools and a whole host of things (that really took me by surprise, I didn't know we had all these things). The children were tasked with creating a scene which would depict the theme for the camp "One in Christ". I was walking around and taking pictures of what was going on, and talking to the kids as they were working. The creations were spectacular as the kids formed people and trees and all sorts of scenery. Amazing, I thought. There was one kid, however, who when we looked upon her work, we noticed that she had made all her characters in the scene with sad faces. This took us aback, because from where we were standing, everybody was having so much fun with the clay that I would never have though that someone would be sad on that day. We asked her why it was that she had all sad faces on her people, and she responded by saying that the people in her scene were the kids at the camp, and they are sad because we will have to leave them soon. This is perhaps the very first time that I was so hurt by something that a child said. The reality had hit them a whole lot sooner than it had hit me that we would soon have to part ways; and little did I know how hard that reality would hit me when that time comes.

During rest time, the kids would be running in and out of the church when the teachers would be preparing for the next activities. Because we were high on the mountains, clouds would be rolling over us when we were outside. Clouds, being made of water, would make the ground soggy and muddy. This mud would then be brought into the church by the shoes of the children when they come cantering in. Before long, the church's floor would be carpeted with mud, and my heart would clench with discomfort. Coming from a church context like mine, a dirty church is an unacceptable church; and children would be heavily scolded for tainting the house of the Lord. But, as I was watching them, watching the little children run about and throw the clay at each other, I couldn't help but think to myself of what I believe Jesus' attitude to this would be. I looked back at the banner which hung from the front of the Church building, and there was a "Jesus" there playing a guitar and dancing, with children dancing around Him, playing different instruments. After looking at that picture, and seeing Jesus loving those children who were brought to Him, it could never be that He would be at all angry with the conditions of the church building. More accurately, I believe that Jesus would be more concerned about the little ones enjoying Him, than the state of a floor that could always be swept. With this in mind, I took up the broom when the kids had gone back outside, and I swept the floor with a smile. I smiled not because I was sweeping the floor (it hurt my back after a while), but because I know that these kids are in Jesus, and we will play with Him in eternity. Moreover, when it was time for them to come back inside, they muddied the floor afresh. And when they left, I swept the floor again…and so it went.

Sometime during the afternoon, it was a little warmer, and I was able to take my jacket off and leave it in the church. I went outside to bond with the children and I noticed that there was a man chopping some wood. Having never really done something like that before, I thought it a good idea to try my hand at it. The gentleman obliged and I took the axe from him. I placed a log to stand vertically like they do in the movies and swung the axe down at it. To my great surprise, two halves of the log flew in opposite directions and the axe lodged into the tree stump beneath. This was followed by the "ooohs" and "aaaahhs" from the people watching as well as the man who had lent me the axe in the first place. After I had hacked open a few more logs, the man wiped his brow and went inside. I remained outside and joyfully finished the pile of logs that was there. A few of the little boys came and tried to chop logs too. Even some of the high school guys that came with us had tried. Sometimes, they would get it done. I felt so good chopping those logs. I felt strong. There was something in me that burned with excitement at the thought of chopping these logs. I ran out of logs before I knew it, and let out a grunt of manly satisfaction. I went inside to the man, and happily reported that all the logs were finished.

Later on that day, the Koreans that were with me went and brushed their teeth and washed their hair at the standpipe close by. All of a sudden, as if with the desire for oral hygiene, a cow appeared out of nowhere, and stood by them as they brushed. He started sniffing around and examining the buckets of water that lay around. Those "city kids" who've never been that close to an animal before (except maybe on a plate) thought it quite strange, but gladly no one ran off the nearby cliff.

Memory betrays me at this point, but I'm thinking that we had the church service after this. It could have been that day, or the following day but according to the time at which the pictures were taken, I would have to say that the church service was in the afternoon of that same day with the cow incident. So, I'll talk about that now: here goes! We all went into the church building, and this time, the other villagers poured in as well. We sat among them as the church service began. For the most part, it was just like any church service I've ever been in. Luckily, they all spoke Mandarin, and this made it feel like my home church in Beijing. They sang some songs in Mandarin, and some in their dialect also. There was even one which was sung in both languages at the same time. It was wonderful.

The pastor welcomed us, and then the Korean pastor who went with us preached passionately. It was so great for me. To see these people here in the furthest parts of the country furthest from me, listening to the same Gospel that saved me, to hear the same songs which I sing in my Western church, and loving the same Jesus who I've been serving from childhood, was truly satisfying. I smiled to myself because I sat next to the same guy with the logs. I imagine that we would be in Heaven together, people of all different shapes and sizes, languages and backgrounds, all praising the same Jesus, and being loved by Him for eternity. The church there even had a CHOIR! And just like choirs where I come from, the little baby came up and stood up in front of them to help them sing. Though it wasn't the same little baby who taught me how to dance just a few days prior, I still smiled as I watched him sheepishly stand there and mumble words as if singing with the choir. After that, what took us all by surprise is that a few of the students had practised and performed a dance for us in thanks for coming to teach them.

After the church service, we mingled outside (as all Christians do after their church services). There was food, talking, laughing and having a grand time. There were other activities which we put on for the children, including a puppet show, a dance and others; all expressing the love the Jesus has for us. Before long, the children were sent home and the teachers gathered again together for another debriefing in the night time. What would usually happen is that we would sit in a circle and share our thoughts in Korean or Chinese (me), and this time I learned that yet *another* one of the students was a non-believer, and this time it was one of the high schoolers that was helping the kids the most. This came as a shock to me, but I wasn't that taken aback for some strange reason. When it was my time to share, even I was surprised with how clearly I expressed myself in Chinese for them. Again, I thank the Lord God for allowing me the talent to carry myself in the languages of others. I am grateful to Him for His gifts to me, especially in this ability. I see this as His enabling to fulfill this commission of His of "going into all the world, teaching them to observe all things whatsoever I have commanded you". While I was thinking these things, I noticed that one of the guys was in the back preparing something. He then brought forth a box with enough cups on it; and another one with pieces of bread. We were about to have communion!

After the wonderfully blissful reminder of the unity in Christ that all believers share, we went outside for some Korean BBQ. This was the fanciest BBQ I ever experienced. We were sitting outside around the fire when we heard a thud. I looked around to see a large slap of pig shoulder upon a log, and some knives were brought out to carve this meat. We scrubbed a shovel clean, and when the meat was carved, it was placed on the shovel and roasted over the fire. I had taken up one of the knives and began "professionally" carving the pork off the bone. The nearby dogs were there standing, and I would throw them some pig fat every once in a while. I thought to myself "if only my father could see me now: chopping wood, slicing meat; man, I'm sure he would be quite the proud dad." While I was yet thinking these things, I felt the knife slide across my thumb. *Gyahhhhh!* I actually didn't think much of it, until I saw the red. Even in the night, I could see that I was bleeding a lot. I moved my thumb to avoid the blood landing on the meat. Someone noticed. People were alerted. There was one girl, I'll call her "Claire" for the time being. She saw me, and was so full of care for me. She only knew that my thumb needed to be above my heart in order to slow down the bleeding that was now, looking more and more serious. She held me. She grabbed my thumb and held it up for me above my heart. She looked up at me with eyes reflecting the radiance of the moonlight above and said, "I don't know what to do. *She was so cute.* So, I will hold it until you stop bleeding." *Oh my*, I thought to myself. Though I would refrain from writing down all of what I thought in that one moment, it was very softening to have someone care for me so much. In a few minutes, some of the others whisked me off into the corridor where there was a light. They hauled out the first aid kit and proceeded to rustle about in it for some stuff to sanitise my wound. They were dabbing and wrapping and applying this ointment and that ointment. Claire stood there the whole time looking at me with the largest eyes I've seen. She didn't know what to do, and she wasn't much help, but she stood there and offered me her moral support, and that was appreciated more than the medical attention that was administered. I tried to convince her that I was okay, but Claire refused to move.

When I went back out, I was glad to see that all the pork was already sliced up before I sliced my thumb, because I was willing to finish cutting up the meat, irrespective of my cut. I walked around and talked with my friends, and stoked the fire, and did everything else that I could do that didn't require the use of my thumb. Turns out, that the others were not planning on sleeping that night, but stay up until the morn, because we had to leave early the next day to make our morning flight.

SUCH SWEET SORROW

Let us not become weary in well-doing, for in due season we shall reap if we faint not.

– Galatians 6:9

The following day was the worst of all; yet the best of all. We were leaving Kunming. I went to sleep with the forced urgency that I had to awaken early the following day. Yet, I still was completely frozen in body and mind. I was still very unwilling to move, but I think I was the last person to awaken. There was one last student who I had got rather close to, that was searching about for his shoes. I helped him look and wrote down my contact information in a book for him, in case he ever got the technology to contact me one day. It was with a heavy heart that I said goodbye to him after helping him find his shoes.

Time was getting closer to departure, and we got ready to leave. I had packed my suitcase the night before, so it was simple (not easy) to get myself ready. We left our rooms and were met with the news that the road that we took to get to the campsite was too muddy for the vans to take us to the airport. This meant that we would have to hike to the part on the mountain that was paved well enough for the vans to travel. An hour. That was how long we had to hike up this mountain with our luggage. I was not pleased at this news. I don't know what happened, but I was feeling extremely tired from the very first step up the mountain. I don't know if it was the high altitude or what, but as soon as I tried hiking, I was feeling very bad. What was encouraging was that the kids were not willing to let us walk with our own bags. They wanted to serve us by taking our bags up the hill for us. Even when we refused, they would go so far as to take them and run with them up the hill, just so they could take our bags for us. That made me smile.

When we got to the end of our trek, the vans were there waiting for us. It was then that the tears started flowing for the last time. The children teared and sniffled as they loaded our luggage onto the vans. Others posed with us as we took photos with them. With each passing minute, the bitter-sweet weight of our impending departure got heavier on my shoulders and I became very quiet. I took a few photos with some of my students, and made sure that all the luggage was loaded up. When that was done, I sat in the van and waited to move off. I was fighting my tears. They were many to come, and I forced them all back. The other teachers got into the vans as well, and the engines started. As the children closed the doors for us, they started crying and waving goodbye, and the first tear began to trickle over the brim of my reservoir. They tried to stop me, saying that they will cry if they see that I am crying. I took a deep breath and reached my hand through the window to touch their little hands one last time before the van moved off. My chest began to quake as I saw them getting smaller in the van's rear-view mirror. They were gone. I wasn't to see them again this side of Heaven. I let go. I opened my mouth and released a gut-wrenching wail loud enough to startle the others in the van with me. Hand in glove, I covered my face to mute the screams and hide the tears. My chest continued to tighten and my stomach cramped after the first fifteen minutes, which felt like the whole ride.

Soon, with each groan, the pain in my stomach got worse until I had to force myself to stop crying just to abate the pain racking my being. It didn't help, however, that when I moved my hands from my face and looked down, the red earth that clung to the children's faces was the main hue on my black gloves. My next thought was that my face was caked in dust like theirs, and that I was united with them. My wrist carried a band which had the inscription, "one with them". I could not help but weep afresh.

[As I pause to reflect on the events in those days, I rub my cross and ponder about all these things. I ponder about why I do all these things, and why I share them with other people.] Our van eventually met up with the other team, and we got out excited to see one another (well, the Koreans all were. Coleman and I just greeted and talked with our Nepali brother and sister). It was another rough and tumble ride home, but we eventually got there. Coleman and I became closer buddies since that trip, and would go on to touch many more lives in the coming months. I would always call to mind the times we had in Kunming, from morning dance routines to Bible studies. I only wish that God would have mercy on me to do more for His Glory.

HY Camp

"...and he took a child, and set him in the midst of them: and when he had taken him in His arms, He said unto them, 'Whosoever shall receive one of such children in My name, receiveth Me, and whosoever shall receive Me, receiveth not Me, but Him that sent Me."

– Mark 9:36

IT WAS THIS verse that was etched in the hearts of this team of ten who took up the call to go to the southern province of Hunan, China to the small town of Maoshi茅市. This group, though small, was made up of persons from many different races and nationalities: Terry from China, Alkesh and Miatta from the UK, Katie and Coleman from the United States, Alexis and Gaby from Malaysia and Indonesia respectively, Stefan from Barbados, Cyril from Ghana; and the superstar of the group: Charles, also from the US. They called him the superstar because he was the youngest one on the trip (15 years). One Sunday after church, the group prayed, got into a van and embarked on a journey to a place and situation to which no one except Terry and Alkesh have ever been before. Some of them had only known about the trip a few days prior, and some of them had even started their final exams for the semester, but took the time between exams to go on what would be a most wonderful expedition. All this, to show total strangers that love that Christ commanded us to share.

Along the way to the train station, the group discussed that which was preached in the sermon just a few hours earlier, and the implications that would have on a

21st century group of believers, namely loving our brother; and how that would reflect in respecting each other's cultural differences while still keeping true to the Scriptures. Regardless of the conclusion, they had all agreed that it was quite the arduous task and lifestyle to maintain, which would require much thought and consideration for others in the Faith. They disembarked and thanked the driver. Then, they checked in at the train station, where they relaxed and waited for their evening train. Coleman had shared of his trips to other camps, and he and Stefan reflected on the trips they had in common. Others didn't have such an experience, and so this would be their first time doing something like this. Miatta writes: *"I had served in Children's Ministries back in London, but I had never experienced teaching English to young adults or anyone else, before. This experience beautifully surpassed all my expectations, and all my prayer requests too. Seeing God work throughout our time there, was incredible."* Whether any of them had experience or not, this trip would prove revolutionary in their view of the world, and their Commission to go into all of it.

While on the 18-hour journey from Beijing to Hunan, some talked, some prepared, some ate and slept; while others just appreciated the soft beds on the train and the excellent service. One thing that was remarked about, regarding the duration of the trip, was that it was the perfect opportunity for the members of the group to get to know one another better, and to form a unity among them that perhaps could not have been forged in a 2-hour flight. A deeper understanding of each other would be of great benefit to the group, especially in times when things wouldn't go according to plan. As the immediate purpose of the trip was to teach English to about 80 middle school students, the group was divided into teams, each team with two teachers. The teachers were assigned to a class, and they had to prepare a lesson to teach them English in a fun and interactive way. The teams were strategically organised to have at least one English teacher (or someone with English teaching experience), or someone with a manageable level of Chinese proficiency, and seeing as there were people from different races, the group reflected that kaleidoscopic image of the Kingdom made up of people "from every race, tribe and tongue" (Revelation 7:9).

At every stop, the resident Chinese, Terry, would give a little summary to those in his earshot about that particular province or city. The train would stop for a matter of minutes only to allow passengers to disembark and others to get on. Soon, the train finally arrived at Hengyang Station. The longer they stayed in the car park, the more Stefan Lorde didn't think it coincidence that the "yang" in Hengyang meant "sunshine", because where he was, was much hotter than where they had just come from. Fortunately, the group didn't have that long to bake in the sun, because their contact, Sue met them at the gate, and provided them with transportation and breakfast.

The first pit stop en route to the camp was the home of the resident Chinese,

Terry. There, the group rested and recuperated, then decided to finish up the plans and preparations for the camp. The group got acquainted with the host family, and Coleman even caught a few fish with Terry's father, while Stefan caught a few Z's on the bed provided. The time spent there, though short, was quite filling both in spirit and stomach, and much appreciated by all in the group. Transportation soon arrived, and the group then embarked on the second and final leg on their trip to the camp.

The gates of Maoshi Middle School opened to this group of multinational English teachers literally and figuratively, as the transport drove up the ramp, onto the compound. From the cars, these excited teachers could see little heads popping out from around corners and above ledges. They were welcomed by the local English teachers who were kind enough to give away their own living quarters for them to sleep. Stefan and Coleman, unable to wait, were the first to reach out to the kids. The heads that appeared earlier further manifested themselves, and it wasn't long before little bodies were surrounding this pair. These little children gathered and crowded in on the two, reminiscent of Paul and Barnabas (Acts 14:11-13). It was remarked that this is probably what the scenes surrounding Jesus looked like, as people were pressing in to touch Him and hear Him speak. Knowing the deeper purpose of going to this camp, added to the uncanny resemblance of the scene with Coleman and Stefan to that of Jesus' experience, brought to their hearts a blessing that came from knowing the Great Commission was being realised in this little corner of the world.

After the group had all settled in and had a small tour of the school, there was dinner. The food was quite different (some may even say better) than what they were accustomed to, and they thanked the cooks daily for such lovely meals. This expression of gratitude came as a great surprise to the cooks, though it seemed like something natural for the team. The more they were surprised, the more the team sought to thank them and tell them how good the food was. All the teachers ate together, and all the students ate together. However, some of the members wanted to sit and spend time eating with the students. What was saddening to them, though, is that the children had little time to eat, before they had to rush off to evening classes. This "rushing off to class" trend was just a small bit of the hard time the students have in certain parts of China. The kids wake up at 5 am, start classes, and continue on until 10 pm. Maybe a shower, maybe some lunch, and they're off again with the studying. Gaby writes: *"I was touched by how limited they were in terms of personal care and how far off they are from the Truth; their mind-set and hard work are to go after money and acceptance…when I trace my sadness, I realise that this is God's heart [that's hurting] and that He put this in me and all the members' hearts. That's why we can love and care for them, because God wants to do something in that town, and I feel so privileged to [be a] part in His good work at Maoshi."*

Gladly, the school had taken about 70-80 kids and allowed them to be a part of our camp. Unfortunately, however, as Alkesh noted, the timing was a little inconvenient. He said that the camp schedule was running concomitantly to the school's teaching period, and so there were about 350 children who weren't going to be able to participate in the camp. Stefan also noted this, and was heartbroken whenever he would see the other children looking on through windows and around corners, unable to join the fun that these few kids were enjoying. This was especially notable during the evening activities we had, as the rest of the school had class. One could see little heads peeking from classroom windows, drawn away from the attention of their books and blackboards, to the love and fun happening on the outside courts. This broke the hearts of all the members of the team. The evening activities we had were water balloon fights, an auction, Frisbee and other sports. These were geared towards showing love to the kids, while using English at the same time for their practice. The kids really enjoyed them, and so did the teachers involved. Miatta writes: *"I particularly loved the evening game activities. I enjoyed seeing the children enjoy a time away from intensive studies, and seeing them experience playful moments together. I thought that the water balloon games were fantastic. Initially, I was worried about "getting my hair wet", but could not miss out on a chance to further connect with the Children, especially the Pink Team that I was leading. The Auction game was also a wonderful addition, and was a great way to emphasise the theme of our camp "Love never fails", and reflecting on what lasts and makes us all special."*

The auction, as Miatta rightly points out was geared with a special purpose. There were many things "for sale", which were really just things printed out on paper. The students were given print-outs of money from the Monopoly board game to use for spending. Things on sale ranged from a basketball signed by China's famous basketball player, Yao Ming, to flights to New York, perfect English, stock investment, gold watches and many more. But, the items on sale were also "love", "joy", "forgiveness" and "peace". What the students never expected was the "nuclear war" that came upon them, and wiped out all the things they worked so hard to buy and accumulate. The "soldiers" came in and snatched up everything that the students had bought, and tore them up in front of their faces. However, when they tried to tear up the "love" and the "joy" and the "peace" and the "forgiveness", they found that they cannot be destroyed. The students, through this, learned a valuable lesson. All the things which they run after can be destroyed and pass away, but only the very important things remained. They then were taught a song called "love never fails". After these evening activities, the kids would be sent off to bed, and the team stayed behind for debriefings and preparations for the following morning's classes.

The morning session was English, of course, but in a new and fun way.

The team used presentations about their countries, world landmarks, sports, and even parables to bring English to this group of children. Underlying the English lessons were the moral lessons of cultural acceptance, loving others, sharing and teamwork; and it was evident from even after the classes, how much the students learned from them. Miatta writes her experience teaching these kids for the first time, and how this was to her. *"I was supported by Charlie, in teaching lessons relating to Wimbledon, Badminton and the World Cup. The Children admired Charlie. He was full of great ideas and Chinese to keep them engaged to understand what was being taught. I was also fortunate enough to have Maoshi English Teachers Sue and Christina assist the class at times too. Their help was valuable for language and exchanging ideas. Seeing them in class also gave me an opportunity to share more and develop a deeper connection with them."*

Alexis adds: *"...through afternoon tutorial sessions by the third day (after Terry's talk on Western culture and Christianity...) my students were asking 'why do all the teachers mention Jesus? Why do they think He's important?', 'Can you tell me what Saviour means?' 'Why is Jesus called the Saviour?' [and] to call these questions mind-blowing would be an understatement. I witnessed how the Lord can bring to mind various things the students learned in different classes and help them to see the big picture: God's love never fails, He cares for them, and thinks they're special and He's important because He is the Redeemer."*

Of course, as Job would ask, shall we accept good from God and not evil also? (Job 2:10). While some of the kids from the camp were enjoying day after day of fun and English learning, others weren't so fortunate. By the second morning, the kids from Stefan and Katie's class were told that they were no longer allowed to participate in the camp, because their local teachers told them that they're not learning anything, and should therefore go back to class. Stefan was on his way to start his lesson when he heard the news. He writes: *"I was confused. I was angry. I started to hold great resentment against those teachers, and because I didn't know which teacher was responsible, I looked at all the local teachers with spite. I couldn't bring myself to look at any of them without feeling the bitter thought come over me 'I loved those kids; and you took them from me'. My precious jewels were taken, and were replaced with other kids that I wasn't prepared to love yet. However, the silver lining is that I got to spread love to more kids, and thereby leave a bigger impact in the student body for God. After a change in mind-set and a deep breath, I let the love of Jesus wash over these new kids, and the newer kids that came in the afternoon."* Those "newer" kids I refer to were another batch of students. Just when Katie and Stefan were getting used to the new kids they got in the morning, they were replaced again by lunch time, and another set were sent in, each set with a lower English proficiency than the one before. Though that was difficult to manage, the kids still had fun playing name games, and getting to practice the little English that they were taught.

During the afternoon sessions, the teachers were tasked with taking one of the students and have a one-to-one time with them to talk (in English) about what they learned about life; and see how their views on life are; and perhaps, if they ask, tell them about why we think Jesus is important. I say "if they asked" because, as Alexis put it, *"...before the camp, we as a team discussed multiple times how much of God and Jesus we should incorporate into our teaching. Coleman and I were in a team, and we decided to teach the parable of the 'Good Samaritan', hoping that the students would learn the values without the lesson being outwardly Christian."*

Even Gaby was slightly cautious. She says that she was always warned about anything resembling religious activities in China. But, she said *"I know I want to do it, and am ready to take the risk to bless these people."* Later on, when the students were sent off to their respective evening classes, the team would meet with the English teachers there to discuss their teaching methods, and see if (from a native speaker's perspective) there would be any need for improvement. Though that was the motive, the time was actually spent chatting casually, albeit awkward at first. This led to the team getting to know the teachers there a lot better, and sharing experiences with each other. Gaby continues: *"... by the time I got engaged with the people there, I started to love them and it hurt my heart greatly that there is no one there who knows the liberating Truth that would light up their darkness."* The bonds that were made during those sessions were as such to encourage the team to come back the following year, and to keep in contact during the year. This time was beneficial for the local teachers there as well.

However, when the students outside playing got too rowdy, trying to peek through the glass above the office door, one of the team members went outside with an idea. His idea seemed to work, because as soon as he emerged from the office, the kids moved along with him to see what he would say/do next. He went into their classroom and began looking at their English books, and would even help them write the correct answer down. Then, one student came with their book and asked him to sign it…about an hour later, this tired teacher was signing away on books that the students brought to him. *"Again, I felt like Jesus,"* he said. *"I felt tired from being in that hot room with all those students crowding around me like a great multitude. My hand was tired, but I didn't want any one of those students going to bed that night without having their book signed, because I read that when Jesus was tired, He still ministered to people. The next day, the idea spread around the whole school, and students from all classes came to all of us to get us to sign their books for them."*

The team was also privileged to go on a tour of the village. Seeing this strange group of people walking through the town sparked great interest in the eyes of the villagers. Some ran, some came up to the team for pictures; and some just sat there and stared. The news of the team spread all through the social media of the town, and before long, everyone in the town knew that they were there. Even the teacher that was giving us the tour got the news. The team, as they walked and talked couldn't help but notice that there were idols and images of worship in almost every house. Incense was lit and blood was spilled all over the place as the idolatry of the town became more and more evident.

After the tour, the team visited the home of one of the local teachers. There, they sat and ate fruits and talked. One of the team members was praised for his knowledge of Chinese characters, and was even (as he would say) coerced into giving a small presentation on how some of the Chinese characters carry Bible stories inside them. As a few of them were traditional characters, some of the Chinese who were there did not even know about them. This was followed by a Chinese song, and some more discussion. After leaving, the team purchased some notebooks to give to the students for completing the camp. Inside every notebook, they would write a special note for every individual student they taught.

The worst part of the camp—the last day. Kids were bringing their books and getting the team to sign them. The team got some gifts for the students, and even for the teachers. Some of the students made some cards and letters by hand especially for the team, and they were all very touched. Many tears were shed as the teachers and students parted ways. The team encouraged their students to write letters of appreciation, and give them to their own family members or local teacher. Though this instruction was very clear, some students still gave the team letters of love and thanks. They were received with thanks, and then the instruction was given again until every student had at least one letter to give away. Many photos were also taken. There was a closing ceremony, and the pictures and videos were shown. This was also an opportunity to share about the crazy love that we have been shown. Teddy joined the whole team to perform a story about a man whose wayward son kills someone and, as judge, must make a terrible choice. Justice requires that he sentence his own son to death. Yet mercy drives him to trade places with the boy just before the execution. He died, so his son may go free – just like Jesus gave us his own life for us.

The team went to the front and gave their final remarks to the students about the camp and their experience. The students were already crying, and the speeches of love by the teachers had the tears rolling all the more. More pictures were taken, and more tears were shed after the closing ceremony. All the preparation and meetings could not prepare them for that- the hardest part of the camp. The bonds formed over those four days proved to etch deep into the being of every member of the team, and every student taught, and no one was willing to leave camp.

That wasn't the end of their time there, however. Though the camp had finished, they still got to spend time with a number of teachers that lived in Hengyang city – including Sue, Teddy, and Terry's former English teacher – Mr Xie. They even graciously drove them down to the city in their own cars. On the way, they gave us a supply of *Maoshi Bing* – the local speciality of roasted pastry with a sweet filling. The team thought they were receiving 50 of them, which seemed like a wonderful gift – as each of us would get 5. Only after Alkesh asked to buy more to give away in Beijing, did Terry clarified the gift was 50 each. When the team said this was excessive, Terry responded that he'd already haggled them down from receiving 100 per person! This is Chinese hospitality in action. Luckily, they didn't easily spoil, so I did not need to keep them in the fridge.

Our hotel in Hengyang gave us the creature comforts that we could easily do without, but had nonetheless missed over the past few days. A mosquito-free, air-conditioned room with soft beds and consistent Wi-Fi. Charlie and I missed no opportunity to re-connect with the students from the Middle School. One girl felt worthless after telling her parents she had performed badly on a test. This was an opportunity for me to remind her that she was special – as someone God had fearfully and wonderfully made.

The team was then invited for a yet another meal of delicious Hunan cuisine with local believers, followed by visiting a local fellowship. It was exciting to see that God 'still had people in this city', however full of idol worship it was. We couldn't stay out too long, however, since Alexis and Gaby had to leave the next morning. Over breakfast we considered our next steps – how we would share God's love not only on this one trip, but in our day-to-day lives in Beijing. Once we bade our farewells and took the morning to rest, we went to lunch with a number of teachers that came on the camp.

The meal was a great time to share with the teachers about our faith. The vice principal explicitly said that we not only "taught the students how to love", but "the love that comes from God." Terry was greatly surprised that this would come out of the lips of a Communist Party member, especially when he even made a toast 'to God'. This made it easy to open up the Bible and spend some time explaining to Teddy, Sue, and a few other interested teachers what it says. Sadly, the conversations couldn't last forever, and we eventually went to the train station. Teddy and Sue thoughtfully (and tearfully) were able to come to the platform itself with us (since everyone knows everyone in China. Teddy and Sue were not riding on the train and they wouldn't normally be allowed to accompany passengers all the way to the platform. But because of a pulled string or two, they were able to.

On the train ride back home we had an opportunity to pray for each other's futures, learning the sudden news that Charlie will probably be leaving Beijing this summer (as are Cyril and Alexis, with Miatta and Gaby uncertain). Terry planned a car to pick us up in advance to take us straight from the train station to BICF. Just as we left directly from worshipping together one Sunday, we came back to worship together the next Sunday. Yet ours had been a whole week of worship to God – giving thanks for what he had done in their lives and ours.

Knowing that we had just four days to interact with the students and local teachers, our pre-trip expectations were mostly just to lay groundwork for future teams. We'd hoped that we might strengthen connections with the school and sow a few seeds. At the end of our trip, it seemed as though we'd met those expectations. But God had also accomplished far more than those relatively low expectations. In just four days, we'd seen students and teachers embrace the idea that they could be loved unconditionally and an eagerness to learn more. We were even able to open the Word with some of the teachers, and they were visibly hungry to understand it more. As a team, our own hearts were grown in learning to love others and the desire to make Christ's love known. We hope and pray that we will be able to return to this school and continue the work begun. But if we never return again, we give thanks for the seeds sown, the hearts softened, and the continued work of the Spirit there.

– Katie

I was really grateful for the opportunity to serve. I learned so much from the Children and the team. I especially loved the leadership of Alkesh and Terry. I appreciated the fact that all plans were linked to glorifying God, Godly wisdom and Scripture. I really enjoyed the West and East lecture created by Terry, despite not understanding the Chinese content. The questions raised on the back of that were great and has led to an opportunity to share more life with school. Overall, despite not being proficient in Mandarin, and speaking too quickly in my British accent, I was still able to share my joy for being there and share enthusiastic encouragement as we learned together. This is definitely the best experience I have had while living in China for almost two years.

– Miatta

The whole camp turned out awesome! I enjoyed my time and experience with all the school members there and Praise the Lord it went smoothly and safely…I can't wait to see what God has in hand for Maoshi, and I hope I can be a part of it.

– Gaby

This camp has opened my eyes to see that when the Lord moves, nothing can stop Him.

– Alexis

What inspired me most was how radically counter-cultural living for Jesus is. Terry left Maoshi for the 'big city' and 'made it'. Yet instead of being the 'big shot' everyone expected, he has chosen to serve God's people. What's more, he has now chosen to go back with his friends to love a town that the world largely doesn't care about. For those of us who have impressive degrees, this is a real challenge to live very differently to social expectations – but to give up our lives for the sake of the Gospel instead.

- Alkesh

Don't cry because it's over; smile because it happened.

- Stefan

Crossing the Bridge of Hope

THOUSAND-WORD INTRODUCTION

WHEN I FIND MYSELF at that 'writer's block' stage in my writing, I sometimes just up and start writing. Sometimes, I find it difficult to find the first few words to begin with; and other times, I can just roll and roll with endless streams of acatalectic verbiage. Today seems like one of those times of fluidity. I guess it's because of the content of this particular chapter. It is likely that the title alone would not give the reader a clear picture of what I'm writing about this time, but I assure you that more and more clues will be provided as the paragraphs roll on.

In 2015, I heard about an organisation called **Gospel for Asia** that evangelises to remote villages in India and Nepal. When people are saved, they get trained as national missionaries, and then tasked immediately with spreading the Gospel to the others in their village, and beyond. People are saved by the Lord, and a congregation grows. This process is then repeated, and the impact is significant. A sub-branch of Gospel for Asia is their Bridge of Hope program. It is so named because of a dream that the owner had. K.P. Yohannan writes that he was standing in front of a huge field looking over a vast multitude of people. He, though he was excited to tell them the good news of Jesus and His salvation, soon realised that there was no way over the raging river that stood between him and the people in need. When he was about to give up hope, there appeared before him a broad bridge over which people could cross from where they were in darkness, into God's marvellous light. Unfortunately, I don't have permission to freely quote his book, so no references will be made here. What I will mention, however, is that the Bridge of Hope program mentioned earlier (or should I say *the aforementioned Bridge of Hope program*) here and after known as BOH, is an expansion of the Gospel for Asia organisation but is more focussed on the children in need, than other aspects of evangelism.

As you can imagine, the situation in India is as such that there are some parts where people do not even dare to touch certain other people, because of the fear of contracting their curse of being poor. The poverty level is so high that 276 million people live on less than US$1.25 per day. That's about 22% of the total population. Food is scarce, water is ridden with unclean bacteria, and clothing, medicines and education are bordering on extinction. What the BOH program seeks to do, is to spread the Gospel to those areas, and then tangibly help them by digging wells, building schools and making clothes for the children to wear. Education wise, the BOH program takes kids off the street and provides them with that very precious gift. Left alone, these kids could suffer attacks from all sorts of criminals that would use them as beggars to gain money for them, often blinding or dismembering the children to make them look more pitiful for potential givers. Some are even set ablaze if they do not match their quota. Health wise, some are so deprived of the bare necessities, that they develop ailments which would be treatable with just a glass of clean water a day. However, safe within the BOH Centre, these children are treated for their medical ailments, given daily meals and educated in love.

Unfortunately, however, as funds are not at all enough for the 14 million or so children who live on the streets of India, their ability to meet the need is vastly outweighed by the need itself, and they require the help of willing and loving people who would spare a little each month to sponsor a child. This is where I come in.

Take your mind back to the latter months of 2015. What were you doing then? Maybe you were pursuing a degree? A job? A relationship? For me, at the time, I only had two out those three things, so I guess I wasn't that bad off. I was a 23-year-old university graduate, and the first Barbadian to work at the Chinese Embassy in Barbados. I was told of an opportunity to go to a student Missions Conference called Urbana. The details of that experience, I have also written down, but I will not be including it here, as it is twenty-five pages long in itself, and this is only page two. In the time you would finish reading about Urbana, you would lose all interest in BOH. Still, I got introduced to BOH through Urbana *seemingly* by chance. They sent me emails updating me on information on the upcoming conference, and every so often, they would send one regarding some missionary organisation or another. Gospel for Asia, here and after known as GFA was the only one they sent that offered me free books. As 2015 was during a time when I had rekindled my love for reading, I desired to get my hands on those free books without delay, so I ordered them. I'll be honest and say that I also used the books as a sort of test, to gauge their legitimacy.

As I sat there in my office looking at the computer, I saw that they had a site, and there were missionaries who needed sponsoring, female missionaries, which was a separate ministry altogether; and the BOH program which needed sponsors for their children. Of course, I was drawn to the section about the children. As suspicious as I was, as I had ordered the books, I took the time to read all the free information that GFA provided about itself and about the ministries in which they serve. My plan was to go to the Missions conference and check out GFA, and then come back to Barbados and sponsor a child, if it is that they were indeed genuine. Due to circumstances beyond my control, however (all of which are described in detail in another document) I decided to remember my trust is in God, and sponsor a child, Kunal Hembrom before even getting to the conference.

Now, the year is 2018. Three years since I have been sponsoring Kunal, writing and receiving letters from him. We have had a long running relationship going, and I thought it was best that I go see him. And so, I did.

VERY INTENSE, STRESSFUL APPLICATION - VISA

As the first letter of the above words would suggest, persons in possession of a certain passports had to apply for an e-visa in order to enter India, and holders of certain other passports weren't allowed in at all. Application and payment were not guarantees of entry into the country, and the flight ticket in and out of the country needed to be bought and produced in order to pass the process. The application form was very long, and asked for a lot of information to be provided. Sometimes, I even had to put the application on hold, so I could ascertain said information, and then continue with the filling out of the form. (Funny enough, we fill out a form by filling it in) Sometimes, I had to send emails back and forth, and wait for replies and such before I could complete this long and tedious form. Then came the payment.

Since the beginning of the year, my CIBC visa debit card had expired, and funds from my account stopped going to Kunal. This both saddened and scared me, as I imagined the worst happening to him, especially since I only found out about the cessation of funds several months after. Luckily, though he was still able to receive education for the time being, but I wanted to get that sorted out as quickly as possible, and even more urgently now that I was going to go look into his face. Plus, I wasn't able to pay for the visa with the Chinese bank card, so using the Barbados debit was my only option. This led to another hectic back-and-forth with the bank in Barbados, and the 12-hour time difference did not make it any better at all. I requested a call back, and had to jump out of bed in the wee hours of the morning to answer the call, and then have them call the particular branch responsible, and have them call me as well, a few days after. During that time, of course, the date for the flight was coming up, and I did not know how long it would take for the application to be processed, and for word to get back to me, so I was feeling a little urgent. I noticed that PayPal was also an option, and so I called around to find someone who had an account with them to see if they could help me.

I found a friend who was more than willing to help me with my plight. I gave him the application numbers for the application website, and he tried for me. I started to relax for a day or two, until he called me back and said he couldn't get through. Furthermore, the website informed him that because he tried so many times, that the entire application form has to be done over and the process must start from the beginning. When he told me that, I could not really put into words what I felt.

So, here I was without an Indian visa, a booked flight already (visa requirement), an expired visa debit card, and a tight schedule. The clock was ticking, and I didn't know what to do. I remember the day well. It was the 19th of September. A Wednesday. I was completely out of ideas. By then, the bank had called, and after about 45 minutes of trying, they said they'd try their best to help me out. I felt like I was backed into a corner. I prayed to God:

"Father, I know You. I do not believe that You would work such a miracle in having me meet Kunal, get me to China- a country so close to his that I could throw a stone from this country to his, and then I miss the chance to see him by this much. I pray that You work this out for me..."

Sure enough, I went to a bible study that night and we looked at the first chapter in Paul's letter to the Romans. After the study, they asked if there were any prayer requests. I, of course, brought up the whole situation about the card and the visa, and they were sure to pray with me about it. When I woke the next morning, I turned on my computer and refreshed all my internet pages. As Providence would have it, the application form for the Indian visa was filled, and didn't have to be refilled, as previously stated. I checked my email, and saw that they had completed my account and I was able to use my card, without having to risk it being shipped to China. I was able to pay for the visa, complete the form, and resume Kunal's sponsorship. I thank and bless the name of God for His goodness that I would get through the day after I prayed.

THE FLIGHT

When it was coming time to go, I got on the plane and left Beijing. The worst thing about the flight was the flight itself, believe it or not. I was to fly from Beijing to Guangzhou, from Guangzhou to New Delhi; and from New Delhi to Ranchi. I was to then take a train from the airport in Ranchi 8 hours to the Deoghar Railway Station, and then get a taxi from there to the Sujani BOH centre where Kunal lives. I only had a maximum of 3 hours to spend with him, and then make that whole trip in reverse, back to Beijing. I sat in the airplane, looking out the window and thinking to myself that this was going to be a very long and tough journey for me. I was glad that I had only packed my backpack, because I know that lugging around with suitcases filled with things will only prove to be a hindrance for me as I journey along.

I looked out the window of the plane. I sighed to myself, and pulled out my notebook to jot down points for this, as I know that I would be writing about it, and it would be a great an exciting part of my story. When holidays come up like this one (Chinese National holiday 国庆节) people always ask each other how they plan on spending the holiday. One person in particular asked me what I had planned on doing. Mr Liu (from GETTING IN THE SWING OF THINGS) asked me if I planned to travel or stay in Beijing. When I told him I was going to India, he of course asked questions, as India is not a place that people usually flock to [Chinese people anyway]. I took the time to answer all his questions, and of course tell him about Kunal and GFA. He called me great. I said that I was just following Christ's example. He then told me "那你跟耶稣一样，太伟大了！" (Then, you're great- just like Jesus is great!) I praise the God of Heaven that an atheist Chinese would be so impressed with the work of Christ. This and many other comments of encouragement seemed to lift my spirits as the wind carried the plane across the skies.

I look through the window to my right, and I see a field divided into quarters. I think immediately of the Chinese word for "field" 田 tián. My brain just flicks the "auto-pilot" on my train of thought, and it ran all through the pictographic characters that look like what they mean. For example, 口 means mouth, looks like an opened mouth; 山 means mountain, which sorta-kinda looks like a mountain. To be honest, as they've gone through so much change in appearance over the last couple centuries, you'd have to be taught what they're supposed to look like before you start seeing the resemblance for yourself.

IDOLATRY ASIDE

I looked to my left and I couldn't help but notice the man sitting next to me. The seat between us was empty, and I believe that he and I were both glad for the extra space. What piqued my interest was that he would grab at his phone within 30 seconds of putting it down. I didn't have to count the seconds, but I know that it was not long after he put down his phone, that it would light up and grab his attention again. The announcement came on for the cellular phones to be switched off or put on airplane mode. It took him a while, but he finally put it on airplane mode when the wheels got up in the air or thereabout. I thought to myself that he was done fiddling with his phone, and I continued writing.

As if he forgot something, the guy reached over and grabbed his phone again and started tapping away. He wasn't playing a game, he wasn't calling or messaging anyone (I love how the word "message" has become a verb now), he was just taking it up and looking through it and putting it down. He would then pick it up again and repeat the process. I thought to myself that he was clearly not the master of his phone. Later on in the flight, he seemed to nod off in sleep, or did he- I can't remember. The phone was in the seat between us, and I was just thinking to myself that he had finally let the phone go, when he seemed to jump out of a daze as if a pin had stuck him in the rear. He reached and grabbed for his phone. Once his hand felt the seat and felt that it was there, he then quieted down.

I examined myself and asked myself if I go for my phone like that. Sure, I'm casting a judging eye on this man, and seeing immediately that his idol is his phone. I can see that he can't put it down. I can see that he is panicking when he can't feel it on him for more than 30 seconds, but the more important question is "am I like that?" "Is this just a reflection of me and my idols?"; "what idols do I have in my life that are keeping me clutched in their grasp?" I started to ask myself a lot of questions. I then thought back to the last time that I used my phone to see if I could outlast my fellow idolater in the seat next to me. I think of how we think ourselves in control, yet are ourselves controlled by the things we have created; and serve them.

FIRST LEG

Within a few hours, the plane had successfully landed in Guangzhou, and I had to wait for about 8 hours in the airport until my next flight to New Delhi. I took the time to talk to my dad on the phone and try my best to pass the time somehow. I had just finished a book that I had bought in Indonesia on my last vacation, and I didn't want to start the other one too soon, as I had only brought two in my backpack. I was feeling calm and relaxed. I was also, however, a little concerned about the island of Barbados, as they had recently been affected by a tropical storm, and many a house was damaged by the heavy rains and flooding. Father and I talked at length, and when he had to go, I tried to sleep. Unfortunately, the seats in the airport are as such that there is no way for anyone to get comfortable enough to do anything, much less sleep. I spent the night writhing and wriggling in the seats provided, until I couldn't take it anymore. When 6 o'clock arrived the following morning, I made my way to try to check in and get on the second leg of the flight. It was a difficult walk, seeing as blood had to start circulating again through my body, and there were parts of me like my neck that felt completely out of whack. While waiting the long hours for the flight to arrive, I was able to get into contact with another friend of mine, and we talked for a while, until the plane arrived. While I was there, I noticed that a lot of Indians were there in the airport with me, and I presumed they were going home after some time spent in China for work or pleasure. When they were checking the boarding passes and passports, it was the first time that I had heard English being spoken for this journey. Here in this line, the Chinese were outnumbered. Well, no. they weren't exactly outnumbered, but there were a relatively large number of Indian people and other internationals. From there, I said goodbye to my friend on the phone, and boarded the plane.

SECOND LEG

When I got into New Delhi the following day, I burst forth from the plane with enthusiasm, and headed to the immigration and security area. I smiled when I looked up and saw the sign that said "Welcome to India". This, however was the part where the difficulties start. As anyone who has been travelling in the past half-decade or so, would have a smartphone with which one would attempt to connect to wireless internet as soon as one lands in the airport. That being said, it was with great alarm and disappointment that I arrived in the airport in Delhi, to find that there wasn't a free Wi-Fi network in sight. Worse, when I tried to get on to the only service offered, they were saying to put in my telephone number and a code would be sent to my phone which I would use to enter the network. However, what had me even more hysterical was that I was getting no signal at all in the airport. It turns out that my Chinese sim card doesn't work over there, even though it works in other bordering countries. Therefore, there was no way to get onto the internet.

I got to the immigration section, and tried to fill out the form. When I got to the "address" part of the form, I racked my brain to remember what the name of the hotel was that I was told to write for the address/contact in India. I tried to explain this to the officer, but before I could say anything I was practically shoved aside, and was not allowed to enter the country. Time after time, I tried to ask for help, but no one would help me. I tried to explain to someone there that because my sim card isn't working in India, I cannot get the code for the Wi-Fi. I was never cut off so fast. A man who kept cutting me off was assuring me that all I needed to do was to get the text message with the code sent to me, and I would be able to log into the internet. I am trying to tell him that I cannot, because I cannot receive any text messages at all, and he continued to assure me. Even when I tried it before his eyes to show him that it wouldn't work, he insisted that I try again. I don't know what to call this situation. Is it service? Is it rude? At that moment, I was standing in the middle of the department idly, just waiting for some miracle to happen.

As if he got tired of seeing me there, the 4th person that I asked came back up to me and asked me what the problem was. Trying to be calm, I spoke slowly and clearly. He understood, and told me that he would help me. He then took me aside and took out his phone. Using small talk to get me to calm down, he then put his number into the site on my phone, and get the code on his. He then told me the number, and I put it in, and got connected. However, though I managed to find the email with the address and finish the form, though I felt that happy sensation of the vibrations on my phone telling me of incoming messages, the joy was short lived.

I had noticed on the site to pop up, and it was also reinforced by the man who had helped me, that the Wi-Fi only works for 45 minutes. That means that I would have only enough time to get on to the internet, get the email with the address in it for the filling out of the form for immigration, and send a short message to Brother Jacobs[26] before the internet cut out on me. I quickly found a seat and sent some voice messages, just in case I don't see anyone when I disembark from the plane and don't know where to go.

Following that, knowing that I am in a strange country, I thought it best to ask the information desk where I had to go next. I told them that I was going to Ranchi in the afternoon, and I wanted to know where to go. Hoping that the information desk lived up to its namesake, I followed their instructions, which were to go outside the airport itself and head to the bus stand #10 and take the shuttle bus to Terminal #1. *Simple; easy to remember.* I went outside to see that there was a sign in front of the shuttle bus stand saying that there are certain requirements needed to ride on the shuttlebus, one of which was my boarding pass. Unfortunately, I couldn't have got the boarding pass printed in China, because I had switched airlines, and would have to get it printed from the new airline, Indigo airlines. Seeing the requirements, I then turned back to get into the airport, and was immediately stopped by security. The guards, though I was only going "right there", instructed me to go upstairs around the back of the airport to get back in. I then took the escalators up to the back part of the airport to get back in, but lo and behold, I was not allowed in without my boarding pass. *Welcome to India.*

I asked what to do, and the guard there told me to go to the entry gate #3 and they will let me in. When I got there, they at #3 told me that the people at entry gate #1 would let me in. When I got there, they told me that the wheelchair access point would let me in. *They can't send me any further left, because there're*

---

26 Brother from GFA. Name changed for privacy and security.

no more entrances. When I got into the wheelchair access point, I looked for the window that corresponded with the airline I was to take. When I started to explain my plight to the guy in the window, he couldn't help me either. He then told me that I had to go…you've guessed it- to shuttlebus stand #10 and take a shuttle bus to Terminal #1. If you find yourself looking up on the page to see if this is the exact instruction I was given earlier, no need. It was! I ran out of the wheelchair access point, and headed downstairs just in time to squeeze myself onto the shuttlebus.

I find myself seated on one of the few remaining seats on this bus. I looked through the window as the bus moved off. In Barbados, this vehicle would be described as a "jigga-jigga pak-pak" because it would be noises that would be heard as the bus went along swiftly along the roads of India. India is a place, that I didn't see much of between Terminal 3 and 1. I guessed I would see more as I landed in Ranchi later that afternoon. The bus continued to drive along, and I couldn't help but notice that we passed a sign saying "Terminal 2", and I tried not to panic that we were going the wrong way. Then something else happened to take my mind off that.

There was a conductor on board. He was coming down the aisle and he seemed to be collecting something from people. It seemed to be a slip of some kind that he was collecting. *What is that? What are they giving him? I don't have one. What if it's a payment slip to ride the bus? They'll put me out here in the middle of the highway and I'll have to walk to Terminal 1 and miss my flight!* Fortunately, that wasn't my lot. I still was concerned, however, that this man was coming down collecting payment slips and I am still without. I thought to myself "maybe he's just collecting from the locals on the bus" but then he tapped the shoulder of the white man with a UK passport and collected a slip from him too. *Oh dear.* I sat there still as a stone. I was almost holding my breath as he collected from the people in front, behind and next to me. I was thinking that I don't know this language. I can't assume that he speaks English, and most importantly, I don't have a slip. What will I do when he taps me on *my* shoulder?

He comes over to my seat, leans himself on the seat on the other side of the bus from mine, and pulls out the money from his little pouch to start counting it. Satisfied that he had counted correctly, he then walks past me again and weaves his way through the crowded bus to get back to his original position. Like clockwork, the bus arrived at the terminal, but it was Terminal 2. Panic seemed to be knocking at my heart as I looked around the bus for changes in face expressions from anyone one the bus. Seeing as no one looked worried, I then thought that the bus would most likely turn around and go to Terminal 1 after some people got off here. I was right, and the bus moved off after a minute or two.

When we finally got to Terminal 1, I hoped against all hope that there would be Wi-Fi here at this terminal. Of course, there wasn't and I just walked around aimlessly, until I found something that caught my eye. The bathroom first (because I had to go) and then a Starbucks. Seeing as I had to wait another few hours before my flight to Ranchi, I decided to have a seat there and perhaps take some notes and read my book. There wasn't any Wi-Fi, so it was the next best thing to do. I guess that's what we humans did before there was wireless internet. There was something troubling me when I was going to the Starbucks, whether my card would work there or not. I mean, the sim card doesn't work, who's to say that the debit card would prove any different? I went to the counter and the young lady flashed me the most welcoming smile. I asked her if I could try my debit card there. I had to order some food first in order to try the card. I ordered some corn and spinach toast bread thingy with a coffee of some sort with it. Even though the price came up to a manageable amount, when the lady swiped the card, it was rejected time and again. She then took the food and smiled ever so brightly, "take it now, and whenever you visit India again, you can pay back." *What an angel!*

I was thrown completely off my rocker. Sure, I appreciate the kindness of this stranger, but I remember to "owe no one anything but love" (Romans 13:8), so I took and ate the food, and got up to look for a money exchange. Of course, I couldn't use the card, and I had no choice but to use the remaining cash in my wallet to exchange to Rupees and run back to Starbucks. After paying them, I went back and sat by the gate to wait for the next flight.

I finally got some sleep on the plane to Ranchi.

HOME ON THE RANCHI

Two hours later, I landed in Ranchi. Somehow the sleep that I had on the plane left me feeling rather revived and rested. Seeing as there was a million percent chance that there wouldn't be any Wi-Fi here either, I didn't even bother to take my phone out of my pocket. I did glance at Brother Jacobs' picture one last time, in case I saw him outside. When I had cleared all the checkpoints, I had just managed to dodge someone who was trying to get me to exchange money with her, and I stepped outside. I was more than convinced that she was too enthusiastic to exchange money with me, and a little too urgent to have me exchange money at her kiosk alone, and no other. I may be foolish at times, but that was not one of those times. It was while I was politely declining her proposal that I noticed there was someone on the outside with a paper held up. "Stephen Lorde" it read, and I told her that my ride was out there waiting on me. Walking and saying goodbye at the same time, I exited the airport. I approached the guy holding the sign, and pointed at it with a smile. Thoughts began to stir as he looked up and saw me. He then roused up two other men around him, and they turned around and smiled at me with a welcoming excitement.

I was escorted to a vehicle, my bag was taken from my hand, and a bouquet of flowers replaced it, along with a handshake. *Welcome to India! I then entered the vehicle as the door was opened for me. If there was a time where I was thinking that my kidneys would be stolen and sold on the Black Market, it would have been now.* I tried to push aside any thoughts of the sort and concentrate on the task at hand, which at this time was trying to take in as much of India as I can, especially now that my level of comfort had risen a bit. I was now in a position where I could take a breath and finally relax. The car took me to a hotel less than 20 minutes away from the airport.

Inside this hotel, they checked me in and gave the key for a room on the 2nd floor. During this time also we took some pictures and talked some more. I was trusting them more and more as we continued to talk about the Lord, about Chinese culture and about myself. There were Brother Lucas and Bro. Buckman[27]. When one of them looked down at their watch, I knew that a very important time was coming…dinner.

We got into the car from the hotel and started to drive towards a mall that had Indian BBQ. On the way, Lucas was in the backseat of the car with me, and he told me that he was very encouraged to see me. When I told him that seeing the things I've only been imagining since learning about Gospel for Asia was quite the experience, he admitted that he felt revived. He's only ever heard of sponsors, and had never seen one before. Yes. I was the first sponsor he had ever seen. I was indeed the first sponsor to have ever visited the centres in that part of India. In expressing himself, he grabbed his chest and said that there was an inexplicable feeling in him that compels him to carry on. I was encouraged. As we were speaking, we arrived at the place where we were to eat.

I was treated like a Prince as they ordered more and more food to add to my plate. I was beginning to feel full when they said "okay, now for the main course". *You've got to be kidding me.* I am on the brink of bursting, and they intend to pack on more food? What I didn't know was that main course was really small, and so the culture is to pack on the starters. While at the table, I learned that only Bro. Buckman would be accompanying me to go see Kunal, as we spoke about the great need that the children have for sponsorship. Though money has its place, the sponsor's letters serve as a great encouragement to them, that they are loved greatly.

Let me express my thanks to God for how I was picked up. Why I would particularly take a paragraph is because when I asked Gospel for Asia about the way in which I would go about visiting my sponsored child, they had given me a detailed travel plan which involved taking a train for 8 hours, taxi rides and all; and I was to leave immediately. However, when I got there, I was picked up with

---

27 Names changed for their safety

escort, taken to lunch, and given a bed. From what was described in the email that I was sent (which was possibly just a general travel plan) compared to the actual situation was certainly a miraculous difference, and I only remembered that email long after.

THE ROAD TO SUJANI

The following morning, I got up and had breakfast. I was anxious to get on the road and go see my boy. However, I woke to the news that all the gas stations in the city had gone on strike. I'll admit that there was a tinge of suspicion in my heart, but as we travelled to the Head Quarters for the organisation in that city, I noticed that the gas stations on the way were all barred off. Traffic in India is crazy. One of their own described the people as uncivilised. The drivers, from my own observation, seem to press their horns more than their brakes. *Imagine that.* It seems to be the case to me that the cars overtake those which are smaller than they. The small vans are overtaken by the larger vehicles, as the horn is blown. It was only when I saw written "use horn please" at the back of the many dozens of trucks that were hauling rubble to and fro, that I realised that it was not as crazy as I had previously thought. Through many road bumps, holes and curbs we finally arrived at the HQ. It was a church.

Inside the church, I was given a tour of the compound. The others were trying to find a way for us to get fuel for our journey. While in the chapel, I was invited to sign the visitors' log, where I wrote my name and 我爱耶稣 (I love Jesus) in the comments section. At the front of the church was a set of bongo-like drums and a tambourine. They asked me if said instruments existed in my country. I pointed at the tambourine, and they invited me to play a rhythm for them. It was of course quite different from what they were accustomed. *Oh, how I miss playing the tambourine. I can almost hear the congregation singing "Deeper, Deeper in the love of Jesus".*

Back in the church office, I got the news that we had acquired fuel, and we should be on our way in a few minutes. I caught a glimpse of a book, "ST. THOMAS AND THE SYRIAN CHURCHES OF INDIA"- K.V. Koshy. This book outlines and discusses the legends of St. Thomas the Apostle, and how his ministry in India continues to this day. I was about to put it back into the shelf when I was told that I can take it along for the ride. I tucked it into my bag, which I didn't have to hold for the entire trip. They put the bag into the vehicle, opened the door for me, and we got in. After saying goodbye to Brother Lucas, we drove off and headed along the 'under construction' highway. The journey was to be 6-8 hours long, and I was wondering if we would make it in time to see anything before it got too dark.

The hours rolled slowly along as we got closer to Deoghar. The further we went away from the city, and the more we digressed from the main roads, the poorer it seemed to get. I thank God that I did not have to take that train that the email said I would have to take, as I felt a lot safer in this van with them, than I would in a crowded train with all my stuff.

MY THOUGHTS AT THIS POINT

I was thinking about Kunal. I was thinking about him, and trying to picture in my mind what it would be like to see him finally. *What would he look like? Would he look the same as he does in the photo? It was taken quite a while ago. What will I say when I see him? I have absolutely no idea what I'm going to do with him for a whole three hours!* I compared the meeting with me and Kunal with the meeting with how I think the Apostle Paul felt, when he wrote in his letters "how I long to see you..." (Romans 1:11-12) how the letters I've written to Kunal were reminiscent of the letters Paul had written to the churches in Asia When we got to a toll station, there was a little boy there, and he seemed to be selling snacks of some kind. Thing is, the two snacks he had in his hand seemed to be the only snacks that he had to sell.

We ended up at another hotel in Deoghar, and met Brother Pilgrim. From there we were to have a bit of a rest (I really wasn't in for all the "resting". *Take me to see my son!*); some dinner, and then we set out to find my boy. It took us like fifteen minutes to get there, but it was still a good way out from the main road, and as it was getting dark so fast, I am glad that it wasn't that long a drive.

THERE HE WAS

The sun finally set as the car approached the Sujani Centre. There was a large crowd gathered outside the vehicle as it pulled up. *What's going on?* I was looking through the window as the car was stopping, and the car door opened for me. There seemed to be a special carpet rolled out just where the car had stopped, and when I stepped out, all the people around me started singing and dancing. There seemed to be two lines of girls performing a traditional cultural dance that was accompanied by the clapping of the villagers that encompassed the vehicle. *This cannot be for me.*

Just when I was thinking that there must have been some mistake, up comes these three older ladies. They bent over before me and began to prepare a bowl and water. I was instructed to remove my shoes, and they proceeded to wash my feet! My heart was racing as I felt their hands on my feet. This was probably not even close to the feeling that Simon Peter felt as Jesus did the same to him two thousand years ago. He said to Jesus that he should not have his feet washed by Him, but that he should wash the feet of Jesus instead. He felt unworthy to be served in this way, and so did I. From where I was standing, I just came here to see my child. I was not expecting this whole fanfare, far less for me to be served. My heart raced some more. As my head bowed watching the women, the girls on the side-lines came up one by one and put reefs around my neck. I was in complete awe. I was speechless. *What if they had the wrong child?* I started thinking to myself. I didn't know what to think. I was at a loss. Even now, as I write this paragraph, I don't exactly know what to say was going through my mind. I continued walking. In my attempt to speed off, Brother Pilgrim instructed me to walk slowly. I was to walk slowly to accompany the dancing that was ushering my along the carpet in the middle of this village. *Is this all real?* As we approached the building, I thought that I would finally escape all this fanfare. What I saw next proved that I was never so wrong.

We turned, and I tried not to be too overwhelmed. Looking around the corner, I heard more claps. I peeked and saw little children sitting on the floor, legs crossed. When I was fully around the corner, it took me aback to see all the children in that centre all seated and waiting for my arrival. They were many different ages. One hundred and twenty students fixed their gaze on me as I came in and sat down. There were a few seats at the front of the little area in which they sat, and I was instructed to come in and sit down. All the while, cameras were flashing and phones were clicking (of those who didn't live there, who had phones) and villagers were gathering in and peeking around the corner to see me. The last child to put a reef on my neck…was Kunal himself.

He was around the same height as the picture, though I thought he would be taller. His hair was also styled very sleekly, and he was wearing the school uniform of the Bridge of Hope centre. His hands and feet were cleaned, and he sat at a distance. He was the same boy as in my picture, and that put all my worries to rest. I finally saw him!

Kunal was 11 years old. The age that I thought he would be was probably was not even close to his actual age. I asked about this, and Brother Pilgrim said that because the village is so uneducated and "backward", or so I'm told, that the parents would not know what date or time around which their children are born; and so they just guess whenever they're asked. He was sitting at a distance when the brothers called him up, and put him to sit with me. All the while, the other hundred and twenty students were gazing up at us. This made Kunal very nervous, apparently because he didn't say anything. He did, however, build me a house. This house which he built me was a three storey house, with a flight of stairs winding up to the second floor, and a ladder on the side heading up to the third. The edges of the outside walls were etched to look like those of a castle, and there was also a lovely guard wall around the property. Of course, this house was made from Styrofoam but I appreciated it all the same. I was told by Brother Pilgrim that the kids learn how to do these kinds of handicrafts at the centre; and without my support, he would not have been able to build me such an edifice.

As we were talking through interpreters, I thought of a way to get his attention. I pulled out my phone, and started showing him pictures of Barbados. He remarked on how lovely the scenery was; and I continued showing him all the other pictures in my phone with me, and scenery and friends and family and school, etc. He seemed pretty interested just to be on a phone. It was then that I handed it to him and had him take a selfie of us. He had said that he can finally put a voice to the picture and the letters that he has been receiving all this time from me.

I then reached into my bag and pulled out the first letter that he had written to me back in January 2016. In it, he had written that he thanked me for sponsoring him, and that he hopes to see me one day. When he and his family saw it, they were (not so) visibly taken aback; and his father went inside somewhere and came back out later with a couple sheets of paper. What I didn't expect in a thousand years was, that which Kunal's father showed me was the first letter that I ever wrote to him! I was completely blown away. I almost snatched them, and my eyes darted across the pages, as I was taken back to when I wrote them to him. I could almost remember what I was doing at the time of writing the letter. While I was yet reading, Kunal also produced a picture of me. This picture had the head of a Stefan Lorde, but the body of someone else. What I mean is that there was a "ping-pong"[28] picture of me that I sent to Kunal during the first few months of our relationship. They had got the photo edited so as to have a body to add to the head. Before this explanation, I was struggling to remember when I would have sent this photo. It was only after the explanation that I realised that only the face on the picture was what I sent him; all the rest was computer edited.

There were testimonies. While I was sitting there, the students also sang a song and said a prayer and a message. When the testimonies were being said, this one girl said that it was only because of coming to the centre that she started noticing a change in herself. Her mother also noticed and started to slowly change as well. When asked about the change, this little girl told her mother about Jesus. After this, the surrounding villagers started to notice the change, and an impact was made in that village for those living in that area.

After this, myself, Kunal and the other brothers from the centre came into a room where we could get away from the crowd. Inside, I took out the first draft to this book which I had printed, and showed it to Kunal. I was proofreading it since I printed it, and gave it to him to see. While I watched him flip through the pages, I told him that people usually go to the author to get the books signed, but I want him to sign my book for me. I am thinking of putting that signature in the final copy as well, somehow. As he wrote, Brother Pilgrim explained to me that without my support, Kunal would not be able to write and read. There, education is not as emphasised as it would be in other parts of the country. For

---

28 Passport-sized photographs

them, if they want to, they would pursue an education, but if they don't, they won't. Thinking about it, I don't think that anyone would pursue an education if they had the option to avoid it. I certainly, seeing that there isn't an immediate result or advantage, would not have opted for an education; but thank God that I didn't have that choice to make. Praise God that my education was always free. Even now, my education in China is paid for by scholarship, and my education in Barbados was always subsidised by the Government. Eternal gratitude!

We got ready to leave, but not before I was encouraged to say a few words to the children gathered there. I was not prepared in the least, but I still tried my best to say something coherent enough for them to take away. Leaving the Sujani centre, we took a load of pictures, and some of the children were very delighted to have me sit with them. My favourite one was with me and Kunal sitting at the front, and the others sitting behind us. I don't know how brother Buckman did it, but he made all the kids laugh just before the picture was taken, and that made it so magical. That was probably the best picture I have taken in a long time.

Back in the car, we waved goodbye to the children and set off from Sujani. I was happy. I was very happy. Jesus says to doubting Thomas "blessed are those who haven't seen, but still believe"[29], but now after I've seen the Centre and Kunal, all the doubts that I would have been having along the way were gone. Seeing is believing more. I believed, but my sight helps my belief. I was talking to Brother Pilgrim, and talked all over my face. I talked and talked all the way back to the hotel. I was all smiles and I spoke about any and everything with those in the car. The next day, we left Deoghar to head back to Ranchi.

When I got back to Ranchi, about 7 hours later, I had asked if I could have a look around at the other centres that are in the surrounding area. The brothers obliged, and soon I was touring the village and marvelling at the stars that I didn't get to see for so long. I went to another centre, and there I received similar treatment. They sang and they danced, and performed as they welcomed me to their home. I was given a tour of the place, and noticed that this centre (maybe because of its close proximity to the city) was a lot better off than the one in Sujani. At this centre, I was given a plaque of appreciation, and got the chance to speak to the children that were there. I was introduced to all the staff, and given some treats and delicacies to try. After fellowship with the brothers and answering all their questions, it was time for me to head back to the hotel, as it was getting late.

Being back in a nice, warm, Wi-Fi flooded zone, I spent the hours chatting with people over WhatsApp, and sending photos to people from all over my friend circle. Even people with whom I was no longer friends, I sent photos too, because I was happier about seeing Kunal than I was feeling about anything else.

29 John 20:29

I was more concerned about encouraging other people to become sponsors, than I was about how I was feeling about them. I was lying in bed, and finally got to rest for a bit.

Time moved along swiftly, and I was soon to leave India altogether. Up until this time, because my debit card didn't work in India, I was left without a means to cover the expenses that I had promised to cover. This was getting more and more frustrating, because I have the money, and I never would have thought that my card would be rejected (as it is one of those "international cards"). We searched and inquired from all manner of banks and agencies, and all to no avail. It was getting frustrating, but when I felt myself starting to worry, I would close my eyes and remember the smile of the little boy I went there to see. Then, I would think that regardless of what trouble would surface throughout the remainder of my trip, it would all be worth it because I had accomplished my purpose. I had asked where I could go to purchase some Indian clothes to take back with me to China. I thought that I wouldn't have to pay as much, and even try my card at the store to see if I can at least get through there. The card didn't work, and the price of the clothes that I bought was almost the same as the price for one night at the hotel. *Oh my goodness!* After having my last supper in India, I was escorted back to the airport. I took a few more selfies and entered the departure lounge.

As the flight takes off from Ranchi, I close my eyes and call to memory that pearly white smile my son flashed. I turn and look through the airplane window and whisper goodbye as the earth beneath me hurried out of sight, and disappears beneath the blackness of the night sky. Thoughts of all that has happened since I landed in Ranchi are still very fresh in my mind, and flash behind my eyes whenever I blink. The humming silence of the flight does nothing but make way for the recollections of song and dance. A friend on social media admonishes thus: "I hope you know that you have changed his life." Maybe the full impact of my visit to Kunal would be felt or noticed later on in life. For now, I sit here in seat 27F, thinking about him.

Missing him…

Loving him….

Nobody made a greater mistake than he who did nothing because he could do only a little.

– Edmund Burke

Bibliography

Bunyan, John. The Pilgrim's Progress. Ed. Rosalie De Rosset. 1678: Moody Publishers, n.d.

Lorde. THE INFLUENCE OF TEACHERS' ATTITUDES . B.A. Thesis. Bridgetown, 2013. Document.

Lynch, Willie. The Making of a Slave. Virginia, 1712. Letter.